A Writing Apprenticeship

Norman A. Brittin

Auburn University

SECOND EDITION

HOLT, RINEHART AND WINSTON, INC.

NEW YORK   CHICAGO   SAN FRANCISCO   ATLANTA   DALLAS

Note to the Second Edition

All authors, no doubt, are gratified when the success of a work warrants a second edition. This new edition of *A Writing Apprenticeship* follows the same principles and the same organization as the original edition. In response to requests from instructors who have used the first edition, however, a larger number of selections by twentieth-century writers has been included, as well as a few longer pieces. Exposition has received more emphasis, and the total number of selections has been somewhat increased. Both author and publisher feel that the new edition will be thought an improvement over the first.

Thanks are due to the following frank and friendly critics of the first edition: Stanley L. Archer of the Texas Agricultural and Mechanical College Station, Catherine R. Gira of the University of Baltimore, Sybil Goldsmith of Wharton County Junior College, Donald Novick of the Mohawk Valley Community College, Doris H. Meriwether of the University of Southwestern Louisiana College, Albert P. Sawyer of Bogar Junior College, and John R. Williams of Southeastern Louisiana College—and as in the first edition to Professor Richard S. Beal of Boston University.

N. A. B.

Auburn, Alabama
January 1968

Foreword to the Instructor

This text is designed as an unpretentious, practical instrument for the teaching of composition. Many students coming to college have not read much, nor have they written much in any of their high school classes. Consequently they have very little idea of how to write English sentences according to standard patterns or how to compose solid and effective paragraphs. They are frequently set to studying material that is over their heads—material far too long and complex to serve as a model for writing. So the students often flounder around, trying to put together five hundred words on topics that are vaguely associated with the material read and that freshmen frequently are as yet too ignorant to write about. The material in this text was carefully chosen so that students would not be thrust into writing situations that are bound to be unprofitable.

As a matter of common sense, it is well to start students off by presenting paragraphs that they can use as models. There is a long and approved tradition of learning to write by imitation. But if students are really to learn by imitation, they must have models brief enough to imitate. Thus one third of the selections in this book contain only one paragraph; more than half of the selections contain no more than three paragraphs.

Along with the imitable model goes the practicable writing assignment. The assignments should permit the student to follow the pattern established by the paragraph. The assignments here call upon students to imitate the models on topics that are within their experience or require only direct observation of life about them.

It is hoped, too, that the very concept of apprenticeship in writing, as explained in the first pages, will produce in students a healthy, common-sense attitude toward composition. The selections in the text are examples of serious, craftsmanlike writing which in a great many respects is easily imitable by beginners. Though the names of many famous authors appear in the table of contents, the selections, which have considerable variety, do not represent the undesirable extremes of either the belletristic or the utilitarian.

The material is arranged so that it gradually becomes more complex, and the assignments naturally sometimes become longer.

The selections are varied enough that the text will suit freshmen of different levels of proficiency. After a while the student should feel that he is making definite progress. By the time the student has had the experience of writing single paragraphs and linked paragraphs of the types assigned, he should have laid a really effective foundation for writing practically anything he will be called upon to write later.

The work sections accompanying the selections apply, of course, to the methods by which the authors composed their work and are designed both to make the student understand some of the standard practices in writing and to inculcate in him the habit of critical reading. As the student directs his attention closely to sentence patterns, paragraph patterns, and diction, in the way that the study questions ask him to do and that the requirement of imitation imposes upon him, he will learn a good deal about efficient reading as well as about writing. In the work sections, necessary terms like *topic sentence* and *transition* are introduced along the way in such a manner that the student should become accustomed to employing them practically and naturally. The attention to diction varies with the vocabulary difficulty of the different selections; but the word-study included should help the student overcome scantiness of vocabulary and set him off on the right foot, by making him more aware of word-roots.

The text was devised with both the experienced and inexperienced instructor in mind. It is believed that the experienced instructor will feel that the strategy of this text is a sound one; it is hoped that the inexperienced instructor will find the text informative and effective.

Foreword to the Student

Writers and people who teach writing often call it a craft. A craft is an art or occupation that requires special skill. A person who wishes to learn a craft, whether it is pottery making, carpentry, weaving, or silversmithing, must have instruction. He must have direction and practice. Before a potter gives his apprentice a ball of clay to turn on the potter's wheel or before a carpenter puts a saw into the hand of his apprentice, he tells him to watch the master's skilled hands handle the clay, handle the saw and the board. So the apprentice tries to do exactly what the craftsman did. He tries to do it with the same smoothness and precision of his master. At first he is awkward, but as he becomes more familiar with the material used, with the tools, and with the problems that his craft has been created to solve, he gradually improves.

People who wish to learn the craft of writing go about it in the same way. They learn by imitating the work of those who are master craftsmen.

Let us remind ourselves that an apprentice is first put to making small pots, not great vessels; he is first shown how to saw boards accurately, not given a house to build. In the early stages of his apprenticeship the projects of an apprentice are small ones; only gradually do they become larger and more complicated. But after he has learned to do the little things well—after he has mastered the basic operations—he can do larger things too with success.

A student who wishes to develop his special skill in writing cannot start by composing an epic or a novel. First he must learn how to compose sentences and paragraphs. He must learn how to value words in terms of their special meanings, and he must learn how to place them in the right spots (paying attention also to the rules of grammar and syntax) so that they will form effective statements. And he must combine the sentences into paragraphs that are effective for various purposes. It has been said that if a person can write a good paragraph, he can write a book. This means, of course, that if a person has enough writing skill to compose a good paragraph, he could, if he acquired enough knowledge, create paragraph after paragraph until he had written a book.

ix

Thus at first a carpenter's apprentice may know very little about saws, hammers, and planes, boards, planks, and nails; but after he has worked steadily with them for a few years and has learned the principles of using them, he may be in a position to build a house. Though perhaps few college freshmen will ever actually write books, they will all certainly write many other things: papers, reports, letters, speeches, articles. And if they have learned through direction and practice how to write sentences and paragraphs, they have learned the essential skills of the writing craft.

This book provides masters and models; it provides direction and practical patterns as guides. A student who does the writing assignments, always imitating the work of some master (and learning through answering questions the principles that have guided master writers), will eventually be able to produce writing that can pass inspection. He will have served his apprenticeship; and he can call himself at least a journeyman writer.

Contents

Thurs. Oct. 1

Section One

Description
and
Narration

*H*uman beings are always interested in other human beings. Perhaps the majority of people are interested in people more than in anything else. Often, in conversation, one hears: "What did she look like?" "What was she wearing?" "What does he look like?" To answer such questions, we describe.

In describing, one notes the details that he has observed, or, more precisely, details that he has been made aware of by the use of all his senses—sight, hearing, taste, smell, touch. All of the environment—the world of people, the world of nature, and the man-created world—comes to one first through the senses; and if an individual is to communicate to others what his experiences in that environment are like, he must report through words what his senses have told him. Even so common an experience as washing one's face in the morning provides numerous sense impressions—the flashing on of the light in the bathroom; the gleam of chromium and porcelain; gray steam rising and clouding the mirror; the scalding feel of over-hot water; the response of the nerves to contrasting cold or lukewarm water; the smells of soap, shaving cream, and toothpaste; and the feel of the soft tubes or of the bar of soap: cold hardness if new, wet slippery smoothness if used. Nor is the ear dull to varied sounds: the splash, hiss, trickle, or gurgle of water, the rubbing of palms, popping and roaring in the ears. Maybe, because of familiarity, one pays little attention to these sense impressions—but they exist, they *are* in their totality the experience that the individual has had, and if he were to become blind, deaf, or nerve-dead, the experience would undergo radical change.

If anyone tries to answer questions about people or about environment—"What does that place look like?" "What kind of house does so-and-so live in?" "So you have been to ———! What is it like? How did you feel when you saw it? Is it pleasant? Is it scary? Is it fantastic? Is it picturesque? Is it beautiful?"—the person asked is often likely, in conversation, to give answers that are not adequate, being too hurried, too broad, too lacking in details. In writing description, however, it is possible to take time to set down details that will show with exactness just how someone looks: the person's height, shape of head, color of hair, way of gesturing or walking, shade of complexion, look of eye, twist of mouth—all these pieces of evidence can be recorded if the writer looks closely enough and if he can think of the correct terms to express them. In order to be accurate and to be interesting, he must notice details and be able to report them in abundance. But a writer must also notice telling details—that is, the particular details that give him his impressions of people and of places. A place may be awesome or dreary or uncomfortable or colorful (and a colorful place may be unpleasantly gaudy or delightfully harmonious) or spacious or crowded, and so forth. To convey the impressions that the senses have given mankind, it is essential to find words that are just right.

In the most exact meaning of the term, *description* is writing that conveys these sense impressions; but writing about people and places may also have informational purposes which are combined with description; description may lead to or be blended with character study; and description is often a necessary element in storytelling.

A large part of our lifetime goes into our associations with other people. We are constantly trying to become acquainted with them, trying to get to *know* them. Description is important in this effort, for it lets us know what sense impressions people arouse. What different pictures are conveyed by the words: "tall, dignified gentleman" and "little roly-poly fellow"! Yet, one would be more fascinated by a further report: "tall, dignified—but stupid"; "little roly-poly fellow—but sharp, even waspish!"

People are interested in surface appearances, but they are even more interested in what lies behind them. "What *kind* of person is this? What are his qualities? What are the elements of his character?" Thus persons are frequently led as they talk or write about human beings to go from description to characterization—after surveying the outward appearance, to penetrate to the inner being, the character. Of course, this calls for more knowledge, more thought, more analysis. But people are always doing it, informally as they make mental notes or chat with friends, formally as they write letters of recommendation and make other appraisals.

Though, as has been said, writing about the environment is often descriptive (it aims to make us *see* a place and sometimes to experience it with our other senses), such writing may also, at times, be as much informational as descriptive. To know that the Washington Monument is 555 feet high does not make a person see the exact look of it, but this information might be a necessary part of an article about Washington, D.C. In practice, description and informational writing, which is called exposition, often go together.

Likewise, in a story an author often tells how both places and people look; the reader generally wishes to know something about the background of the place where the story happens. Often, too, the author relates in stories how both places and people affect the feelings of other people. That is, description and storytelling (or narration) usually go together.

In the section that follows, the apprentice writer is given models for these several kinds of descriptive writing. Since everyone is in continual communication with people, it will be easy to observe them. To describe people will be one of the simplest writing exercises with which to start. And writing description will be an excellent discipline for the writing apprentice because it will begin to train his powers of observation and to show him the value of sharp, clear details. Some of the selections provide examples of characterization; some provide models for the description of places and for things seen in certain environments, such as animals. Some of the models come from stories; the section ends with readings that have more of narration than of description.

🌼 *Kittredge of Harvard*

ROLLO WALTER BROWN

1   The sight of him as he came to the ten-o'clock class was in itself something that had to be recognized as dramatic. In the pleasant autumn or spring, men stood high on the steps or out on the turf in front and watched in the direction of Christ Church to see who could catch the first glimpse of him.

2   "There he comes!" somebody called, and then everybody who was in a position to see watched him as he hurried breezily along—a graceful, tallish man in very light gray suit and gray fedora hat, with a full square beard at least as white as his suit, who moved with energy, and smoked passionately at a big cigar. Students used to say that he smoked an entire cigar while he walked the short distance along the iron fence of the old burying ground and across the street to Johnston Gate. But as he came through the gate he tossed the remnant of his cigar into the shrubbery with a bit of a flourish, and the students still outside hurried in and scrambled up the long stairway in order to be in their places—as he liked—before he himself entered. If any of them were still on the stairway when he came in at the outer door like a gust, they gave way and he pushed up past them, and into the good-sized room and down the aisle to the front, threw his hat on the table in the corner, mounted the two steps to the platform, looked about with a commanding eye, and there was sudden silence and unrestrained expectancy.

STUDY QUESTIONS

Organization and Content

1. Why is paragraph 1 so short?
2. Why did Brown decide to start paragraph 2 where he did and as he did?

3. Paragraph 2 has four sentences. What determines the order in which they are arranged? Does the paragraph have a beginning, a middle, and an end?

Sentence Structure

1. Sentence 1, paragraph 1, is almost exactly balanced before and after *was*. Describe the pattern of balance in terms of subject, predicate nominative, and modifying clauses and prepositional phrases.
2. Does the author have any purpose in placing the word *dramatic* at the end of sentence 1?
3. How does Brown proceed in sentence 1, paragraph 2, from the observers to the subject of his description (Kittredge), and then to the physical details that begin the description of the subject?
4. What purpose is served by placing *But* (an important word in our language) at the beginning of sentence 3, paragraph 2?
5. What is the relation of the second half of sentence 3 to the first half? Could the second half just as well come first?
6. Sentence 4, paragraph 2, is the longest sentence in the description (seventy-one words). Why should it be so long? If it were divided into two or three shorter sentences, how would the effect be changed?
7. How does Brown manage the attention given to the students and to Professor Kittredge in sentence 4, paragraph 2?

Diction

(The vocabulary given in this section throughout the book is taken from the text in the exact form in which it appears and in the order of appearance within the article.)

1. What is the key word of paragraph 1 (and of the whole description)?
2. Would there be any difference if *grass* or *ground* were used instead of *turf*? *Look, observation, sight,* or *view* instead of *glimpse*?
3. What is the meaning of *breezily*, of *passionately*?
4. Which adjectives help you most to visualize Kittredge?
5. What effect do these phrases have: "with a bit of a flourish," "like a gust"?
6. There are more than a dozen verbs in sentences 3 and 4, paragraph 2. What is the effect of having so many, and which are the most specific?
7. What effect do the last two adjectives have?

Assignment

Describe the approach of one of your teachers to his classroom or office, or of a businessman to his place of work. Your problem is to convey the special and specific look, walk, and manner of your subject.

Charles Bradlaugh

A Journalist

Mr. Bradlaugh is a tall, muscular man, who stands firm on his legs, with broad shoulders, between which is a massive, square, powerful head. He dresses in plain black, relieved only by an ordinary display of linen and a slender watch chain. He is closely shaven as a Roman priest. His features are large and open, his eyes are of a greyish hue, and his hair, which is fast turning grey, falls back from a brow on which intelligence, perception, and power are strongly marked. He has a face which can be very pleasing and very stern, but which conceals the emotion at will. As he sits listening to the denunciations of his opponent, the smile of incredulity, the look of astonishment, the cloud of anger, pass quickly over his countenance. Rising from his seat, and resting one hand upon the table, he commences very quietly, in a voice which, until the ear is accustomed to it, sounds unpleasant and harsh, but which, when it becomes stronger, loses much of its twang, and sounds almost musical. His enunciation is singularly distinct, not one word being lost by the audience. He addresses himself to all parts of the house—gallery as well as body. When warmed by his subject, he advances to the centre of the platform and looking his audience full in the face, and with right hand emphasising every important sentence, he expresses himself in tones so commanding and words so distinct that his hearers may be hostile or friendly, but cannot be indifferent. One may retire horrified at his sentiments, even disgusted at his irreverence and audacity—from a Christian's standpoint—but no one would go to sleep under him. He can be complimentary and humorous, but is more at home in sarcasm and denunciation. He is never ponderous; nevertheless, the grave suits him better than the gay. Cheering does not seem to affect him, though he is by no means indifferent to it, but he is quick to perceive disapproval, and is most powerful when most loudly hissed. With head erect, face coloured with a flush which has in it a little of defiance as well as earnestness, now emphasising with his right hand, now with folded arms, now joining the tips of his fingers as if to indicate the closeness of his reasoning, as he would have the audience to believe it, he stands defying opposition, even going out of his way to increase it, and revelling in his Ishmaelism.

From *The Darlington and Stockton Times* (1876).

STUDY QUESTIONS

Organization and Content

1. This description of Charles Bradlaugh as a public speaker is more detailed than the preceding description. More attention is given to the dress, expressions, movements, and bearing of the subject. Point out which sentences deal with each of these topics.
2. What specific details are given in sentences 1, 2, 3, and 4?
3. Explain how the details in the last sentence of the paragraph are presented so as to convey the idea of defiant vigor.
4. Using this description only, what would you take Bradlaugh's beliefs and profession to have been?

Sentence Structure

1. The subject of the first three sentences is the same: Mr. Bradlaugh (he)—followed by a verb. How may we say, then, that these sentences are linked to one another?
2. In sentence 4 what are the key words?
3. Note how the modifiers are arranged in sentence 4. They are adjectives, an adjective phrase, and two adjective clauses. Identify them.
4. Point out the balanced clauses in sentence 5.
5. The variety of sentences in this paragraph is noteworthy. The first five sentences all begin with independent elements. The next two sentences begin with dependent elements, the first with a dependent clause, the next with two participial phrases. How do sentences 8, 9, and 10 begin?
6. Some of the arrangements of the sentence parts within the sentences are also noteworthy: the parallel subjects, each with its adjective phrase for modifier, in sentence 6; the parallel *which*-clauses in sentence 7, and the pair of verbs making up the predicate of the second clause; the parallel main clauses in sentence 10, "he advances" and "he expresses."

Diction

1. The majority of words of this paragraph are simple, commonly used terms. Among them are a few less common ones, long words of Latin origin. Contrast the meanings of: *denunciation* and *enunciation, incredulity* and *astonishment.*
2. What is the etymology of *astonishment?*
3. Look up *perception, sarcasm, ponderous.*
4. *Ishmaelism* is a word made up from a proper noun, as one might say *Daniel Boone-ism.* Find out what there was about Ishmael that made his name suitable for the writer's purpose here.

Assignment

Imitate this paragraph by writing one about a professor, politician, preacher, or another person addressing a group.

✿ *Sherlock Holmes*

SIR ARTHUR CONAN DOYLE

1   Holmes was certainly not a difficult man to live with. He was quiet in his ways, and his habits were regular. It was rare for him to be up after ten at night, and he had invariably breakfasted and gone out before I rose in the morning. Sometimes he spent his day at the chemical laboratory, sometimes in the dissecting rooms, and occasionally in long walks, which appeared to take him into the lowest portions of the city. Nothing could exceed his energy when the working fit was upon him; but now and again a reaction would seize him, and for days on end he would lie upon the sofa in the sitting-room, hardly uttering a word or moving a muscle from morning to night. On these occasions I have noticed such a dreamy, vacant expression in his eyes, that I might have suspected him of being addicted to the use of some narcotic, had not the temperance and cleanliness of his whole life forbidden such a notion.

2   As the weeks went by, my interest in him and my curiosity as to his aims in life gradually deepened and increased. His very person and appearance were such as to strike the attention of the most casual observer. In height he was rather over six feet, and so excessively lean that he seemed to be considerably taller. His eyes were sharp and piercing, save during those intervals of torpor to which I have alluded; and his thin, hawk-like nose gave his whole expression an air of alertness and decision. His chin, too, had the prominence and squareness which mark the man of determination. His hands were invariably blotted with ink and stained with chemicals, yet he was possessed of extraordinary delicacy of touch, as I frequently had occasion to observe when I watched him manipulating his fragile philosophical instruments.

STUDY QUESTIONS

Organization and Content

This is the first description of one of the most famous characters of modern literature—Sherlock Holmes—given shortly after Dr. Watson had met him and the two men had decided to room together. However,

From Sir Arthur Conan Doyle, *A Study in Scarlet* (1887).

there are other elements here than description. These other elements make us aware of Holmes's habits and thus make us think about his character. Therefore, these paragraphs represent a combination of description and characterization. Both the description and the characterization are accomplished by means of selected details.

1. The first sentence of each paragraph is its topic sentence. The rest of each paragraph gives support to the topic sentence, or sets forth *reasons to believe that the topic sentence is true.* Give six reasons why Holmes was not a difficult man with whom to live.
2. In paragraph 2 what are the main reasons that support the idea expressed in the topic sentence?
3. Paragraph 1 is largely informational; it presents very little that we can *see.* Which details in the last two sentences allow us to form a picture in our imagination?
4. Paragraph 2 has more details that help us to form a visual image of Sherlock Holmes. Name five such details.
5. With what qualities of character has the author linked the descriptive details?
6. With these indications of Holmes's character, what terms would you use to express the kind of man that you think he is?

Sentence Structure

1. Point out parallel elements of sentences 2, 3, and 4 of paragraph 1.
2. Sentence 5 has a semicolon. What do you think is its function?
3. The last three sentences of paragraph 2 all begin in the same way. What is the effect of these three similar beginnings?

Diction

1. Conan Doyle's vocabulary is easy here. Perhaps it is necessary to look up *torpor, manipulating, fragile.*
2. If you can discover what *natural philosophy* is, you ought to know what *philosophical instruments* are.

Assignment

Imitate this description in two paragraphs. In the first paragraph tell about the habits of a person; in the second, relate the appearance of the person to his character. Include at least half a dozen informational details in the first paragraph and the same number of visual details in the second.

Choose for the subject someone that you know well, such as your roommate, a laboratory partner, a member of a team, a hunting companion, or a relative.

It will probably be useful, *before writing* the paragraphs, to make lists of the details that give life to the subject and fullness to the paragraphs.

Domna Rejnev

MARY McCARTHY

Domna Rejnev was the newest member of the Literature Department, a Radcliffe B.A., twenty-three years old, teaching Russian literature and French. To deter familiarities, she wore a plain smock in her office that gave her something of the look of a young woman scientist or interne. Her grandfather had been a famous Liberal, one of the leaders of the Cadet party in the Duma; her father, a well-educated man, a friend of Cocteau and Diaghileff, sold jewelry for a firm in Paris. She herself was a smoldering anachronism, a throwback to one of those ardent young women of the Sixties, Turgenev's heroines, who cut their curls short, studied Hegel, crossed their mammas and papas, reproved their suitors, and dreamed resolutely of "a new day" for peasants, workers, and technicians. Like her prototypes, she gave the appearance of stifling in conventional surroundings; her finely cut, mobile nostrils quivered during a banal conversation as though, literally, seeking air. Her dark, straight, glossy hair was worn short and loose, without so much as a bobby-pin; she kept ruffling an impatient hand through it to brush it back from her eyes. She had a severe, beautiful, clear-cut profile, very pure ivory skin, the color of old piano keys; her lips, also, were finely drawn and a true natural pink or rose. Her very beauty had the quality, not of radiance or softness, but of incorruptibility; it was the beauty of an absolute or a political theorem. Unlike most advanced young women, she dressed quietly, without tendentiousness—no ballet-slippers, bangles, dirndls, flowers in the hair. She wore dark suits of rather heavy, good material, cut somewhat full in the coat-skirts: the European tailor-made. Only her eyes were an exception to this restraint and muted gravity of person; they were grey and queerly lit from within, as by some dangerous electricity; she had a startling intensity of gaze that never wavered from its object, like that of a palmist or a seer. Her voice, on the contrary, was low, concise, and even; a slight English boarding-school accent overlaid a Russian harshness.

STUDY QUESTIONS

Organization and Content

1. Is there a principle governing the order of the sentences in the paragraph? Consider, for example, what each of the following three sections contains: sentences 1–5, 6–8, 9–12.
2. What do the grandfather and the father have in common? In what sense is sentence 4 a contrast to sentence 3?
3. How are the last two sentences related to the preceding ones?
4. Point out five details that help us to form a visual image of Domna Rejnev. What sentences characterize her rather than describe her? Which sentences both describe and characterize?
5. What topic idea is the author trying to support in this paragraph?

Sentence Structure

1. Explain how items of information are arranged in sentences 1, 3, and 4.
2. Sentence 3 has two equal parts. To what is each part devoted?
3. Sentences 5–8 all have two parts separated by a semicolon. In each sentence what is the relation of the second part to the first?
4. Each sentence has at least one word that refers to Domna Rejnev and thus links the sentences. Point out these words.
5. How much variety and how much sameness are there in the way the sentences begin? Has the author avoided monotony in the sentence openings?

Diction

1. Look up *Radcliffe, Duma, Cocteau, Diaghileff, Turgenev*. For what purpose does the author use these references?
2. Look up *anachronism, crossed, reproved, prototypes, banal, absolute* (noun), *tendentiousness, seer*.
3. In sentence 4 what is the connection between "smoldering anachronism" and "ardent young women of the Sixties"? Why is "a new day" in quotation marks?
4. May *impatient* properly be applied to a hand (sentence 6), *concise* to a voice?
5. Which words contribute the most to the consistency of this character portrait? (Some significant terms occur even as early as sentence 2.) Which are concrete and which are abstract?

Assignment

Write a one-paragraph description-characterization of someone you know whose whole appearance, manner, and dress are consistent with the character of the person. Follow approximately the same arrangement of material as in the model.

Mrs. Jack Gardner

CLEVELAND AMORY

1 For a Boston Society which has never lacked for grandes dames to have to admit that its greatest was not a Bostonian at all but a New York import is a stern story indeed. Furthermore this greatest of grandes dames was a lady who persisted in regarding herself as a sort of dedicated spirit to wake up Boston. The daughter of a New York dry-goods merchant named David Stewart, she was christened Isabella. In the year 1860 she married John Lowell Gardner, son of the last of Boston's East India merchants, and moved to Boston. From then until her death in 1924 at the age of eighty-five Isabella Stewart Gardner proceeded to do everything that Proper Boston women do not do, and then some. "In a Society," wrote Lucius Beebe, "where entertaining Major Higginson at tea and sleigh-riding on the Brighton Road on Sunday afternoon were the ultimate public activities endorsed by decorum, she soon became far from anonymous."

2 Mrs. Gardner didn't drink tea; she drank beer. She adored it, she said. She didn't go sleigh-riding; instead, she went walking down Tremont Street with a lion named Rex on a leash. She gave at-homes at her Beacon Street house and received her guests from a perch in the lower branches of a mimosa tree. Told that "everybody in Boston" was either a Unitarian or an Episcopalian, she became a Buddhist; then when the pleasure of that shock had worn off she became such a High-Church Episcopalian that her religion differed from Catholicism only in respect to allegiance to the Pope. Advised that the best people in Boston belonged to clubs she formed one of her own named the "It" Club. In Boston one coachman was enough for anybody. But Mrs. Gardner soon showed she wasn't anybody. She kept two footmen as well as a coachman and rarely drove out in her carriage without all three of them in full livery. Warned that a woman's social position in Boston might be judged in inverse ratio to her appearance, she spent thousands of dollars a year on the latest Paris fashions. She saw Cabots and Lowells leave their jewels in their safe-deposit boxes; she picked out her two largest diamonds, had them set on gold wire springs and wore them waving some six inches above her hair like the antennae of a butterfly. Mrs. Gardner

even told risqué stories and told them in mixed company—at the same time, her bout with Buddhism behind her, each Lent with much fanfare she piously atoned for her misdeeds by scrubbing the steps of the Church of the Advent and sending out black-bordered invitations to Holy Communion.

3   Hypnotic was the word for this woman. She had a way with her. Plain of face to the point of homeliness and short of stature, she had a strikingly curvaceous figure and attracted artists by the score, most of whom offered to paint her merely for the pleasure of doing so. When she finally chose John Singer Sargent to do her portrait, she once more showed her scorn for Bostonian propriety by having him paint her in a black low-necked dress with a rope of pearls around her waist and a black shawl drawn tightly around her hips. Exhibited at the gentlemanly St. Botolph Club in the winter of 1888–89 the picture caused so much comment that her husband had it removed and declared it would never be exhibited again as long as he lived. So far as it is known this is the only occasion he or anyone else ever told Mrs. Gardner what to do. "To dominate others," writes her biographer and present-day executor, Morris Carter, "gave Mrs. Gardner such pleasure that she must have regretted the passing of slavery."

STUDY QUESTIONS

Organization and Content

1. What is the main theme that continues throughout this account of the famous Mrs. Gardner?
2. Paragraph 2 does not have any general statement to serve as a topic sentence. What idea would cover the many details mentioned in paragraph 2?
3. What relation does paragraph 2 have to paragraph 1?
4. How does the principal thought of paragraph 3 contrast with that of paragraph 2?

Sentence Structure

1. Note that the author begins many of his sentences with dependent phrases or clauses. He uses the participial modifier like the "Told that everybody in Boston' . . ." in paragraph 2, the appositive as in "The daughter of a New York dry-goods merchant . . ." in paragraph 1, the adjective plus modifiers in the "Plain of face to the point of homeliness . . ." in paragraph 3, and a series of prepositional phrases in the "From then until her death . . ." in paragraph 1. Does he overdo the opening with dependent elements?

2. However, the first several sentences of paragraph 2 are of a different type. Explain what their difference is.
3. What is the effect of this "change of pace" in the early part of paragraph 2?
4. To what extent would you say that Amory has achieved variety in his sentence style in these paragraphs?

Diction

1. Look up *grandes dames, ultimate, decorum, livery, risqué, fanfare, atoned, propriety.*
2. What are the chief differences among the beliefs of Unitarians, Episcopalians, and Buddhists?
3. Comment on the effect of these terms: *and then some, bout, curvaceous.*

Assignment

Write two or three paragraphs about an unconventional person. To do justice to your model, Mrs. Jack Gardner, choose the most unconventional person you have ever known, one who has seemed "wild" and who has delighted in challenging social conventions wherever he or she has lived.

Note that though there is some description here, the author places most stress upon Mrs. Gardner's activities and personality. He does not say much about her character or temperament. Sentence 2 of paragraph 1 gives necessary information in this respect and so does the last sentence of paragraph 3. Paragraph 2 is devoted entirely to the actions of Mrs. Gardner. Do the same in your paragraphs; an honest report of facts is generally very effective.

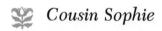

Cousin Sophie

ALFRED KAZIN

1   Our cousin Sophie was a difficult case. Because she had always lived with us, and had often taken care of me as a child when my mother was ill, I could have thought of her as my other mother, but she always seemed too young, restless, tormented. Although she was certainly not pretty—her long face usually looked sad or bitter,

and when she was gay, wildly and almost desperately gay—she radiated, as if it were warmth from her body, a passionate and angry vividness. All my life I had seen her, with the long black hair which had never been cut, her embroidered Russian blouses and velvet skirts, against the background of a tiny rectangle room scented with musk, with patchouli, while above the bed covered with a tickly India spread there hung, side by side, two pictures. One (I learned their names only much later) was Sir George Frederic Watts's *Hope*—a blindfolded young lady with bare feet sat on a globe earnestly listening for the vibration of the single string on her harp; the other was Pierre-Auguste Cot's *The Storm.* As the lovers raced before the storm, their heads were apprehensively yet exultantly turned back; and the cloak that the godlike lover was tenderly holding over the woman's shoulders, so light and flimsy that it barely covered her nakedness, seemed woven in its lightness and transparency of "love" itself, so that the gauze veil which together they held over their heads, though too flimsy to shield them from the storm, carried some deeper knowledge of desire that explained the shyness of the woman and the confident and protective smile of the man. As they ran together, just ahead of the storm, they seemed to be running not only under the same veil, but with the same feet.

2   I had looked at Sophie under those two pictures all my life, just as I had looked at her blouses, her skirts and her petticoats—there was no closet—or could smell from her warm and fragrant flesh, as soon as she came near me, the musk and sandalwood, or could feel her presence again whenever I touched her velvet skirts on the hangers and the stiff crinkly surface of the India spread on her bed. She was never easy with anyone, never tender; there was something about her long sweeping hair and the ungraspable scent of her body that was like the resistance of velvet, which retreats back into itself, in soft and recessive lines, after you have touched it. As a child I had often watched her, while she sat doing her hair in front of the mirror, suddenly in despair let the great mane fall over her face; or else she would sit coldly coiling her hair, doubling and then binding with long black hairpins each sheaf she caught up in her hand. Her moods were always extreme. The whole long day for her was like a sundial, either washed in sunlight or cold-gray in shadow; the moody, somber Sophie, in whose face one saw the control of her despair, alternated with a Sophie reckless, agonized, violently gay, who as she threw her great hair back, or bent over the mandolin with the little black pick in her hand, or coldly stared at some possible suitor stiffly seated at our dinner table whom my mother had hopefully brought in, impressed herself all through my

boyhood with that proud and flashing loneliness that I was to recognize immediately when I first saw *Carmen.*

3   Sophie was not just the unmarried cousin who had always lived with us; her unmarriedness, her need of a husband, of some attachment, was our constant charge and preoccupation. To this my mother gave as much thought as she did to us, and at the center of our household, whether she was off in her room under the picture of the two lovers fleeing from the storm, or in the kitchen with her friends from "the shop," drinking tea, eating fruit, or playing at the mandolin, one always saw or felt the vividly resentful figure of Sophie—Sophie beating at the strings of that yellow-shining, deep-bosomed, narrow-waisted mandolin, Sophie standing in front of the great mirror in the kitchen combing up her black black hair. As I watched with amazement, she kept one plait of hair suspended in her hand and then unceasingly and rhythmically, with the curved comb glistening in rhinestones, drew it with her long bony fingers through her hair, back and forth, until, when she had sifted and coiled and piled it up again, she would gather out the last straggle-thin threads in her hand as if it were a claw, and with a last sidelong look, manage with one gesture to throw a little ball of hair away and to give herself one last approving glance in the mirror. How natural it had always been to stand behind Sophie and to watch her combing her hair; or to steal into her room to smell the musk, the patchouli, the stingingly sweet face powder, the velvet skirts whose creases seemed still to mark the pressure of her body, the slips whose straps seemed just to have slipped off her shoulders. In the sepia dusk of the old prints, the lovers still ran rapturously before the storm, *Hope* held up her harp, and the bony gnarled wicker bookstand was filled with romantic English novels like *The Sheik* and Russian novels in stippled blue bindings which Sophie and Sophie alone could have brought into the house. And as if the difference had not already been made sufficiently clear between a mother who always seemed old to me and Sophie forever sultry and vivid, it was brought closer by the fact that my mother was at home all day and that Sophie appeared only in the evenings; when she was home, she was often elaborately sick in bed, with a bed jacket, while my mother brought her soft-boiled eggs and toast. The difference in their status was established by the way my mother worked, and waited on her, and told us to be quiet when Sophie was ill; we knew from my mother's constant expression of anxiety over her, from her anguished sulky looks of demanding love, that Sophie lacked something that everyone else in the world possessed.

STUDY QUESTIONS

Organization and Content

1. What are the main items supporting the idea that Cousin Sophie was "a difficult case"?
2. What key terms provide the focuses for a consistent impression of her appearance and character?
3. Half of paragraph 1 is devoted to Sophie's two pictures. Why does Kazin give so much space to them?
4. What does paragraph 2 tell us about Sophie that we did not learn in paragraph 1? And paragraph 3 that we did not learn in paragraph 2?
5. Kazin refers to his mother early in the portrait and again toward the end. What is the significance of these references?
6. Sophie's hair, her clothing, and the musk she used are mentioned in all three paragraphs. What variations prevent monotony? How do these things illustrate Sophie's personality?
7. Certain items function as symbols in the characterization: the pictures, velvet, the mandolin, and Sophie's books. Explain their symbolic value.
8. Which portrait is more subjectively presented, that of Cousin Sophie or that of Domna Rejnev?

Sentence Structure

1. How does Kazin manage to place an important word at the end of sentences 1–4 in paragraph 1?
2. Sentences 3 and 4 are opposite in their arrangement of independent clauses and dependent material. Explain this contrast.
3. Why is it good to omit *and* after *restless* in sentence 2? Why has Kazin placed *or* or *and* between adjectives in sentence 3? In what other places has he used *and* between pairs of adjectives? Has he done this too much?
4. How many simple sentences does this selection contain? Identify them.
5. One of the things to be noted about sentence management in this selection is the use of "interrupters"—terms that are set off by commas, dashes, or parentheses, such as the material between dashes in sentence 3. Point out other examples of interrupters.
6. Several sentences are extremely long: for example, sentence 6, paragraph 1; sentence 5, paragraph 2; sentences 2 and 3, paragraph 3. Point out the basic subject-verb-complement structure of these sentences.
7. Show how elements with parallel grammatical structure help to communicate the thought clearly in spite of the interrupters and the length of the sentences.
8. To write about two people and keep the references to both entirely clear is difficult. Mark the noun and pronoun references in the last two sentences to show how Kazin has accomplished this task.

Diction

1. Kazin's vocabulary is easy. You may need to look up *patchouli, sepia,* and *stippled.*
2. What terms has Kazin used to tell of Sophie's hair?
3. Explain the significance of the two similes in paragraph 2. Explain how the metaphor of "sheaf" in sentence 3, paragraph 2, is more economical than the similes.
4. What words tell of the two aspects of Sophie's nature?
5. Which of Kazin's words are the most precise and effective: adjectives, adverbs, nouns, verbs? Of these, which seem to convey best the quality of intensity?
6. Contrast the terms describing the lover in sentence 6, paragraph 1, with those describing the suitor in sentence 5, paragraph 2.
7. What extra connotative value is communicated by *angry* (sentence 3, paragraph 1), *flashing* (sentence 5, paragraph 2), *bony* (sentence 5, paragraph 3), and *sultry* (sentence 6, paragraph 3). Look up *connotation* and *denotation.*

Assignment

Combine description and characterization in an account of a person you know who is unhappy, troubled, or eccentric. You may give, as Kazin does, a certain amount of analysis of the personality, but provide also enough physical details so that the reader can visualize the person. You might try to include something symbolic. Use exact words, and imitate Kazin with at least one long sentence containing interrupters.

 **A Kitchen**

JAMES BALDWIN

Their mother, her head tied up in an old rag, sipped black coffee and watched Roy. The pale end-of-winter sunlight filled the room and yellowed all their faces; and John, drugged and morbid and wondering how it was that he had slept again and had been allowed to sleep so long, saw them for a moment like figures on a screen, an effect that the yellow light intensified. The room was narrow and dirty; nothing could alter its dimensions, no labor could ever make it clean. Dirt was in the walls and the floorboards, and triumphed beneath the sink where roaches spawned; was in the fine ridges of the pots and pans, scoured daily, burnt black on the bottom, hanging above the stove; was in the wall against which they hung, and revealed itself where the paint had cracked and leaned outward in stiff squares and fragments, the paper-thin underside webbed with black. Dirt was in every corner, angle, crevice of the monstrous stove, and lived behind it in delirious communion with the corrupted wall. Dirt was in the baseboard that John scrubbed every Saturday, and roughened the cupboard shelves that held the cracked and gleaming dishes. Under this dark weight the walls leaned, under it the ceiling, with a great crack like lightning in its center, sagged. The windows gleamed like beaten gold or silver, but now John saw, in the yellow light, how fine dust veiled their doubtful glory. Dirt crawled in the gray mop hung out of the windows to dry. John thought with shame and horror, yet in angry hardness of heart: *He who is filthy, let him be filthy still.* Then he looked at his mother, seeing, as though she were someone else, the dark, hard lines running downward from her eyes, and the deep, perpetual scowl in her forehead, and the downturned, tightened mouth, and the strong, thin, brown, and bony hands; and the phrase turned against him like a two-edged sword, for was it not he, in his false pride and his evil imagination, who was filthy? Through a storm of tears that did not reach his eyes, he stared at the yellow room; and the room shifted, the light of the sun darkened, and his mother's face changed. Her face became the face that he gave her in his dreams, the face that had been hers in a photograph he had seen once, long ago, a photograph taken before he was born. This face was young and proud, uplifted, with a smile that made the wide mouth beautiful and glowed in the enormous eyes. It was the face of a girl who knew that no evil could undo her, and who could laugh, surely, as his mother did not laugh now. Between the two faces there stretched a darkness and a mystery that John feared, and that sometimes caused him to hate her.

STUDY QUESTIONS

Organization and Content

1. From whose point of view is this description presented? If the observer were a child of three or a man of sixty, would the altered point of view make a difference in the content?

2. In what way does "end-of-winter sunlight," a detail mentioned in sentence 2, influence the description?
3. What is the dominant impression created by this description? What items support this impression?
4. Note the physical point of view in sentences 8 and 9. Where is the eye of the reader led?
5. What change occurs in the presentation in sentence 10? Is the paragraph organized in terms of two main parts, or more?
6. Should the part about the mother be in a separate paragraph or not? Answering this question requires consideration of the question: Does the paragraph have unity?

Sentence Structure

1. Explain how sentence 2 in its second part resembles sentence 1 in structure.
2. If sentence 3 had periods instead of the semicolon and comma, what different effect would be produced?
3. What pattern of verb-plus-prepositional phrases helps Baldwin to get so many details into sentence 4?
4. What subject-verb pattern is repeated in sentences 4–6? What effect does Baldwin secure by this repetition?
5. How does the use of the *and*'s in sentence 11 compare with that in sentences 2, 4, and 12?
6. Do the appositives serve a purpose in sentence 13? Would it be better not to repeat *face* and *photograph*?
7. How does Baldwin put emphasis on *face* in sentences 13–15? Is the word *face* important enough to deserve such emphasis?
8. Point out the parallel clauses in sentences 15 and 16.

Diction

1. The vocabulary is not difficult, but Baldwin uses words with great skill to create a dominant impression or a certain *atmosphere* for his setting. Which words through repetition contribute most to this atmosphere?
2. Consider how different the connotations would be if *diseased* replaced *morbid* in sentence 2, and if *reproduced* replaced *spawned* in sentence 4.
3. The verb *be* does not suggest vigor. Writers are often advised to avoid it and use instead verbs of action. In sentences 3–6, however, Baldwin uses *was* several times. Are the sentences weakened by this usage? What is contributed by other verbs, such as *triumphed* and *leaned* (sentence 4), *lived* (sentence 5), *roughened* (sentence 6), and *crawled* (sentence 9)?
4. Baldwin uses some terms which suggest that the thing he is writing about is something else, or is like something else: "like lightning," for example, in sentence 7. His language is "figurative"; that is, he uses metaphors and similes. Identify his figures of speech. Does he use more similes or more metaphors?

5. Should *triumphed* (sentence 4), *lived . . . in delirious communion* (sentence 5), *veiled* (sentence 8), and *crawled* (sentence 9) be regarded as metaphors?
6. What idea is communicated to the reader by *scoured* (sentence 4), *scrubbed* and *cracked and gleaming* (sentence 6)?
7. In the latter part of the description both adjectives and verbs are important. Which are the most significant ones in sentences 11, 12, and 14?

Assignment

Imitate this paragraph by writing one that describes a room with a person or persons in it and conveys a dominant impression. Be sure to include abundant details, as Baldwin does. Use striking adjectives and verbs and some figurative language. You might take a laboratory, an operating room, a hospital waiting room, a police station, a room prepared for a party just before the guests arrive, or the same room just after the party is over.

 A Schoolhouse

VERN WAGNER

1   My first glimpse of the White Star School in its weed-grown and treeless yard facing north on the south side of a shallow basin is an indelible memory. The building was alone on the prairie, a little gray, white-trimmed, peaked-roof schoolhouse with two windows on the east and two on the west, fronted by an enclosed entry with a shed roof. A white star was painted on the gable of the building; a short flagpole was fastened above that to the ridgepole. Back of this were two other buildings, an open shed for children to tie their horses in if they rode to school, and the coal house with the boys' toilet on one end and the girls' on the other. In the yard was the pump.
2   The inside of the schoolhouse was calcimined a pale blue with a whitish ceiling. The floor was a worn gray. Desks and seats were scattered about, the kind that are usually screwed to the floor, with iron grill work on the sides and legs. There was a small teacher's desk, an old round coal stove in the middle of the floor with a pipe going up then back to the chimney at the south end, a water cooler on a stand, a large wooden cupboard where books and supplies were kept, a glove hanging from one corner of the ceiling on a pulley,

Vern Wagner, "The White Star School," *Western Humanities Review,* Vol. 11 (Autumn 1957).

a map case. There was a blackboard across the front of the room, a kerosene lamp in a bracket on the wall, no blinds at the windows, a picture of Lincoln and another of Washington on the back wall. A dusty American flag was fastened above the blackboard. There was also the flagpole outside, a prow on the front gable. There was a windup phonograph with six records, an organ rendition of "Always," the "William Tell Overture," a record to teach the identification of various instruments, and three lesser numbers. The school smelled of stale, locked-in air, as distinctive an odor as that of a beer parlor.

3   The school and its yard were haunted with echoes from a quarter century's children, their pulses and shapeless dreams. It was worn, tragic, a country school on the first day following a summer's glad forgetfulness by its young. It had been patient and deserted then but for rare derisive forays made by passing youngsters all through the heat of June, July and August. The building stood there. It did not sit. It stood as the wooden weapon against ignorance and defeat, the house of community hope and of the future. It stood alone on the high upland prairie, braving cold and heat, a land ship on a motionless voyage of discovery into human possibility. It was wholly inspiring. Only in separated views was it depressing. At nineteen, scared as I was, I felt how, above all, upright it was. I was at last a teacher housed in my own school.

STUDY QUESTIONS

Organization and Content

1. What three things about the schoolhouse does the author take up in his three paragraphs?
2. Paragraph 1 lists many details. Which of these details best convey an impression of the school facilities and location?
3. Paragraph 2 also gives many specific details. What feeling do they give you about the schoolhouse?
4. Which of the details are purely informational? Which have something to do with color, shape, or condition?
5. Besides information and sense impressions, what feelings does the author succeed in conveying about the school in paragraph 3?
6. What interpretation does the author give of what the building represented? Explain how metaphor helps in the interpretation.

Sentence Structure

1. By what means has the author made some sentences especially long—for example, sentences 2 and 4 of paragraph 1, sentences 4 and 5 of paragraph 2?

2. What similarity of pattern do these four sentences have?
3. Point out the shortest sentences in the paragraphs.
4. Do these very short sentences have any special purpose or effect?

Diction

1. Look up *indelible, derisive, forays.*
2. Are the adjectives more important for their denotative or for their connotative value?
3. Do the adjectives appeal to any senses other than sight?
4. Which are more important in this description, the verbs or the adjectives? Why?
5. Is there a difference in the vocabulary of paragraph 3 and that of paragraph 2?

Assignment

Write three paragraphs on a building—the first paragraph on the exterior, the second on the interior, and the third on the feelings that the building created in an observer. Take a church, a country store, a barracks, a camp, a bank, or a hotel. It might be best to select as the subject either a rather new building or an extremely old one. Be sure to note a great many specific details.

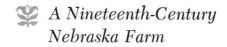

A Nineteenth-Century Nebraska Farm

WILLA CATHER

1   Early the next morning I ran out-of-doors to look about me. I had been told that ours was the only wooden house west of Black Hawk—until you came to the Norwegian settlement, where there were several. Our neighbours lived in sod houses and dugouts—comfortable but not very roomy. Our white frame house, with a storey and half-storey above the basement, stood at the east end of what I might call the farm yard, with the windmill close by the kitchen door. From the windmill the ground sloped westward, down to the barns and granaries and pig-yards. This slope was trampled hard

From Willa Cather, *My Ántonia.* Reprinted by permission of the publisher, Houghton Mifflin Company.

and bare, and washed out in winding gullies by the rain. Beyond the corncribs, at the bottom of the shallow draw, was a muddy little pond, with rusty willow bushes growing about it. The road from the post-office came directly by our door, crossed the farmyard, and curved round this little pond, beyond which it began to climb the gentle swell of unbroken prairie to the west. There, along the western sky-line it skirted a great cornfield, much larger than any field I had ever seen. This cornfield, and the sorghum patch behind the barn, were the only broken land in sight. Everywhere, as far as the eye could reach, there was nothing but rough, shaggy, red grass, most of it as tall as I.

2   North of the house, inside the ploughed fire-breaks, grew a thick-set strip of box-elder trees, low and bushy, their leaves already turning yellow. This hedge was nearly a quarter of a mile long, but I had to look very hard to see it at all. The little trees were insignificant against the grass. It seemed as if the grass were about to run over them, and over the plum-patch behind the sod chicken-house.

3   As I looked about me I felt that the grass was the country, as the water is the sea. The red of the grass made all the great prairie the colour of wine-stains, or of certain seaweeds when they are first washed up. And there was so much motion in it; the whole country seemed, somehow, to be running.

STUDY QUESTIONS

Organization and Content

1. Cather describes a much larger area than Baldwin or Wagner did. What general plan does she use to make clear the arrangement of the items in space?
2. The observer is a ten-year-old boy. If you made a map of the area described, at what point would you place him?
3. What item is emphasized at the end of paragraph 1? What receives most emphasis in paragraph 2? How does paragraph 3 differ in content from paragraphs 1 and 2?
4. Make a statement about the intentions of the author when she wrote this three-paragraph description.
5. Cather mentions more than fifteen items. Can you visualize them or sense them in other ways more precisely or less precisely than the items mentioned by Baldwin and Wagner? Why?

Sentence Structure

1. By what steps, in sentences 5–11, paragraph 1, does Cather lead the eye of the reader farther and farther from the starting point? What

words indicate each step? What position do the words have in the
sentences? Why do they have that position?

2. Why do some of sentences 5–11 begin with phrases or adverbs and
some with subjects of clauses?

3. Why does Cather use a comma after the first word in sentences 9
and 11?

4. What sentence elements keep the reader aware of the point of view
in paragraphs 2 and 3?

5. What is the advantage, for the management of the whole sentence,
of using inverted order ("grew . . . trees") in sentence 1, paragraph 2?

Diction

1. What is the difference between *storey* and *story?* What is the meaning
of *draw, unbroken, broken?*

2. Does paragraph 1 create an impression of beauty, ugliness, or some
other quality? Which words are mainly responsible for creating this
impression? Are they adjectives, adverbs, nouns, or verbs?

3. Does Cather use more or fewer adjectives than Baldwin and Wagner?
To what extent is the effect of her description different from that of
theirs?

4. In her last four sentences Cather makes comparisons. Point them out.
Why should figurative language be needed here but not in paragraph 1?

Assignment

Imitate Cather by describing a farm or landscape or other interesting
area of considerable extent within which you show the arrangement of
various items. Be careful to indicate directions (for example, north-south,
left-right) and make the space-pattern perfectly clear to the reader. End
with a dominant impression as Cather does.

 *A College Campus*

Ralph Ellison

It was a beautiful college. The buildings were old and covered
with vines and the roads gracefully winding, lined with hedges and
wild roses that dazzled the eyes in the summer sun. Honeysuckle
and purple wisteria hung heavy from the trees and white magnolias

From Ralph Ellison, *Invisible Man* (New York: Random House, Inc.).

mixed with their scents in the bee-humming air. I've recalled it often, here in my hole: How the grass turned green in the springtime and how the mocking birds fluttered their tails and sang, how the moon shone down on the buildings, how the bell in the chapel tower rang out the precious short-lived hours; how the girls in bright summer dresses promenaded the grassy lawn. Many times, here at night, I've closed my eyes and walked along the forbidden road that winds past the girls' dormitories, past the hall with the clock in the tower, its windows warmly aglow, on down past the small white Home Economics practice cottage, whiter still in the moonlight, and on down the road with its sloping and turning, paralleling the black powerhouse with its engines droning earth-shaking rhythms in the dark, its windows red from the glow of the furnace, on to where the road became a bridge over a dry riverbed, tangled with brush and clinging vines; the bridge of rustic logs, made for trysting, but virginal and untested by lovers; on up the road, past the buildings, with the southern verandas half-a-city-block long, to the sudden forking, barren of buildings, birds, or grass, where the road turned off to the insane asylum.

STUDY QUESTIONS

Organization and Content

1. Which sentence is the topic sentence of the paragraph?
2. How many different things does Ellison name in this paragraph by using nouns? Which nouns are general, and which specific?
3. Which details are the most concrete?
4. Which terms refer to color, sound, movement, size, and shape?
5. Why should the five sentences of the paragraph be arranged in this order?
6. What do the items named in sentence 3 have in common? Those of the *how*-clauses of sentence 4?
7. How does Ellison provide a moving point of view from which to present descriptive details? Contrast this point of view with that in the Cather selection.
8. Should the last detail of the paragraph (the insane asylum) be regarded as literal or symbolic?

Sentence Structure

1. Sentence 2 exemplifies the loose sentence; if it stopped after *old,* it would be complete. How does Ellison add so many more elements after *old?*
2. Contrast the structure of sentences 3 and 4.

3. Sentence 4 has several parallel elements. Indicate them.
4. Sentence 5 is very long and has many parallel elements. What words make the reader aware of the parallelism? Which phrases modify *walked* and which modify *winds?*
5. What is the function of the *with*-phrases in sentence 5? Note how the adjectives (modifiers) are arranged both before and after *cottage*. How does the material between semicolons operate in sentence 5?

Diction

1. Such words as *buildings, vines,* and *roads* are general. What terms does Ellison use to make his description more concrete? Are the adjectives or the verbs more important in making the description concrete?
2. Of the verbs in sentence 4, which are the most effective in suggesting sense impressions?
3. In terms of description what is the difference between "precious short-lived hours" and "bright summer dresses"?
4. Which words in sentence 5 have connotative power in addition to their denotations?

Assignment

Imitate this paragraph by writing a similar one about the campus of your school. Avoid sentimentality and include many details perceptible by the senses. Try to suggest, without speaking of them directly, what feelings the campus arouses in you.

 Camping in Louisiana

THOMAS SANCTON

There was a relatively high, sandy point near the mouth of the bayou, where we camped. The sun went down red into the lake and left a long, clear twilight. A few stars came out. A salty wind blew in from the Mexican Gulf; it came out of the south every night. The breeze swept over the rushes and made small waves break on the sandy, grassy shore. There was a red beacon light on weather-beaten piles out in the lake and its long reflection shimmered in the water. We sprayed our mosquito netting with citronella and built

From Thomas Sancton, "The Silver Horn," *Harper's Magazine* (February 1944). Reprinted by permission of Harper's Magazine, Inc.

up a driftwood fire and lay down on canvas bedrolls spread upon the thin, tough grass and sand. The trade wind blew through our tents throughout the night. We listened to the waves. We could smell the vast salt marshes far below us. A yellow moon came out of the gulf. Far down the lake we could see the lights of a railroad bridge. We felt the beauty of this wilderness like a hunger.

STUDY QUESTIONS

Organization and Content

1. What principle of organization governs the arrangement of the details in this paragraph?
2. In sentences 7, 9, 10, 12, and 13 *we* is the subject. Is there any difference between these sentences and the others in regard to content and effect?
3. Sancton projects images before the reader as if they were a series of photographs. What would be gained and lost if he used more commentary or interpretation?
4. Should the last sentence come at the end, or is there a better position for it?

Sentence Structure

1. How does this paragraph compare with "Domna Rejnev" and "A College Campus" as to number of words and sentences?
2. Two of Sancton's sentences have only five words each. Are they too short?
3. Only sentence 1 is a complex sentence. Which of the others are simple? Which compound? Suppose that sentences 5, 6, and 7, for example, were complex. How would the effect be altered?
4. Indicate as precisely as you can the effect that the sentence structure produces.

Diction

1. Why do you think Sancton used such a simple vocabulary?
2. Does he use a high proportion of adjectives?
3. Which adjectives are the most expressive? Which verbs?
4. How many abstract terms does Sancton use?

Assignment

Describe a place that made a deep impression upon you. Keep your sentences uncomplicated, and use abundant details. The impression need not be one of beauty. It might be, for example, loneliness, desolation, ugliness, or awe.

🌸 *Animals*
on the Western Plains

FRANCIS PARKMAN

But in the meantime my ride had been by no means a solitary one. The face of the country was dotted far and wide with countless hundreds of buffalo. They trooped along in files and columns, bulls, cows, and calves, on the green faces of the declivities in front. They scrambled away over the hills to the right and left; and far off, the pale blue swells in the extreme distance were dotted with innumerable specks. Sometimes I surprised shaggy old bulls grazing alone, or sleeping behind the ridges I ascended. They would leap up at my approach, stare stupidly at me through their tangled manes, and then gallop heavily away. The antelope were very numerous; and as they are always bold when in the neighborhood of buffalo, they would approach to look at me, gaze intently with their great round eyes, then suddenly leap aside, and stretch lightly away over the prairie, as swiftly as a race-horse. Squalid, ruffian-like wolves sneaked through the hollows and sandy ravines. Several times I passed through villages of prairie-dogs, who sat, each at the mouth of his burrow, holding his paws before him in a supplicating attitude, and yelping away most vehemently, whisking his little tail with every squeaking cry he uttered. Prairie-dogs are not fastidious in their choice of companions; various long checkered snakes were sunning themselves in the midst of the village, and demure little gray owls, with a large white ring around each eye, were perched side by side with the rightful inhabitants. The prairie teemed with life. Again and again I looked toward the crowded hill-sides, and was sure I saw horsemen; and riding near, with a mixture of hope and dread, for Indians were abroad, I found them transformed into a group of buffalo. There was nothing in human shape amid all this vast congregation of brute forms.

From Francis Parkman, *The California and Oregon Trail* (1849).

STUDY QUESTIONS

Organization and Content

1. Francis Parkman tells in this paragraph of the animals he saw while riding on the Western plains in 1846. What is his point of view?
2. Though Parkman was alone and temporarily lost, his ride was certainly not "a solitary one"! How many different kinds of animals does he mention?
3. Of what significance is the last sentence?

Sentence Structure

1. How many of Parkman's sentences start with a subject-verb construction? How many have some sort of modifier before the subject?
2. Do any of the sentences begin with a dependent clause?
3. What is the effect of having a majority of sentences constructed like Parkman's?

Diction

1. Notice that Parkman describes the characteristic movements of animals. He does this by means of carefully chosen verbs. Count the verbs in the paragraph. Which three verbs have the greatest force?
2. This paragraph makes an extremely strong appeal to the eye—to the sense of sight. However, not all of this appeal comes from verbs. What details expressed by means of nouns and adjectives appeal to the eye?
3. Look up *declivities, supplicating, vehemently, demure, teemed, congregation, squalid.*
4. What is the effect of mentioning the "squalid, ruffian-like wolves" between the antelope and the prairie-dogs? What is the connotation of *squalid?*

Assignment

Few people today could have the same experience that Parkman had. But one should be able to create a similar paragraph with a moving point of view based on city sights or on movements of things observed during a windy day. At certain seasons almost anyone could write such a paragraph describing birds rather than animals. In your paragraph use sharp, precise verbs to convey the exact look of the movements you describe.

✿ Herding Buffalo in India

RUDYARD KIPLING

Then Mowgli picked out a shady place, and lay down and slept while the buffaloes grazed round him. Herding in India is one of the laziest things in the world. The cattle move and crunch, and lie down, and move on again, and they do not even low. They only grunt, and the buffaloes very seldom say anything, but get down into the muddy pools one after another, and work their way into the mud till only their noses and staring china-blue eyes show above the surface, and there they lie like logs. The sun makes the rocks dance in the heat, and the herd-children hear one kite (never any more) whistling almost out of sight overhead, and they know that if they died, or a cow died, that kite would sweep down, and the next kite miles away would see him drop and would follow, and the next, and the next, and almost before they were dead there would be a score of hungry kites come out of nowhere. Then they sleep and wake and sleep again, and weave little baskets of dried grass and put grasshoppers in them; or catch two praying-mantises and make them fight; or string a necklace of red and black jungle-nuts; or watch a lizard basking on a rock, or a snake hunting a frog near the wallows. Then they sing long, long songs with odd native quavers at the end of them, and the day seems longer than most people's whole lives, and perhaps they make a mud castle with mud figures of men and horses and buffaloes, and put reeds into the men's hands, and pretend that they are kings and the figures are their armies, or that they are gods to be worshipped. Then evening comes, and the children call, and the buffaloes lumber up out of the sticky mud with noises like gunshots going off one after the other, and they all string across the gray plain back to the twinkling village lights.

STUDY QUESTIONS

Organization and Content

1. Kipling's paragraph tells about a certain customary activity in the out-of-doors: herding buffalo in India. What are the main subtopics that are dealt with in the paragraph?

From Rudyard Kipling, "Tiger, Tiger!" in *The Jungle Book* (1894).

2. What things do the herders see? Hear? Do?
3. Is this paragraph rich in details or not? Explain.
4. Why does the day of the herders seem long and tedious?

Sentence Structure

1. Notice that Kipling's sentences contain many coordinating conjunctions. Mark the coordinating conjunctions in sentences 3–7.
2. Which is the longest sentence of the paragraph?
3. What is the effect of lengthening sentences with many coordinating conjunctions?

Diction

1. Count the verbs in the paragraph. Is the number large or small?
2. Make a list of the verbs. How do these verbs compare, for precision and vigor, with those of Parkman in the preceding reading?
3. Which are the most effective of Kipling's adjectives?

Assignment

Write a similar paragraph about herding in an American scene, or about the succession of things experienced while hunting, or about trying to make the time pass anywhere when one is a bored child. Or you might achieve the same effect of monotony plus activity by telling about the day of a convalescent or about the evening of a babysitter. Cram your paragraph with details, and stress verbs!

Nightfall on a Tropical Island

Gilbert C. Klingel

1   The tide had fallen and near the top of the beach lay a long pile of seaweed that had been washed ashore and was strewn in narrow arcs as far as the eye could see. The sun turned cherry red, then became elliptical, and in an angry blaze settled behind the clouds, sending a momentary flash of green light before it disappeared. This green luminescence was almost a nightly occurrence and lasted for

From Gilbert C. Klingel, *The Ocean Island* (*Inagua*) (New York: Dodd, Mead and Company, Inc.)

fifty or sixty seconds at the exact moment of the sun's sinking. Shortly after the sky became gray and then purplish.

2   Then in the darkness, from the piles of seaweed at my side came a faint rustling, like the swishing of fine silk. As I listened the sound became stronger, reached its maximum and continued steadily. I lit a match and looked downwards. There on the beach were hundreds upon hundreds of beach hoppers, little translucent crustaceans a half inch or so in length. They were hopping and jumping over the sand in a frenzy. It was the combined scrapings and bumpings of millions of these creatures that blended to make the rustling. Where were they a bare fifteen minutes ago? What brought these myriads of crustaceans climbing upwards through the damp clinging sand at the exact moment of nightfall? What invisible crustacean time signal told them their hour of activity was at hand down in the wet and the dark? Yet there they were, swarming where all day had been only blank sand and swirling water. Then, even as I watched, a number, disapproving of my presence, dug themselves in again, sinking smoothly and evenly as though let down by an invisible elevator.

3   The coming of nightfall was the signal for the coming of other nocturnal animals. The bushes and grasses began rustling with the movements of the hermit crabs; whirring moths swept past my ear and went on into the dark; beetles droned across the glades and blundered into my hair; a few mosquitoes sang busily, taking the places of the flies that had buzzed all day and were then asleep on the under surfaces of leaves. Back in the interior the low notes of a pair of night herons echoed across the surface of the saltpond and faintly I could hear them splashing in the shallows. High in the zenith the faint geese-like notes of a flock of flamingos came filtering down; every evening after dusk they circled the beach and then settled on the far side of the lake back of the settlement. Here they spent the night gabbling to each other; their tones were reminiscent of the chatter of old ladies at a sewing circle.

STUDY QUESTIONS

Organization and Content

1. Gilbert C. Klingel is a naturalist and prize-winning nature writer who was shipwrecked on the island of Inagua in the Bahamas and who observed fauna and flora there. Does his description contain terms or ideas that the descriptions by nonscientists lack?

2. If this material were prepared for a scientific journal, would alterations be required? Additions? Deletions?
3. To what topic is paragraph 1 devoted? What are the topics dealt with in paragraphs 2 and 3?
4. Which of the paragraphs has a topic sentence? How many items does Klingel use to support the topic idea? Why does he not have topic sentences for the other two paragraphs?
5. Is it reasonable to place the three paragraphs in the order that Klingel uses?

Sentence Structure

1. What is the advantage of inverted order ("lay . . . pile") in the first sentence? In sentence 1, paragraph 2?
2. Why does the structure of sentence 2, paragraph 2, suit the thought it conveys?
3. In sentence 2, paragraph 2, why not have commas after *listened* and *maximum?*
4. What is the purpose of the three interrogative sentences in paragraph 2?
5. How does the last sentence of paragraph 2 differ in structure from sentence 2, paragraph 1?
6. Only in paragraph 3 does Klingel use semicolons. What is the purpose of this punctuation?

Diction

1. Description has to do with the effects of things on our human senses—on sight, smell, hearing, taste, touch. Klingel emphasizes colors, sounds, shapes, and movements. List the words that describe these four aspects of things.
2. Which terms give the sharpest, most precise impressions of colors? Sounds? Movements?
3. What is the difference between *luminescence* and *luminosity?* What is the relation of *luminescence* to *adolescent, obsolescence,* and *senescence?*
4. Look up *translucent, crustaceans, myriads, nocturnal, zenith.*
5. Where has Klingel used figurative language?
6. There are words formed to imitate sounds—such as *clang, hiss, moo.* Forming words of this sort is called onomatopoeia. Identify the onomatopoetic words in paragraphs 2 and 3.
7. Compare Klingel's verbs, for precision and vigor, with those of Parkman.
8. To get a sharper idea of their connotations, look up *angry* (paragraph 1), *blank* (paragraph 2), *filtering* (paragraph 3).

Assignment

Describe nightfall in the country, at a beach, at a lake, in the mountains, or any other place where you can detect the change that comes with night. Emphasize sounds, and be sure to select exact words to represent the noises that you describe.

New York City in Summer

SAUL BELLOW

There was still a redness in the sky, like the flame at the back of a vast baker's oven; the day hung on, gaping fierily over the black of the Jersey shore. The Hudson had a low luster, and the sea was probably no more numbing in its cold, Leventhal imagined, than the subway under his feet was in its heat; the trains rushing by under the gratings and along the slanting brown rock walls seemed to set off charges of metal dust. He passed through a small park where the double circle of benches were jammed. There were lines before each drinking fountain, the warm water limping and jetting into the stone basins. On all sides of the green square, the traffic of cars and cabs whipped endlessly, and the cumbersome busses crawled groaning, steering down from the tall blue oblong of light at the summit of the street through a bluish pallor. In the bushy, tree-grown corners, children played and screamed, and a revivalist band sang and drummed and trumpeted on one of the sidewalks. Leventhal did not stay long in the park. He strolled homeward. He thought he would mix a cold drink and lie down beside an open window.

STUDY QUESTIONS

Organization and Content

1. Divide the paragraph into its logical divisions.
2. What main impression is made in each division?
3. How are these divisions related to the point of view of the observer? Which sentences show observations and thoughts of the observer, which his actions?
4. Compare Bellow's description of the sunset with Klingel's.
5. Would "Summer in New York City" be a better title?

Sentence Structure

1. Sentences 1 and 4 begin with *There,* so that the subject comes after the verb. Where are the modifiers of the subject placed? Is this a favorable position?

From Saul Bellow, *The Victim* (New York: Vanguard Press, Inc.). Copyright © 1947 by Saul Bellow.

2. What is the purpose of the opening words in sentences 5 and 6? How do the rest of the sentences begin?
3. Does Bellow use verbs in passive voice or active voice?

Diction

1. What terms have the most vivid descriptive effect in sentence 1?
2. How does the diction of sentence 2 contrast with that of 1?
3. Note the importance of verbs in this description. Which of them are present participles, verbs ending with the suffix *-ing?* Which are the most specific?
4. Why can it be said that the following are examples of figurative language: *gaping* (sentence 1), *limping* (sentence 4), *whipped, crawled, groaning* (sentence 5)?

Assignment

Imitate Bellow by writing a paragraph in which you describe what you see, hear, and feel on a short walk through a town or city. *Before* writing, *list* the details that will make your description vivid. Use the most *specific* terms you can find.

 **A Desert Storm**

Edward Abbey

1   In July and August, here on the high desert, come the thunderstorms. The mornings begin clear and dazzling bright, the sky as blue as the Virgin's cloak, unflawed by a trace of cloud from the Book Cliffs on the north to the Blue Mountains eighty miles south, from the Sierra La Sal on the east to the notched reef of the San Rafael one hundred miles west. By noon, though, the clouds are beginning to form over the mountains, coming it seems out of nowhere, out of nothing, a special creation. They merge and multiply, cumulinimbi piling up like whipped cream, like mashed potatoes, like seafoam, building upon one another into a second mountain range greater in magnitude than the terrestrial range below. The massive forms jostle and grate, ions collide, and the sound of thunder is heard on

the sun-drenched land. More clouds emerge from empty sky, anvil-headed giants with glints of lightning in their depths. An armada forms, advances, floating on a plane of air that makes it appear, from below, as a fleet of ships must appear to the fishes in the sea.

2   At my observation point on a sandstone monolith, the sun is blazing down as intensely as ever, the air crackling with dry heat. But the storm clouds are taking over the sky and as they approach the battle breaks out. Lightning streaks among the clouds like gunfire; volleys of thunder shake the air. So long as the clouds exchange their bolts with one another no rain falls, but now they begin bombarding the ridgetops and buttes below. Forks of lightning, like illuminated nerves, link heaven and earth. The wind is rising and for anyone with sense enough to get in out of the rain, now is the time to seek shelter. A lash of lightning flickers over Wilson Mesa, scorching the brush, splitting a pinyon pine. Northeast, over the Yellow Cat area, rain is already sweeping down, falling not vertically but in a graceful curve, like a beaded curtain drawn lightly across the desert. Between the rain and the mountains, among the tumbled masses of vapor floats a segment of a rainbow. But where I stand the storm is only beginning.

3   Above me the clouds roll in, unfurling and smoking billows in malignant violet, dense as wool. Most of the sky is lidded over but the sun remains clear, halfway down the west, shining beneath the storm. Over my head the clouds thicken, then crack and split with a roar like that of cannon balls tumbling down a marble staircase; their bellies open—too late to run now!—and suddenly the rain comes down.

4   *Comes down:* not softly, not gently, with no quality of mercy, but like heavy water in buckets, raindrops like lead pellets smashing and splattering on the flat rock, knocking the berries off the juniper, plastering my shirt to my back, drumming on my hat like hailstones, running like a waterfall off the brim. The ˙pinnacles and arches and balanced rocks and elephant-backed fins of sandstone, glazed with water but still exposed to the sun, gleam like old gray silver in the holy—no, unholy—light that slants in *under*, not through, the black ceiling of the storm.

5   For five minutes the deluge continues under a barrage of lightning and thunder and then trails off quickly, diminishes to a shower, to nothing, while the clouds, moving off, rumble in the distance. A fresh golden light breaks through and now in the east, over the turrets and domes, appears the rainbow sign, a double rainbow with one foot in the canyon of the Colorado and the other far north in

Salt Wash Valley. Behind the rainbow, framed within it, I can see jags of lightning play among the stormy skies beyond.

6   The afternoon sun falls lower; above the mountains and the ragged black clouds floats the new moon, pale fragment of what is to come; in another hour, at sundown, Venus will appear, planet of love, to glow bright as chromium low in the western sky. The desert storm is over and through the pure, sweet, pellucid air the cliff swallows and the nighthawks plunge and swerve, with cries of hunger and warning and—who knows?—perhaps of exultation as well.

STUDY QUESTIONS

Organization and Content

1. Abbey provides five or six indications of time during which the storm occurs. What are they? According to what principle of order is the material organized?
2. Explain what each paragraph accomplishes in the total account of the storm.
3. At what point does the climax of the storm come? (Look up *climax*.)
4. What determines the beginning (sentence 1) and the end (sentence 2, paragraph 6) of the description?
5. Abbey makes numerous references to sun, clouds, lightning, and rain. Which of these elements dominate the interest in the individual paragraphs?
6. What is Abbey's point of view?
7. Which receives more attention—color or sound?

Sentence Structure

1. Does sentence 1, paragraph 1, with its inverted order, have a more emphatic effect than it would have with normal order?
2. Four types of sentences are much used: (1) simple sentence, often short; (2) balanced sentence (compound); (3) loose sentence (complex, with subject-verb-complement first and modifiers at end); (4) periodic sentence (complex, with introductory modifiers at beginning and main clause at end). About half of Abbey's sentences are of one of these types. Which one?
3. Another feature of Abbey's sentence style is his use of parallel grammatical elements, such as the *from* . . . *to* phrases in sentence 2, paragraph 1, and similar phrases in sentences 3 and 4. Point out other examples of parallelism. What effect does this parallelism produce?
4. Abbey also makes use of present participles. Where do they usually appear in his sentences?
5. Abbey uses a few appositives (as in sentence 6: "clouds . . . , anvil-headed giants . . ."). Point out two appositives in paragraph 6.
6. Is Abbey's sentence structure monotonous, or does he use enough variety of sentence structure?

Diction

1. Look up *magnitude, terrestrial, armada, monolith, buttes, malignant, turrets, pellucid.* Which of them come from Latin roots? Learn the meaning of the Latin roots.
2. Does the vividness of this description come mainly from specific adjectives, verbs, or figurative language?
3. Point out the verbs and adjectives with most specific meaning.
4. The selection is rich in similes. How many does Abbey use? Are any of them trite? Choose four which you regard as the freshest and least trite.
5. Explain how these metaphors function: "anvil-headed giants" (sentence 6, paragraph 1), "bombarding" (sentence 4, paragraph 2), "lash . . . flickers" (sentence 7, paragraph 2), "lidded over" (sentence 2, paragraph 3), "play" (sentence 3, paragraph 5).

Assignment

1. In one paragraph describe the beginning of a storm.
2. In three paragraphs describe the beginning, the climax, and the ending of a storm.
3. If you have no chance to observe a storm, write one paragraph describing a sunrise.

Whatever you write, try to make use of figurative language after the manner of Abbey. Pay attention to both colors and sounds.

 Autumn in the Woods

John Hersey

The hills beyond the first step of the ridge are round, and they're easy, not too steep, so they'd had farms on them in former years, and I went along their shoulders and eventually left the tarred road and walked down the unmaintained dirt track that leads to the abandoned knife-and-scissors works on Chestnut Burr Creek—through patches of woods of various stages of growth, depending on when the farmers who'd been there had given up and quit, past newly grown-up sprout land of sumacs and hardhack and meadow cedars

and young wild cherries, and past other sections—of course you had
stone walls dividing these growths, right through the woods—other
sections with middle-sized popples and sapling elms and dirty birches,
and then past adult forests, great maples, hickories, ashes, oaks, and
I tell you, all these woods were dressed in colors you simply couldn't
imagine. That afternoon was a climax. I don't know if there'll be
but two or three more such days this year, and maybe none that
bright, and I guess there won't ever be another one in my whole
lifetime exactly like that one, because October around here, as you
know, is just a mass of colors in constant motion; the colors are fugi-
tive, you can't stop them from changing and running away. Even
every minute that afternoon they changed. There was a blue haze
hanging on the hills, and above that there were some small soft gray
clouds, and when one of them blew across the sun, all the colors
in the woods changed their tones, and the yellows took charge over
the softer reds which, just a few seconds before, in the full sunlight,
had had the intensity of the center of fireplace flames. I've read in
books about the sadness of autumn, the way time turns down toward
death in the fall, but I was happy through and through; I saw the
colors, and they made me happy. I don't know what's happened these
last few days; I'm utterly bewildered. I only know I'll never be as
happy again as I was the other afternoon in the woods. The white
oaks made a kind of backdrop, because, you know, they hold their
leaves the longest, like small leather gloves, still solid green; while
the elms and hickories had gone brown early in the dry August we
had this year, and in the wind on Ella's train the week before they'd
been almost stripped, and their skeletons made a blackish mesh, so
the displays of the other trees seemed even more prodigal: deep
coppers of the sumac and dogwood, pure yellow of birches and, here
and there, ironwood and sassafras, and, best of all, the incredible
orange glow of hard maples—like the inside of a Halloween pumpkin
when the candle's lit. There was a dry breeze blowing, and leaves
of all colors were falling slantwise across the old track where I was
walking. On the stone walls there were some white lichens that stood
out sharply because of all the color around. Once in a while I passed
an old cellar hole, with a big lilac bush or overgrown privet bush
standing in front of it, incongruous in the woods, remnants of civilization—you know? I came to the ruin of the knife works and walked
along the bank of the millpond, and there it was as if I saw two
autumns—one real and the other reflected, until for a second a breeze
sort of stepped on the water and moved both the mirrored and the
floating leaves on the surface a little. I walked to a big dead trunk
of a fallen tree lying on the ground at the upper end of the pond,

and I put my social-studies book down on it, and it seems as if putting my book down was the beginning of my troubles. Anyway I just sat on the log and watched and waited.

STUDY QUESTIONS

Organization and Content

1. In addition to description proper this selection contains an element of personal thought and action. Which element is given more space?
2. The paragraph contains fifteen sentences. Can they be divided into obvious or logical groups? How is the paragraph organized?
3. The speaker mentions many kinds of trees. On what basis does he group those mentioned in sentence 1?
4. On what basis does he group those of sentence 9? Are they the same kinds mentioned in sentence 1?
5. How does sentence 2 contrast with sentence 1? Explain the relation of sentence 2 to sentences 1 and 3. How is sentence 5 related to sentence 4?
6. What is the relation of sentences 10 and 11? What different element is introduced in sentences 12 and 13?
7. Does sentence 5 have material more general or more particular than sentence 9?
8. Are there any images except visual ones? Any except those of color and shape?

Sentence Structure

1. The speaker here is a boy who is responding to questions. We are aware of a speaking voice. The style is more *colloquial*—that is, conversational—than in earlier selections. (Look up *colloquial,* and learn the roots from which it comes. Do not confuse it with *locality.*) Even though the first sentence is long, its very length is evidence of a colloquial style. Why? To appreciate the difference between formal writing and colloquial writing, explain the difference in difficulty and effect between "thus they are easy, not too declivitous; therefore they had had farms . . ." and "and they're easy, not too steep, so they'd had farms. . . ."
2. How many *and*'s does sentence 1 contain? What does your answer tell you about the grammatical complexity of the sentence?
3. What is the function of the three dashes in sentence 1? How are they related to colloquial style?
4. What evidence shows that sentence 4 is colloquial? Why is sentence 9 less colloquial, in its sentence structure?
5. Compare the complexity of sentences here with that of the sentences in the Kazin selection.

Diction

1. Look up *sapling, prodigal, lichens, privet, incongruous. Prodigal* and *incongruous* are less colloquial than most of the diction. Why?
2. Which of the following phrases seem more formal, and which less formal: "had given up and quit"; "colors you simply couldn't imagine"; "had the intensity of the center of fireplace flames"; "hickories had gone brown early in the dry August we had this year"; "incredible orange glow"; "for a second a breeze sort of stepped on the water"?
3. Compare the use of similes and metaphors here with that in the storm description by Abbey.

Assignment

Describe the things you see on a walk—through woods, in a park, along a road, or across the campus. Include plenty of details, and write in a colloquial style, but do not use slang.

❧ A Family Reunion

JOHN UPDIKE

The twins bring down from the barn the horse-shoes and the quoits. Uncle Jesse drives the stakes and pegs in the places that, after three summers, still show as spots of depressed spareseness in the grass. The sun, reaching toward noon, domineers over the meadow; the shade of the walnut tree grows smaller and more noticeably cool. By noon, all have arrived, including the Dodge station wagon from central Pennsylvania, the young pregnant Wilmington cousin who married an airline pilot, and the White Plains people, who climb from their car looking like clowns, wearing red-striped shorts and rhinestone-studded sunglasses. Handshakes are exchanged that feel to one man like a knobbed wood carving and to the other like a cow's slippery, unresisting teat. Women kiss, kiss stickily, with little overlapping patches of adhesive cheek and clicking conflicts of spectacle rims, under the white unslanting sun. The very insects shrink toward the shade. The eating begins. Clams steam, corn steams, salad wilts, butter runs, hot dogs turn, torn chicken shines in the

© Copyright 1964 by John Updike. Reprinted from *The Music School*, by John Updike by permission of Alfred A. Knopf, Inc. This story originally appeared in *The New Yorker*.

savage light. Iced tea, brewed in forty-quart milk cans, chuckles when sloshed. Paper plates buckle on broad laps. Plastic butter knives, asked to cut cold ham, balk. Children underfoot in the pleased frenzy eat only potato chips. Somehow, as the first wave of appetite subsides, the long tables turn musical, and a murmur rises to the blank sky, a cackle rendered harmonious by a remote singleness of ancestor; a kind of fabric is woven and hung, a tapestry of the family fortunes, the threads of which include milkmen, ministers, mailmen, bankruptcy, death by war, death by automobile, insanity—a strangely prevalent thread, the thread of insanity. Never far from a farm or the memory of a farm, the family has hovered in honorable obscurity, between poverty and wealth, between jail and high office.

STUDY QUESTIONS

Organization and Content

1. Into what main sections would you divide the paragraph?
2. Updike shows us a group of people in a setting. What part does the sun play in the setting? What part does the food play in the account of the people?
3. From what point of view is this paragraph written?
4. Some of the people are briefly described, but a few are mentioned without description (for example, those from central Pennsylvania and the Wilmington cousin). Why?
5. Which element predominates: story, information, or description?

Sentence Structure

1. What is the effect of putting all the verbs in present or present perfect tense?
2. What is the effect of having nearly all the verbs in the active voice? Why is the passive voice used in sentences 5 and 14?
3. What is the proportion of monosyllabic words in sentences 9–12? How many words of more than two syllables occur in these sentences? What is the grammatical structure of these sentences? Explain what effect Updike achieves by composing such sentences with such words in such structure.
4. Explain how the rhythm of sentences 13–15 differs from the rhythm of sentences 9–12. What causes this difference?

Diction

1. What is the historical relation between *sparseness* and *spark; bankruptcy* and *interrupt; prevalent, valiant,* and *valuable; obscurity* and *shower?*

2. Which terms most vividly describe how people look? What they do? Which terms are most important for the setting?
3. Updike uses similes in sentences 4 and 5. What do they suggest about the people besides their appearance and the tactual impressions they had?
4. Which sentences contain the most alliteration?
5. How many metaphors do you find in sentence 14? What is the difference between these and the metaphor in sentence 10?

Assignment

Imitate this paragraph rather closely by writing a paragraph in which you describe a group of people in a setting: for example, guests at a party, members of a club at a meeting, a political gathering, or a big family dinner. Tell how some of them look and what they do. Pay particular attention to verbs, differing sentence lengths, and sentence rhythms in your paragraph.

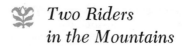

Two Riders
in the Mountains

WALTER VAN TILBURG CLARK

Gil and I crossed the eastern divide about two by the sun. We pulled up for a look at the little town in the big valley and the mountains on the other side, with the crest of the Sierra showing faintly beyond like the rim of a day moon. We didn't look as long as we do sometimes; after winter range, we were excited about getting back to town. When the horses had stopped trembling from the last climb, Gil took off his sombrero, pushed his sweaty hair back with the same hand, and returned the sombrero, the way he did when something was going to happen. We reined to the right and went slowly down the steep stage road. It was a switch-back road, gutted by the run-off of the winter storms, and with brush beginning to grow up in it again since the stage had stopped running. In the pockets under the red earth banks, where the wind was cut off, the spring sun was hot as summer, and the air was full of a hot, melting pine smell. Rivulets of water trickled down shining on the sides of the cuts. The jays screeched in the trees and flashed through the sunlight in the clearings in swift, long dips. Squirrels and chipmunks chittered in the brush and along the tops of snow-sodden logs. On the outside turns, though, the wind got to us and dried the sweat under our shirts and brought up, instead of the hot resin, the smell of the marshy green valley. In the west the heads of a few clouds showed, the kind that come up with the early heat, but they were lying still, and over us the sky was clear and deep.

STUDY QUESTIONS

Organization and Content

1. This is the opening paragraph of a novel of 1940. It quickly suggests "story," some details giving us necessary information about the past and others suggesting action in the future. What are these details in sentences 1–5?
2. Along with the story details the paragraph contains many descriptive details. Which ones make us see the characters doing things? Which ones tell us how they felt? Which ones let us see the things that the cowboys observed?
3. What kind of descriptive detail predominates?
4. Does the description of the setting produce a dominant impression on the reader?
5. Does the paragraph follow any principle of organization?

Sentence Structure

1. Are the verbs in the active voice or the passive voice?
2. How does Clark link sentences 1–5, making it easy for the reader to proceed from one to the next?
3. What repeated word does Clark use to provide the link between sentences 5 and 6?
4. Sentences 7–10 do not have such repetitions. What assumption makes us able to do without them?
5. In which sentences has Clark begun with some element other than the subject?
6. Why should sentences 8–10 all begin in the same way?
7. Is the sentence construction too simple? How does it compare with that of the Hersey selection?

Diction

1. Is there any etymological connection between *sombrero* and *somber, rivulets* and *river, chittered* and *chattered?*
2. This paragraph is in the words of a storyteller, Gil's companion, and we hear his voice. Does he talk formally or informally? Give evidence: choice of words, use or nonuse of contractions, sentences with or without involved relationships between the parts.
3. Is this paragraph as colloquial as the one by Hersey?
4. Most of the words are specific rather than general. Which are the most effective in the description because they are very specific—which nouns, adjectives, verbs?

Assignment

1. Write a paragraph describing a view from a hill or mountain. Divide your attention between distant details and details near at hand. Be very specific.
2. Write a paragraph describing the look, feel, and smell of an area in a park or along a road or street. Stress details that are characteristic of the season—spring, summer, fall, or winter.

 *Cats, Dogs, and a Boy*

John Steinbeck

He closed the screen door after him and went out into the cool blue morning. The birds were noisy in the dawn and the ranch cats came down from the hill like blunt snakes. They had been hunting gophers in the dark, and although the four cats were full of gopher meat, they sat in a semi-circle at the back door and mewed piteously for milk. Doubletree Mutt and Smasher moved sniffing along the edge of the brush, performing the duty with rigid ceremony, but when Jody whistled, their heads jerked up and their tails waved. They plunged down to him, wriggling their skins and yawning. Jody patted their heads seriously, and moved on to the weathered scrap pile. He selected an old broom handle and a short piece of inch-square scrap wood. From his pocket he took a shoelace and tied the ends of the sticks loosely together to make a flail. He whistled his new weapon through the air and struck the ground experimentally, while the dogs leaped aside and whined with apprehension.

STUDY QUESTIONS

Organization and Content

1. From what point of view is this scene presented?
2. What determines the order in which the sentences are presented?
3. State in one sentence what the paragraph is about.
4. Is the main emphasis here on action or on description? Which descriptive details seem most precise and vivid?

Sentence Structure

1. Do the sentences have mainly a subject-verb-complement pattern or some other pattern?
2. By what transitional links are sentences 1–3 connected? Sentences 4–6? Sentences 7–9?
3. Does Steinbeck use too many coordinate elements (those connected by *and* and *but*) in his sentences?
4. In which sentences do subordinate clauses provide variety?
5. Is Steinbeck's sentence style like Clark's or unlike it?

Diction

1. Do nouns, verbs, or adjectives seem most important to the strength and effect of this paragraph?
2. Which words communicate details of color, sound, and movement?
3. Is "blue morning" a figure of speech? What does the simile "like blunt snakes" communicate that would require more words in nonfigurative language?
4. Compare the sentence you wrote on the content of the paragraph with Steinbeck's sentences. Is there a difference in terms of general and specific diction?

Assignment

Make notes on the activities of a child in a particular setting. Then write a paragraph like Steinbeck's, expressing as vividly as possible the movements and actions of your subject. Include an animal or two if you can.

🌼 *A Stagecoach Trip*

CHARLES DICKENS

1   The coachman mounts to the box, Mr. Weller jumps up behind, the Pickwickians pull their coats round their legs and their shawls over their noses, the helpers pull the horse-cloths off, the coachman shouts out a cheery "All right," and away they go.

2   They have rumbled through the streets, and jolted over the stones, and at length reach the wide and open country. The wheels skim over the hard and frosty ground: and the horses, bursting into a canter at a smart crack of the whip, step along the road as if the load behind them: coach, passengers, cod-fish, oyster barrels, and all: were but a feather at their heels. They have descended a gentle slope, and enter upon a level, as compact and dry as a solid block of marble, two miles long. Another crack of the whip, and on they speed, at a smart gallop: the horses tossing their heads and rattling the harness, as if in exhilaration at the rapidity of the motion: while the coachman, holding whip and reins in one hand, takes off his hat with the other, and resting it on his knees, pulls out his handkerchief, and wipes his forehead: partly because he has a habit of doing it, and partly because it's as well to show the passengers how cool he is, and what an easy thing it is to drive four-in-hand, when you have had as much practice as he has. Having done this very leisurely (otherwise the effect would be materially impaired), he replaces his handkerchief, pulls on his hat, adjusts his gloves, squares his elbows, cracks the whip again, and on they speed, more merrily than before.

3   A few small houses, scattered on either side of the road, betoken the entrance to some town or village. The lively notes of the guard's key-bugle vibrate in the clear cold air, and wake up the old gentleman inside, who, carefully letting down the window-sash half-way, and standing sentry over the air, takes a short peep out, and then carefully pulling it up again, informs the other inside that they're going to change directly; on which the other inside wakes himself up, and determines to postpone his next nap until after the stoppage. Again the bugle sounds lustily forth, and rouses the cottager's wife and children, who peep out at the house-door, and watch round the blazing fire, and throw on another log of wood against father comes

From Charles Dickens, *The Pickwick Papers* (1836–1837).

home; while father himself, a full mile off, has just exchanged a friendly nod with the coachman, and turned round to take a good long stare at the vehicle as it whirls away.

4   And now the bugle plays a lively air as the coach rattles through the ill-paved streets of a country-town; and the coachman, undoing the buckle which keeps his ribands together, prepares to throw them off the moment he stops. Mr. Pickwick emerges from his coat collar, and looks about him with great curiosity; perceiving which, the coachman informs Mr. Pickwick of the name of the town, and tells him it was market-day yesterday, both of which pieces of information Mr. Pickwick retails to his fellow-passengers; whereupon they emerge from their coat collars too, and look about them also. Mr. Winkle, who sits at the extreme edge, with one leg dangling in the air, is nearly precipitated into the street, as the coach twists round the sharp corner by the cheesemonger's shop, and turns into the marketplace; and before Mr. Snodgrass, who sits next to him, has recovered from his alarm, they pull up at the inn yard, where the fresh horses, with cloths on, are already waiting. The coachman throws down the reins and gets down himself, and the other outside passengers drop down also: except those who have no great confidence in their ability to get up again: and they remain where they are, and stamp their feet against the coach to warm them—looking, with longing eyes and red noses, at the bright fire in the inn bar, and the sprigs of holly with red berries which ornament the window.

STUDY QUESTIONS

Organization and Content

1. In this selection Dickens tells of one of the famous trips by stagecoach that Mr. Pickwick and his companions made to Dingley Dell. Perhaps the emphasis is more on narrative (story) than on description proper. But how much do we *see* and *hear* while the coach is journeying through one of its stages?
2. *Story* implies a series of events. How does the author make us aware of the passage of time?
3. Try to identify the elements in the writing that make the reader feel action, movement, and adventure.
4. Paragraph 1 consists of a single sentence. Why is it so short?
5. What topic is paragraph 2 mainly about? Paragraph 3? Paragraph 4?
6. How does Dickens distribute the attention which he gives to the coach-

man, the passengers outside, the passengers inside, the horses, the surroundings?

7. Where does Dickens introduce little touches of humor? Is he laughing at the people of whom he writes?

Sentence Structure

1. Sentence 1 has six clauses. What type of sentence is it, simple, compound, or complex?
2. What is the effect of sentence 1?
3. Does the selection contain any other sentences of the same type?
4. The selection contains a number of *and*'s. Count them. What effect does Dickens achieve by using them?
5. Compare this effect with that of the Kipling selection, which also has numerous *and*'s.

Diction

1. Look up *exhilaration, precipitated.*
2. Most of the words in this selection are short. Was Dickens right in using so many short words?
3. Why are the verbs especially significant? Which verbs are the most emphatic?
4. Which adjectives and nouns do the most to create a vivid effect?

Assignment

Write four paragraphs telling of a journey in a modern vehicle—a bus, a train, or a ship. In a brief first paragraph show the start, in paragraph 4 the arrival, and in paragraphs 2 and 3 something of the journey in between. Imitate Dickens by emphasizing action and movement.

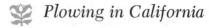 *Plowing in California*

Frank Norris

1   The ploughs, thirty-five in number, each drawn by its team of ten, stretched in an interminable line, nearly a quarter of a mile in length, behind and ahead of Vanamee. They were arranged, as it were, *en échelon*, not in file—not one directly behind the other, but each succeeding plough its own width farther in the field than

From Frank Norris, *The Octopus* (1901).

the one in front of it. Each of these ploughs held five shears, so that when the entire company was in motion, one hundred and seventy-five furrows were made at the same instant. At a distance, the ploughs resembled a great column of field artillery. Each driver was in his place, his glance alternating between his horses and the foreman nearest at hand. Other foremen, in their buggies or buckboards, were at intervals along the line, like battery lieutenants. Annixter himself, on horseback, in boots and campaign hat, a cigar in his teeth, overlooked the scene.

2   The division superintendent, on the opposite side of the line, galloped past to a position at the head. For a long moment there was a silence. A sense of preparedness ran from end to end of the column. All things were ready, each man in his place. The day's work was about to begin.

3   Suddenly, from a distance at the head of the line came the shrill trilling of a whistle. At once the foreman nearest Vanamee repeated it, at the same time turning down the line, and waving one arm. The signal was repeated, whistle answering whistle, till the sounds lost themselves in the distance. At once the line of ploughs lost its immobility, moving forward, getting slowly under way, the horses straining in the traces. A prolonged movement rippled from team to team, disengaging in its passage a multitude of sounds—the click of buckles, the creak of straining leather, the subdued clash of machinery, the cracking of whips, the deep breathing of nearly four hundred horses, the abrupt commands and cries of the drivers, and, last of all, the prolonged, soothing murmur of the thick brown earth turning steadily from the multitude of advancing shears.

4   The ploughing thus commenced, continued. The sun rose higher. Steadily the hundred iron hands kneaded and furrowed and stroked the brown, humid earth, the hundred iron teeth bit deep into the Titan's flesh. Perched on his seat, the moist living reins slipping and tugging in his hands, Vanamee, in the midst of this steady confusion of constantly varying sensation, sight interrupted by sound, sound mingling with sight, on this swaying, vibrating seat, quivering with the prolonged thrill of the earth, lapsed to a sort of pleasing numbness, in a sense, hypnotized by the weaving maze of things in which he found himself involved. To keep his team at an even, regular gait, maintaining the precise interval, to run his furrows as closely as possible to those already made by the plough in front—this for the moment was the entire sum of his duties. But while one part of his brain, alert and watchful, took cognizance of these matters, all the greater part was lulled and stupefied with the long monotony of the affair.

5   The ploughing, now in full swing, enveloped him in a vague, slow-moving swirl of things. Underneath him was the jarring, jolting, trembling machine; not a clod was turned, not an obstacle encountered, that he did not receive the swift impression of it through all his body, the very friction of the damp soil, sliding incessantly from the shiny surface of the shears, seemed to reproduce itself in his finger-tips and along the back of his head. He heard the horse-hoofs by the myriads crushing down easily, deeply, into the loam, the prolonged clinking of trace-chains, the working of the smooth brown flanks in the harness, the clatter of wooden hames, the champing of bits, the click of iron shoes against pebbles, the brittle stubble of the surface ground crackling and snapping as the furrows turned, the sonorous, steady breaths wrenched from the deep labouring chests, strap-bound, shining with sweat, and all along the line the voices of the men talking to the horses. Everywhere there were visions of glossy brown backs, straining, heaving, swollen with muscle; harness streaked with specks of froth, broad, cup-shaped hoofs, heavy with brown loam, men's faces red with tan, blue overalls spotted with axle-grease; muscled hands, the knuckles whitened in their grip on the reins, and through it all the ammoniacal smell of the horses, the bitter reek of perspiration of beasts and men, the aroma of warm leather, the scent of dead stubble—and stronger and more penetrating than everything else, the heavy, enervating odour of the upturned, living earth.

STUDY QUESTIONS

Organization and Content

1. What "extended metaphor" dominates paragraph 1? What terms make us aware of this figure of speech?
2. Vanamee is mentioned in sentence 1. Why is it important to mention him? Where else is he mentioned?
3. What is the function of paragraph 2? How is this function related to its length?
4. Paragraph 3 falls into two parts. What kind of descriptive detail is stressed in part 2?
5. What is the point of view through paragraphs 1–3? How does the point of view change slightly in paragraph 4?
6. Does the material of paragraph 5 differ in any respect from that of paragraph 4? How does the material of these paragraphs differ from that of paragraph 1?

7. Which three paragraphs have topic sentences? In which one does the topic sentence come at the end?
8. What terms make us aware of the passage of time?
9. What are the main divisions of the selection?

Sentence Structure

1. In some of Norris' sentences (*a*) modifiers are tucked away between subject and verb; in others (*b*) they precede the subject or (*c*) come at the end, after subject-verb-complement. Identify the sentences of each group in paragraphs 1–3.
2. Does Norris use enough variety of sentence structure to avoid monotony?
3. In sentence 5, paragraph 3, what words are in apposition with *multitude?* How does Norris introduce the list of sounds? How does the organization of this sentence contrast with that of sentence 5, paragraph 4?
4. Paragraph 5 is the longest of the five paragraphs, yet it has only four sentences. By what grammatical means does Norris handle the many descriptive details of sentence 3, paragraph 5?
5. In sentence 4, there are two lists of details; those of the first one are all visual. How does Norris move within the same sentence to the second list?

Diction

1. Look up *shears, buckboards, lapsed, trace-chains, hames, sonorous, enervating.* Some of these are simple concrete terms, but they may be unfamiliar because of technological changes.
2. Norris, in 1901, used the term *en échelon;* a present-day writer would say *in echelon.* Why? What is the difference between *echelon* and *file?* How are *echelon* and *scale* related?
3. Explain the element of metaphor in one member of the following pairs of verbs: *stretched* (sentence 1, paragraph 1) and *held* (sentence 3, paragraph 1); *galloped* (sentence 1, paragraph 2) and *ran* (sentence 3, paragraph 2); *repeated* (sentence 2, paragraph 3) and *rippled* (sentence 5, paragraph 3); *wrenched* (sentence 3, paragraph 5) and *streaked* (sentence 4, paragraph 5).
4. List the words that refer to sounds. Which of them are onomatopoetic?
5. List the words that refer to sights and smells.
6. An unusual number of terms in this selection describe kinesthetic sensations; examples are *straining, vibrating.* Kinesthetic sensations are those relating to muscular movement, position, and tension. List these terms. Are they chiefly verbs or nouns?
7. Vanamee's richly sensuous experience is called "steady confusion" in paragraph 4. What other terms are approximately synonymous with this?
8. Where does Norris refer to the earth? Why are the references to the earth important? What is the significance of the allusion to "Titan's flesh" in sentence 3, paragraph 4?
9. Omit all the adjectives as you read through the selection. What do

you lose by omitting them? Is the selection better without them? Which paragraphs have the most adjectives? Which adjectives are most effective? Does Norris use too many adjectives?

Assignment

Few people today can duplicate the experience Norris describes, but it is possible to approximate at least part of it. Some suggestions:

1. If you have driven a tractor or large truck, a military vehicle or road-building equipment, describe your sensations as a driver.
2. Imitate the first two and a half paragraphs by describing the arrangements of units just before a parade or an athletic contest.
3. Describe how activities are synchronized for a surprise party or a shower.
4. Describe the "steady confusion" of your experience if you have operated a machine in a cotton mill, steel mill, or other large shop.

A Man Observing a Woman

WILLIAM SANSOM

1   One moment the window was empty, a dark square—and the next this strange new woman was standing against the sill.

2   Her appearance was as sudden as if a blind had been snapped up.

3   There she stood exactly in the centre of her little theatre of sashes and sill and darkness beyond. One expected her to bow.

4   He backed away from his own window like a thief.

5   In between them a wild spring wind drove through the trough of back-gardens, raising sudden birds of white paper, waving the trees, whipping a storm of movement between all the rows of quiet shut windows. But that was outside. In, it was still.

6   He stood back in the room alone and breathless, still slightly crouched, not daring to move about. So quiet alone among the furniture! Sounds from outside echoed in loud to accuse his secret second—a lumber cart rumbling to its cockney cry, a blackbird's sudden pipe, the thrash of a beaten mat. His heart beat loud as a clock, faster than the mat. He thought: Not until that cart has called three

times more, I won't move till then—when a blackbird pounded down with a taffeta swish on the window-box, raised its long tail and slowly lowered it in a long breath of arrival, then cocked its head to stare straight in at him.

7   He blushed. He had begun blushing before. Now the pricking flooded pink round his ears: and staring back into the bird's worm-crazy glare he saw how absurd this was and did what he had all this long second been impelled to do—stepped quietly forward again towards the window; but making, though that woman was a full thirty yards away across the short gardens, carefully no sound. The blackbird looked amazed, gave a gulp and flew off. He started— the little wings thrashed loud like a silk fan—and, with his body carefully turned away from the window opposite, he picked up a book. He opened it, and thus appeared to be reading as now slowly he swivelled round and let his brow-sheltered eyes reach up off the print, keeping his head carefully lowered.

STUDY QUESTIONS

Organization and Content

1. These paragraphs are the opening of an English novel of 1956. The chief character looked out of the window of his apartment and was surprised at the sudden appearance of the woman mentioned in paragraph 1. What feelings and reactions are expressed in the first four extremely short paragraphs?
2. If the author had put the material of the first four paragraphs into one paragraph, what difference in effect would be noticed?
3. Narration and description are combined. Does the selection impress you as mainly narrative or mainly descriptive?
4. There is a stronger psychological element in this selection than in previous ones. Where does the author communicate the psychological reactions of the observer?
5. How would you describe his psychological state?
6. What contrast between indoors and outdoors is made? Why does the author make it?

Sentence Structure

1. Comment on the structure of the three sentences of paragraph 5.
2. What is the function of sentence 2 in paragraph 6?
3. Note how interruptive some of the sentences are: sentence 5 in paragraph 6, sentences 3 and 5 in paragraph 7. Do these interruptive sentences bring the reader closer to the strange experience the man is

having—make it easier to follow—or keep him further off, on the outside of it?

4. How does the structure of sentences 1, 2, and 3 of paragraph 7 reflect the content of those sentences?

Diction

1. Point out which verbs are vivid and emphatic.
2. Does the passage contain any vivid or unusual adjectives?
3. The author makes use of figurative language. Explain how these metaphors function: "theatre" in paragraph 3, "birds" in paragraph 5, "taffeta swish" in paragraph 6, "pricking flooded·pink" and "eyes reach up" in paragraph 7.
4. Indicate three similes in the passage.

Assignment

Imitate the selection rather closely. Imagine someone (yourself, if you like) looking out of a window and seeing something that surprises, or shocks, or excites him very much. Use one-sentence paragraphs at first. Make a contrast of some kind between indoors and outdoors. Have vivid verbs and metaphorical language. This assignment will allow you to use a good deal of imagination. Try to write with high imaginative voltage.

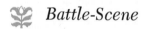 *Battle-Scene*

AUDIE MURPHY

1   A sergeant in the first platoon senses the predicament. If his men are isolated, they will likely be destroyed. He makes his decision quickly. Motioning his men to follow, he rises and with a submachine gun charges head-on toward one of the enemy positions two hundred yards away.

2   On the flat, coverless terrain, his body is a perfect target. A blast of automatic fire knocks him down. He springs to his feet with a bleeding shoulder and continues his charge. The guns rattle. Again he goes down.

3   Fascinated, we watch as he gets up for the third time and dashes straight into the enemy fire. The Germans throw everything they have at him. He falls to the earth; and when he again

From Audie Murphy, *To Hell and Back* (New York: Holt, Rinehart and Winston, Inc., 1949).

pulls himself to his feet, we see that his right arm is shattered. But wedging his gun in his left arm-pit, he continues firing and staggers forward. Ten horrified Germans throw down their guns and yell, *"Kamerad."*

STUDY QUESTIONS

Organization and Content

1. This selection is from a famous story of World War II first published in 1949. Certainly it is primarily narrative. Does it contain any parts that might be called descriptive?
2. The three paragraphs are short. Are such short paragraphs suitable in this instance?
3. The three paragraphs are arranged in the order of climax. Explain what each paragraph tells of and why paragraph 3 is the climactic paragraph.
4. The charging sergeant is attacking enemy forces. How does the author represent the two forces in the conflict?

Sentence Structure

1. The sentences are prevailingly short. Are the short sentences suitable?
2. How many of the sentences are simple sentences?
3. How many of them begin with the subject? How many have some modifier before the subject?
4. Do the sentences follow one another smoothly, or is their effect rather choppy?

Diction

1. In a story of action one might expect verbs to be very important. Are the verbs strong and effective? Which verbs are most effective? Which least effective?
2. How high a percentage of adjectives does the author use? Compare the percentage of adjectives with that of the three preceding selections.

Assignment

Write three short paragraphs arranged in the order of climax about some tense moment of action. This might have to do with an incident of military training, an athletic event, a hunting, fishing, or swimming experience, an automobile accident, or an emergency like a storm, fire, or flood. Check your verbs to make certain that they are effective. In each paragraph underline the sentence that you consider to be the most forceful.

Section Two

Exposition

One of the most important and most often used types of writing is explanation. People are constantly being requested or urged to explain something or other. Explain what was done; explain what it was like; explain how it operates; explain the sequence of happenings; explain what it means; explain how it developed; explain how you felt; explain your position; explain what you think; explain yourself!—these demands for explanations crowd upon all, day after day. These same demands account for the frequency of use and the vast importance of explanatory writing—which, in discussions of composition, is more commonly called exposition.

Though it may certainly deal with things which may be observed by means of the senses, exposition appeals more, however, to the mind than to the senses. Understanding, achieved by the mind, rather than the immediate experience conveyed by the senses, is the chief goal of the expository writer. It is not so much the look or smell or feel of things that the reader gains from exposition as an idea of how they originated, how they developed, how they are organized. how numerous or how complicated they are, how they are related to other things, how significant they are, or what they mean. Description has to do with concrete phenomena and concrete experiences; exposition very often goes beyond the concrete into the region of abstractions, the realm of ideas.

Providing instruction and meeting the needs of the human race for knowledge and understanding—these are the purposes of exposition. Everything found in encyclopedias, handbooks, and dictionaries is exposition. An infantry manual, a manual on constructing family fallout shelters, a handbook explaining the basic movements of square dancing, a pamphlet on methods of insect control—all are examples of exposition; as are likewise such works as a textbook of surgery or a grammar of the French language.

Expository writing concerns itself with practical matters; all the reports that provide information for executives, congressmen, mayors, deans, military officers, school superintendents, diplomats, stock analysts, and prime ministers—all these systematic accumulations of data that help in getting the world's work done are pieces of expository writing. Therefore, it may be stated that exposition is practical writing. But, though exposition deals with every practical matter in the world, it is not limited to practical affairs in the workaday sense of the term. The writer of exposition may present ideas on the most theoretical matters too. Books on physics or philosophy, on metaphysics or evolution, highly theoretical, are exposition; but, of course, they are written to satisfy men's practical demands for understanding in all these areas.

Whatever may be the subject of exposition, the writing itself must be systematic and well organized. The simplest type of exposition is an enumeration, a very common and useful way of developing expository paragraphs. Many explanations simply comprise a list of details (with or without actual numbers) to show what something is like or how something is done.

More complex methods of exposition are analysis and definition, which involve classification and division. Whether one is explaining the operation of an airplane or of a frog, he will have to do some analyzing, that is, tell what the parts are and how they are related for purposes of functioning. Likewise, if a student is defining a frog, he must first classify it: obviously it does not belong in the class of vegetables or any nonanimal group. After he has properly classified it, he must then show how it is different from other members of the same class; he must explain what points of difference separate frogs from toads and salamanders.

In all expository writing it is advisable to use examples, analogies, comparisons, and contrasts, particularly when the subject is an abstract one. The reader will be able to understand an unfamiliar subject better if it is somehow related to a thing with which he is already familiar. The concept of relativity, for example, can be approached by way of two trains moving at different speeds. Understanding is helped too by systematic comparisons and contrasts: two different groups may be compared or contrasted, two different periods, or men, or theories, or methods of agriculture, or government, or medical treatment. The reader is very likely to learn, to be enlightened, by reading a thoughtful comparison. A comparison or contrast, based on various points of resemblance or difference, will have been made possible by an act of analysis.

All of these matters will become clearer as the apprentice writer studies the examples given in the various sections of the text. Though some of the selections in the section on description have contained a small amount of exposition, the readings in the present section contain very little that is not expository.

Enumeration

The writer of exposition must understand his material thoroughly enough to be able to organize it clearly according to some scheme which the reader can follow and understand. It has been noted that the simplest type of exposition is enumeration: a certain number of things exist or are our concern. These are the things, or the parts, or the steps: one, two, three, four. Much the same is the arrangement of items in chronological order, one, two, three, four, from the earliest to the latest. When we are dealing with a systematic arrangement of things in space rather than in time, we can take them up according to a spatial order: one, two, three, four from right to left or from left to right, from top to bottom or from bottom to top. Such an arrangement may seem rather arbitrary, but it has the great virtue of clarity. A reader will hardly get lost during the explanation.

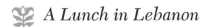

A Lunch in Lebanon

RALPH AND MOLLY IZZARD

Observing the size and bulk of our hosts, we had reasoned that they kept a good table. We were not disappointed. Mme. Kanaan, flushed and perspiring in her pink silk *peignoir*, had been busy in her kitchen ever since our arrival, and through the bathroom walls we had caught many shrill chidings and upbraidings and a clattering of pots from the kitchen next door. We lunched alone in a vast deserted dining-room, sparsely furnished with an elaborate sideboard and a chandelier. The spotless tablecloth was covered with a multitude of *hors d'oeuvres,* the characteristic *Meze* of the Levant. This alone was the equivalent of an entire coffee-shop lunch. Next came a favourite dish: a great platter of snowy rice, accompanied by another platter of French beans in a gravy of braised tomatoes and titbits of tender lamb. A smiling maid encouraged us all to have second helpings, and, this done, we were then presented with a steak each, chips and a large bowl of salad. A certain glaze began to appear over the eyes of the party and the two men had recourse to the small bottles of *arak* to stimulate their appetite. A rice pudding next appeared, sweetened with rosewater, as a treat for the children, Elias rashly having informed our hostess that the children were very fond of this Arab sweet. Then came water-melons, grapes and enormous apples, and hot, sweet cups of coffee, and at last we were done.

STUDY QUESTIONS

Organization and Content

1. How much description is in this paragraph? How much narration? How much exposition?
2. How much of the paragraph is concerned with people? How much with the place where the lunch was served?
3. How many main items of lunch are listed?
4. How many other things are itemized?
5. Instead of first, second, third, and so on, what terms do the authors use to indicate the separate items?
6. What problem of organization did the authors solve? How did they know what to place first in the paragraph? Last?
7. Compare the handling of the material here with that in the paragraph by Updike.

Sentence Structure

1. Participial phrases appear in sentences 1, 3, and 4. Is there any reason why each of them should be in a different position in the sentence?
2. How much variation is there in the length of the sentences?
3. How much variety of sentence structure is there?
4. Does the paragraph contain an excessive number of *and*'s connecting parts of sentences?

Diction

1. Which words give an impression of the dining-room?
2. Which words give an impression of people?
3. Look up *peignoir, hors d'oeuvres, arak (arrack).* Why are they italicized in the text?
4. Look up *chidings, upbraidings, Levant, braised, titbits.*
5. Is there any difference between *size* and *bulk?*

Assignment

Write one solid paragraph about a meal, enumerating the different courses or servings of food. Give the reader some impression of the place where the meal was served and of the people who prepared and/or served it. The material will probably not be interesting unless you write about a meal that is extraordinary; it may seem interesting because of its length, richness, or strangeness. You might write about a family picnic, a Christmas dinner, or some special feast, perhaps one with unusual foreign dishes.

 The United States Capitol

ALLEN DRURY

"This building," one of the Capitol guides was telling the day's first batch of tourists, listening attentively in the great rotunda, "stands on Capitol Hill 88 feet above the level of the Potomac River, on a site once occupied by a subtribe of the Algonquin Indians known as the Powhatans, whose council house was located at the foot of the hill. The building covers an area of 153,112 square feet, or approximately 3½ acres; its width, including approaches, is 350 feet. It has a floor area of 14 acres, and 435 rooms are devoted to offices, committees, and storage. There are 679 windows and 554 doorways. The cornerstone of the Capitol was laid on Sept. 18, 1793. The northern wing was completed in 1800, and in that small building the legislative and judicial branches of the government, as well as the courts of the District of Columbia, were housed in that year when the government moved here from Philadelphia. The southern section of the

Capitol was finished in 1811, the House of Representatives then occupying what is now known as Statuary Hall. At that time a wooden passageway connected the two wings. This was the situation when the Capitol was burned by the British on August 24, 1814, entering up the narrow, winding steps known as the British Stairway which you will see later in your tour."

STUDY QUESTIONS

Organization and Content

1. Which parts of this paragraph would you call description? Narration? Exposition?
2. What things are itemized in the first four sentences?
3. What idea governs the order in which sentences 5–9 are arranged?
4. Do sentences 5–9 also contain itemizing?
5. What elements of sentences 5–9 cause them to differ in content from sentences 1–4? Does the difference cause the paragraph to lack unity?
6. Contrast the purpose and the effect of this paragraph with the purpose and effect of the one on "A Lunch in Lebanon."

Sentence Structure

1. What does the parenthetical material about the guide and the tourists accomplish in sentence 1?
2. Is there any advantage in placing this material where it is? Would it be more effective if placed in a different position?
3. Sentence 1, rather long, is a "loose" sentence; the thought is completed early, and the sentence continues with a string of modifiers. Is the sentence too long? Does it seem unlikely that any one would speak so long a sentence?
4. The sentences of the paragraph are linked together by constant references to what?
5. Why should sentences 2–5 be as short as they are?

Diction

The vocabulary is not difficult. Look up the roots of: *rotunda, legislative, judicial.*

Assignment

Write a paragraph in which you give similar information about a building—a public building in your town, a university building (perhaps the oldest building on the campus), or some other one about which you gather material. Some of it you can obtain by your own observation.

Methods of Developing Great Minds

GILBERT HIGHET

1   No, we can never tell how great minds arise, and it is very hard to tell how to detect and encourage them when they do appear. But we do know two methods of feeding them as they grow.

2   One is to give them constant challenge and stimulus. Put problems before them. Make things difficult for them. They need to think. Produce things for them to think about and question their thinking at every stage. They are inventive and original. Propose experiments to them. Tell them to discover what is hidden.

3   The second method is to bring them into contact with other eminent minds. It is not enough, not nearly enough, for a clever boy or girl to meet his fellows and his teachers and his parents. He (or she) must meet men and women of real and undeniable distinction. That is, he must meet the immortals. That brilliant and pessimistic scoundrel Plato died just over 2,300 years ago, but through his books he is still talking and thinking and leading others to think; and there is no better way, none, for a young man to start thinking about any kind of philosophical problem—human conduct, political action, logical analysis, metaphysics, aesthetics—than by reading Plato and trying to answer his arguments, detect his sophisms, resist his skillful persuasions, and become both his pupil and his critic. No one can learn to write music better than by studying *The Well-tempered Clavier* of Bach and the symphonies of Beethoven. A young composer who does so will not, if he is any good, write music like Bach and Beethoven. He will write music more like the music that he wanted to write. A man may become a routine diplomat by following the rule book and solving every problem as it comes up, but if he is to grow into a statesman he must read his Machiavelli and consider the lives of Bismarck and Lincoln and Disraeli. The best way toward greatness is to mix with the great.

4   Challenge and experiment; association with immortal minds: These are the two sure ways of rearing intelligent men and women. And these two opportunities for greatness are, or ought to be, provided by schools and colleges and universities.

From Gilbert Highet, "The Unpredictable Intellect," in *Man's Unconquerable Mind* (New York: Columbia University Press, 1954), pp. 40–41.

STUDY QUESTIONS

Organization and Content

1. Paragraph 1 has two sentences. Explain the function of each sentence. What is the function of the paragraph?
2. What are the topic sentences of paragraphs 2 and 3?
3. Highet uses several sentences in paragraphs 2 and 3 in order to illustrate the topic idea. What is the difference in the illustrative material of the two paragraphs?
4. What books by Plato and Machiavelli would stimulate the minds of young people? Why should "Bismarck and Lincoln and Disraeli" be grouped together?
5. What is the function of paragraph 4?
6. In one well-written sentence explain how this selection functions as an example of enumeration.

Sentence Structure

1. What is the effect of the successive short sentences that the author uses in paragraph 2?
2. Show how parallel phrasing and repetition provide both emphasis and good linking among sentences of paragraph 2.
3. In what way has Highet gained emphasis in sentence 2, paragraph 1; sentences 2 and 5, paragraph 3?
4. In sentences 3 and 4, paragraph 3, certain words are placed in emphatic positions. What are they?
5. Sentence 5, paragraph 3, is long. Is it simple, compound, or complex? Draw a diagram illustrating the parallel structure that is used in the sentence.
6. Good writers repeat important words for emphasis. What words are thus repeated in the last part of paragraph 3?
7. Why did Highet use the semicolon and the colon in sentence 1, paragraph 4?

Diction

1. What is the difference between a *challenge* and a *stimulus?*
2. Is there a difference between *eminence* and *distinction?*
3. Which two areas of philosophy are represented by *metaphysics* and *aesthetics?*
4. Distinguish among *sophism, philosophy,* and *sophisticate.*

Assignment

Enumerate, with illustrations: methods of developing character; physical strength; agility; sound health; an appreciation of music; an interest in reading, art, geography, mathematics, or science.

🌸 *Qualities of the American Business Man*

Harold Laski

The American business man has certain remarkable qualities in an exceptional degree. His vitality is extraordinary. He lives his business from morning to night; he gives to it the devotion that a medieval saint gave to his religion. He is almost always experimental about it, eager to take a chance, anxious to change from one vocation to another if the latter seems to offer additional opportunities. He believes profoundly in the possibilities of machinery; and he is almost always willing to take the long rather than the short view. He knows, as no other people but the Germans and, since 1917, the Russians know, the value of *expertise* and research. He assumes that success in a business calling is of itself a title to influence, and since there are few men who do not desire influence, he agrees with but little difficulty that the successful business man ought to be respected. There is, indeed, an important sense in which it is true to say that for most Americans the acquisition of wealth is a form of religious exercise; that is why, perhaps, a well-known advertiser could write, in the twenties, of Jesus Christ as a successful business man without the public feeling that there was some incongruity in the thesis.

From *The American Democracy* by Harold Laski. Copyright 1948 by The Viking Press, Inc. Reprinted by permission of The Viking Press, Inc.

STUDY QUESTIONS

Organization and Content

1. What expectation does the first sentence arouse in the reader?
2. What is the key word in the first sentence?
3. If you were to number the items that the author presents for proof of his main idea, how many numbers would you have to use?
4. Which statements explain what the businessman does? What he believes? What judgments he makes about the importance of business?
5. Is the last sentence properly placed? If you think so, explain why it should appear last and not earlier.
6. Why might the author think that the idea of Jesus Christ as a successful businessman is incongruous?

Sentence Structure

1. How are the sentences linked together?
2. What words provide the links?
3. Most of the sentences begin in the same way. What advantage has the author gained by beginning them thus?
4. The last two sentences are the longest, each divided into two parts. Explain how each part is organized.

Diction

1. Look up *vitality, medieval, profoundly, expertise, incongruity, thesis.*
2. How many adjectives has Laski used in his discussion? How vivid are the adjectives?
3. Are adjectives, nouns, or verbs the most significant words of the paragraph?

Assignment

Write a similar paragraph listing the qualities of someone who is not a businessman: a farmer, a lawyer, a civil service worker, a truck driver, a professor, a grammar school teacher, or some other representative of an occupation. Include as many qualities as Laski does in the model paragraph.

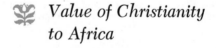 *Value of Christianity to Africa*

GEORGE W. CARPENTER

1   As regards the value of the church and of Christian faith in African society there are at least four such values which are of major importance:

2   1. Christianity provides a simple yet inexhaustible standard of personal moral conduct: *"thou shalt love."* This is within the understanding of everyone, it is the test of every relationship, it is applicable within any Culture. Yet it progressively transforms personalities and social situations wherever it is applied. It demands

From George W. Carpenter, "The Role of Christianity and Islam in Contemporary Africa," in Charles Grove Haines, ed., *Africa Today* (Baltimore: The Johns Hopkins Press, 1955).

and develops the highest personal integrity. It does not solve any moral issues directly—people may not even agree as to the solution which most nearly meets its requirements—but it creates relationships in which any social problem becomes soluble.

3   Of course, those who do not practice the ethic of love are not in a position to urge it on others. It is essentially a religious principle because it can only legitimately be presented as God's commandment, not man's; and as such it challenges all alike. Africans are quick to detect the hypocrisy of those who hold that "Christianity is good for the African" but who reject it for themselves.

4   2. The Christian church, as the fellowship of those who have committed themselves to the Christian way, is a focus of social integration of the utmost importance to Africa. Because it reaches from the individual and the local group out through the community and nation to the whole world, because it reaches back through the past and forward through the future, because it is a living fellowship involving personal commitment, group acceptance, and action together under religious sanctions, it is uniquely able to replace, for its adherents, the old tribal groupings which cannot survive changed conditions. Here, however, there is a dilemma which Western Christianity has never solved: how can the church meet the need to be *universal*, to embrace the whole community, and to be at the same time *pure*—that is, a living fellowship of those who are personally committed to Christ? It may be that African Christianity, with its strong sense of community, will help find an answer.

5   3. The Christian tradition, arising in Hebrew-Judaic life, which was closely akin to African cultures, affords a cosmology which meets African needs for an intelligible universe. It is becoming clear that man cannot live without myths, that he suffers frustration when his world fails to make sense. Our Western passion for verbal exactitude has closed our eyes to great values in the Hebrew-Christian Scriptures which the imaginative African grasps without effort. He may yet help us recover our appreciation of the basic insights on which our culture is based by taking them for his own.

6   4. Christianity is compatible with the total Western cultural pattern which is becoming a world culture. It has already faced the issues posed by nationalism, science, and technology and does not fear to face any new issues which may arise. Hence, adoption of Christianity imposes no limitation on the general social evolution of an African individual or group. The ethical tensions of Christianity, insofar as they influence personal and group behavior, operate as a social force within any culture whatever, Western as well as African. The permanence of Christianity is not that of a fixed unchanging system but of a creative energy, a kind of life.

STUDY QUESTIONS

Organization and Content

1. What is the function of paragraph 1?
2. What enumerative indicators does Carpenter use?
3. What main idea does Carpenter give evidence to prove or reasons for believing?
4. What is the function of paragraph 3? Explain the progress of thought in the second half of the three sentences of paragraph 3.
5. Give an example to illustrate each part of sentence 2, paragraph 4.
6. Can Western Christians expect African Christians to contribute anything of value to Christianity?
7. What problems are posed in our century by nationalism, science, and technology?

Sentence Structure

1. Why does paragraph 1 end with a colon? After this punctuation what does a reader expect?
2. What similarity of beginnings do you observe in the paragraphs that the author has numbered (paragraphs 2, 4, 5, and 6)? What is the use of such similarity?
3. Pronoun repetition provides transition in paragraphs 2 and 4. To what does *it* refer?
4. How is the parallel structure of introductory dependent clauses made clear to the reader in sentence 2, paragraph 4? How is the order of climax used here?

Diction

1. Look up *inexhaustible standard, integrity, soluble, social integration, sanctions, uniquely, adherents, dilemma, cosmology, myths, Western, ethical tensions.*
2. Explain the effect of the contrasting connotations of *system* and of *life* in the last sentence.

Assignment

Prepare a list of reasons why something has proved to be good or bad, and treat them in the same way as George W. Carpenter treats the material in your model. You might write about:

1. A policy of neglecting studies or of carefully preparing lessons
2. Joining a church or deciding not to join one
3. Cooperating with parents or being independent
4. Working while in college or not having to give one's time to a job
5. Exercising systematically or ignoring exercise
6. Smoking tobacco or using drugs such as LSD

❧ *Hindrances to the Enlargement of Man's Range of Values*

RALPH BARTON PERRY

1   There are four chief hindrances to the enlargement of man's range of values. The first of these is simple apathy. The second is the individual's preoccupation with his own subjectivity. A fellow creature is a means or an obstacle to one's own pre-existing ends—a value, positive or negative, only in terms of what one already desires for oneself. Viewing him in this light one tends to overlook that which is good in him—the object of *his* liking or aspiration. In the glaring light of one's own felt interests the vast field of interests all about, the hopes and fears and joys and sorrows of other men, are invisible. One thus lives in a provincial world, embracing only a minute fraction of the values of the larger world. The only remedy for this blindness is sympathy—the power of feeling to penetrate to the centers of other men and share the outlook of *their* emotional life.

2   The third hindrance to the enlargement of the field of values is preoccupation with the means to a given end. This limitation may be imposed by circumstance. A man who is in peril of his life can choose only among the means of self-preservation. When the struggle for existence is hard and relentless, the options are restricted to food, drink, and shelter. When the enemy is present in arms and a man's fighting blood is aroused, he has no choice but the manner of dealing or receiving blows. A similar impoverishment results from the hasty adoption of an end, or from yielding to suggestion, or from a headlong impetuousness, or from an intensity of absorption. An end usurps control without having been deliberately chosen, and all choices henceforth are limited to its means. The maximum of freedom requires that there shall be at least moments of life in which a man freely chooses that ultimate goal which prescribes the chain of subordinate choices with which the greater part of his life is necessarily concerned. To exercise this faculty of ultimate choice requires a discriminating taste and a familiarity with what life has to offer. It implies ,detachment from the importunity of appetite, from sectarian zeal, the pressure of need, the passion of the mob, the slavish adher-

George Braziller, Inc.—from *The Humanity of Man* by Ralph Barton Perry. Reprinted with the permission of the publisher. Coypright © by George Braziller, Inc., 1956.

ence to custom and vogue, or any other force that deadens the heart to wide tracts of the realm of values.

3   A fourth force which works perpetually to narrow the range of values is the tendency of means to usurp the place of ends. A man who leaves his country on account of religious persecution and settles in the wilderness to worship God finds that in order to worship God he must live, and that in order to live he must subjugate the wilderness. In time he is likely to forget God, and devote himself with his whole heart to the acquisition of material goods. Christmas celebrates the spirit of giving, but the business of giving tends to degenerate into the discharge of obligations or the tying and untying of bits of string. Such a change is not always a degradation of values, but there is, in any case, an oblivion of values and a reduction of alternatives.

STUDY QUESTIONS

Organization and Content

1. Does Perry follow any principle of organization for the order of his paragraphs? Could the sequence of his four points just as well be reversed?
2. Why does Perry pay less attention to the first hindrance than to the other hindrances?
3. In paragraph 2 what kind of situation illustrates limitation "imposed by circumstance"? What two more specific examples illustrate this situation?
4. Sentence 6, paragraph 2, has four parallel phrases. What do these parallel elements illustrate?
5. What further point does Perry make in the second half of paragraph 2? What illustrations does he provide to make this point clear?
6. Compare the examples which are used in the development of the three paragraphs. Which paragraph has the most examples? Which has the most concrete examples? Which has the most general examples?
7. Explain the relation of sentence 5, paragraph 3, to the previous discussion.
8. Complete the following sentence: In order to have the broadest possible range of values, a person should. . . .

Sentence Structure

1. Which sentences express the enumeration? What is the basic structure of these four sentences?
2. In paragraph 1, three sentences contain dashes. What is the function of the dash in each? How does your answer help to explain something about Perry's habit of mind?
3. In sentences 2–5, paragraph 2, do the final words deserve the emphasis they receive by appearing at the end of the sentences?

4. Sentences 4 and 5, paragraph 2, begin with *when*-clauses. Why should they both begin in the same way?
5. Sentence 10, paragraph 2, has several parallel elements introduced by *from*. Perry repeats the *from* before the second element. What possible misunderstanding does he avoid by repeating it?
6. What transitional terms does Perry use to link the sentences in paragraph 3?

Diction

1. Look up *range, values, apathy, subjectivity, aspiration, provincial, sympathy, circumstance, impetuousness, absorption, usurps, discriminating, importunity, sectarian, mob, vogue, subjugate, degradation, oblivion.* What particular meaning of *circumstance* and *mob* is indicated by the context?
2. What is the difference between *apathy* and *sympathy*? Learn the meanings of the roots of these words.
3. What is the meaning of the roots of *subjectivity* and *subjugate*?
4. Why did *provincial* come to have the meaning illustrated by Perry's use of it here?
5. Is Perry's diction chiefly concrete or abstract? Give evidence for your answer.

Assignment

1. Write a paragraph in which you enumerate the effects of one of the hindrances listed in sentence 6, paragraph 2.
2. Write a paragraph enumerating examples of appetite, zeal, and other forces, as mentioned in sentence 10, paragraph 2, and showing the effects of such a restrictive force.
3. Write a paragraph or two in which you enumerate hindrances to your own success as a human being.

 *Japanese Characteristics*

FOSCO MARAINI
(ERIC MOSBACHER, TRANS.)

1   Summing up the experience of many years in Japan, I should say that there are at least five important Japanese characteristics which throw light on their success in the world, the modern world which they did not help to create.

From *Meeting with Japan* by Fosco Maraini. Coypright © 1959 by Hutchinson and Company (Publishers) Ltd. Reprinted by permission of The Viking Press, Inc.

2   The first is their sense of communion with nature. As we shall see later, the relations between man and his environment in the Far East are profoundly different from our own. Matter is not regarded as something inert and passive to be dominated, but as life, to be understood, loved, possessed. This, of course, is not consciously present in the mind of an operator using a machine-tool in an engineering shop, and if you questioned him about it he would probably be at a loss for an answer, but, like all other men, he is much more than he is consciously aware of. In each one of us there lives the civilization in which we were brought up; behind that workman there are thousands of years of mystic relationship with things, the subtleties of a profoundly monist philosophy, all the poetry of a popular religion according to which the divine suffuses everything, of an art which regards matter as a sister, not as a slave. These realities, on the level of an entire people, count; they give the Japanese, whether designer, director, artist, or simply workman, a lead of several lengths over others.

3   The second characteristic, closely connected with the first, is the extraordinary manual skill, particularly in little things, widespread among Japanese of all regions and all classes. Examine an eighteenth century *inrō* (medicine box), a sixteenth or seventeenth century *tsuba* (sword guard), a plate, any lacquered object, a wicker basket, above all a sword blade; consider the skill and care with which boats, wooden boxes, lanterns, cheap paper-and-bamboo umbrellas are made, and you will immediately appreciate that this standard of workmanship, when harnessed to modern industry, is equivalent to a fabulous gold-mine on which to draw. For centuries the level of excellence required for native products has been such that these skills have become second nature. Examining the work of western craftsman after one has grown used to Japanese standards is like passing one's hand over articles of furniture chopped with an axe after caressing the work of a first-class cabinetmaker. To get some idea of Japanese standards, one must think of Swiss watches, Italian Renaissance armour, certain English furniture and clothing; bearing in mind, however, that in Japan the high standard of craftsmanship applies not only to expensive products, but also to cheap articles of everyday use.

4   The third characteristic is the traditional specialization of the classes. In Japan the feudal system was abolished in 1868; only the day before yesterday, so to speak. For three centuries Japanese society had been rigidly stratified. At one extreme were the 262 *daimyo* (great names) and their families; at the other the *eta,* social pariahs condemned to what in a society under Buddhist influence

were such degrading tasks as tanning hides and butchery. In between, starting from the top, came the Samurai (warriors, about 7 per cent of the population), *hyakushō* (peasants, about 85 per cent), *shokunin* (craftsmen, about 2 per cent) and *shonin* (traders, about 3 per cent). [N. Skene Smith, *Tokugawa Japan,* Tokyo, 1937, p. 31.] It should be noted that traders were at the bottom of the scale, only a little way above the pariahs; a fact which explains the low Japanese commercial morality which prevailed, particularly during the long period at the end of the nineteenth century and the beginning of the twentieth, when the descendants of the best families preferred the professions or state employment to commerce or industry. There is still something degrading associated with money in Japan, and this often leads to hypocritical behaviour of the kind which with us is associated with sex. To return to class divisions; being so close to a past of specialization imposed from birth leads to ready acceptance of the limitations imposed by the requirements of modern industry. In the brief space of three or four generations there has been no time to develop a complete human nature, a rounded personality; thus a working life confined to the perpetual repetition of a few movements tends less strongly to stimulate resentment; it harmonizes with the atmosphere of family memories handed down by word of mouth; and that makes the condition seem more tolerable.

5   Some of the characteristics of the Japanese of which everyone has heard should also be remembered—their frugal and Spartan habits. These are favoured by the fact that life is organized in such a way that the fundamental human needs are satisfied both cheaply and pleasingly. Housing, food, clothes, baths, are all much cheaper than they are with us; a man can be surrounded by beautiful objects without much expense. Luxury, as I have already remarked, is regarded as vulgar. Even middle-class habits are Spartan. People get up early, put up patiently with cold, and are not demanding in such matters as food, dress, and entertainment.

6   Finally, there is a group of characteristics which I perhaps should have put first, characteristics that are to be noted in all fields of Japanese life; the lack of outstanding personalities, the natural need to collaborate, the docility of groups to their leader. . . . One of the things which strikes foreigners, particularly Latins, most vividly is that when you meet the Japanese you rarely have the impression of meeting an outstanding personality, with an above-average intelligence, though when you meet Japan (the product of some labour, a work of art, an event) you are so often carried away by the warmest admiration. With us it is nearly always individuals who are interesting, brilliant, or witty, while collectively they are a poor thing. In Japan

the reverse is true, and the whole is superior to the sum of its parts. Japanese of real talent may perhaps be few, but evidently the system carries them to the top; the others follow and the organism works.

STUDY QUESTIONS

Organization and Content

1. What is the function of paragraph 1? Compare it with paragraph 1 of Perry.
2. To what phase of Japanese life does Maraini's list of characteristics apply?
3. What terms does Maraini use to indicate his enumeration?
4. What is the relation of sentence 3, paragraph 2, to sentence 2? Explain the important contrast brought out in sentence 3.
5. In sentence 5, paragraph 2, Maraini lists four elements that influence a Japanese workman. Identify them.
6. Sentence 5 has a simile: "an art which regards matter as a sister, not as a slave." How effective is this simile? Try to express in nonfigurative terms what this simile, with its connotations, expresses. To do so, how many words do you require?
7. Sentence 2, paragraph 3, lists ten things. What do they exemplify? What is the difference between the four items after the semicolon and those that precede it?
8. With what simile does Maraini express the difference between Japanese craftsmanship and Western craftsmanship?
9. Why did Maraini select certain products of Switzerland, Italy, and England to mention in sentence 5, paragraph 3? What relation does sentence 5 have to sentence 2?
10. What is the significance of the Japanese feudal system in its relation to modern industry?
11. How are sentences 4 and 5, paragraph 5, related to the topic discussed in that paragraph?
12. How is paragraph 5 related to Maraini's main point about the Japanese? Paragraph 6?
13. What is the meaning of "the system" and "the organism" in paragraph 6? Are these terms metaphors or not?
14. In paragraph 6, Maraini mentions characteristics which he says he "perhaps should have put first." Is there a justification for the order of characteristics that he uses? Do you think there is a better order than his?

Sentence Structure

1. What is the arrangement of the dependent material and the independent material in sentence 1, paragraph 1?
2. Point out the elements that are balanced and parallel in sentence

3, paragraph 2, and those that depart from parallelism to provide variety. What would be the effect of placing *and* before *possessed?*

3. To what extent has Maraini used varied sentence structure in paragraph 2 by using sentences of different types—simple, compound, and complex?

4. What are the main terms in the series of elements listed in sentence 5, paragraph 2?

5. Sentences 5 and 6, paragraph 2, use semicolons. Why?

6. To what extent is sentence 1, paragraph 3, symmetrically arranged? How has Maraini handled interrupters here?

7. In sentence 5, paragraph 3, and in sentences 2 and 3, paragraph 4, semicolons appear. For what different purposes are they used? Which of these sentences is a balanced sentence?

8. Why does sentence 4, paragraph 4, have inverted order?

9. A transitional phrase is used after a digression in sentence 7, paragraph 4. What is it? Where did the digression begin?

10. Sentence 8, paragraph 4, has several parts separated by semicolons. What does each part contribute to the thought of the sentence?

11. Both sentences 1 and 2, paragraph 6, are fairly long. Which one exhibits the greater dexterity in the managing of complex sentence materials?

Diction

1. Look up *inert, mystic, subtleties, monist, popular, suffuses, feudal, stratified, pariahs, frugal, Spartan, vulgar, collaborate, docility.*

2. Is there any etymological connection between *mystic* and *mysterious, feudal* and *feud?*

3. Learn the roots of *popular, suffuses, stratified, collaborate.* In what other words do these roots appear?

4. Explain how each of the following metaphors functions in the discussion: *lives* (sentence 5, paragraph 2), *lead* (sentence 6, paragraph 2), *goldmine* (sentence 2, paragraph 3). Which one has the most force and is the most imaginative?

5. Why is *caressing* (sentence 4, paragraph 3) an especially effective word?

Assignment

1. Imitate Maraini by enumerating characteristics of the American or some variety of American, such as the New Englander, Southerner, or Californian.

2. If you are acquainted with any of the following groups, similarly write on the Italians, Jews, Armenians, Negroes, Indians, Puerto Ricans, Latin Americans, Mexicans, Russians, Scandinavians, English, or Germans.

3. Like Maraini, list the characteristics of one of these groups that pertain to one phase of life, such as art, craftsmanship, or business.

4. Enumerate characteristics of aged people, children, or adolescents.

Analysis

Another method of exposition, somewhat different from the mere listing of details, is called analysis. One may wish to set down a record of something, that is, to make a list: for example, these are the tools of a miner, these are the generous acts of Herod, these are the typical activities of Catherine II. On the other hand, one may wish to explain what conclusions he has reached by thinking about some subject in an analytical way. The process of analysis is a process of taking something apart—not ripping it apart and throwing the parts about helter-skelter but taking it apart in a thoughtful, systematic manner so that one can see the parts clearly and understand how they are related to each other. It is rather like "factoring" a problem. Analysis is one of the chief ways by which the human mind deals with the world. The mind can seldom understand anything immediately as a whole; it cannot "take in" an undivided subject very conveniently. It does not feel satisfied that it has properly done its work of thinking unless it knows that it has divided whatever *can* be divided or has classified whatever *can* be classified.

So the writer, when he explains something by the method of analysis, "thinks out" his subject; he divides a thing into parts, or he arranges items according to some scheme of classification. It would be difficult to explain the construction or the operation of an airplane, for example, without mentioning the different parts of the airplane. Merely listing all the parts (as if one were making up a catalogue of supplies) will not help a reader to understand the construction or operation of an airplane. A writer will have to cut up the airplane, as it were—that is, show what chief functioning areas an airplane designer must take into consideration: the power plant, the fuselage, the guiding apparatus, the landing gear, the instruments. Then, of course, he can subdivide and explain what the parts of each main area are and how they relate to each other. Thus, we may see that analysis, as a form of expository writing, goes beyond enumeration although it also makes some use of enumeration.

The process of analysis as it might be applied to the topic of *an airplane* has just been illustrated. But suppose the topic is *air-*

planes. In this case the writer will take his subject apart in a different fashion—by means of classification. He will tell about airplanes according to types: such as heavy, medium, and light; or fighters, bombers, passenger planes, and cargo planes; or propeller-driven planes, turboprop planes, and jet-propelled planes. When one is classifying, the important rule that he must follow is to use principles that are logically parallel for his "files" or "bins" of classification. There would be an illogical hodgepodge if it were stated, "Airplanes fall into the following classification: jet-propelled, passenger, and medium." The three principles of method of propulsion, function, and weight would be mixed up. Such illogical classifying would not help the reader; it would only confuse him. Classification, then, must be made according to logical principles.

Both of these methods of explanation, analysis by partition and analysis by classification, are very commonly used. When one is discussing topics such as those mentioned above or explaining, for example, how something is made, he will use analysis. If one has to explain how steel is produced or how paper is made, he will analyze the process of production, that is, divide it into its parts and explain each step. It is readily evident how enormous is the field of exposition by analysis. It is, therefore, extremely important that the apprentice writer train himself to be efficient in this type of writing.

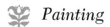 *Painting*

LEON BATTISTA ALBERTI

Painting is divided into three parts, a division we have taken from nature. Since painting tries to represent seen things, let us observe in what way objects are seen. In the first place, when we see an object we say it is a thing that occupies a place. The painter describing this space will call this marking of the edge with a line *circumscription* or outline. Then, looking it over, we observe that many surfaces in the seen object connect, and here the artist, setting

From E. G. Holt, ed., *Literary Sources of Art History* (Princeton, N.J.: Princeton University Press). Copyright 1947.

them down in their proper places, will say that he is making the *composition*. Lastly, we determine more clearly the colors and the qualities of the surfaces. Since every difference in representing these arises from light, we may call it precisely the *reception of light* or illumination. Thus painting is composed of *circumscription, composition,* and the *reception of light*. In the following, each will be discussed briefly.

STUDY QUESTIONS

Organization and Content

1. What is the topic sentence of this paragraph?
2. The three parts into which Alberti divides the process of painting are related by means of what?
3. How has the author emphasized the key terms of his explanation?
4. What is the function of the next-to-last sentence? Of the last sentence?

Sentence Structure

1. What words are used as signals to provide transition in the paragraph?
2. Sentence 2 and two other sentences begin with dependent clauses. Explain what advantage there is in beginning these sentences with dependent clauses.
3. *Painting* is the subject of two main clauses. Is there any advantage in choosing other terms as the subjects of all the other clauses?

Diction

1. Look up the roots of *circumscription, composition, reception, illumination.*
2. From what language are these words borrowed?
3. Give other words using the same roots.

Assignment

Write a paragraph explaining your analysis of some kind of work, a paragraph that might serve as an introduction to a more detailed discussion of the subject. You might write on studying, showing the essential activities that a person must perform in order to study effectively. Or, in the same way as Alberti, write a paragraph indicating the basic operations involved in preparing a meal, making a garden, planting a tree, having a successful meeting.

🌼 Smoking Animals Out of a Tree

GERALD M. DURRELL

The smoking of a tree is quite an art and requires a certain amount of practice before you can perfect it. First, having found your tree and made sure that it is really hollow all the way up, you have to make sure whether there are any exit holes farther up the trunk, and if there are, you have to send a man up to cover them with nets. Having done this, you drape a net over the main hole at the base of the tree, and this has to be done in such a way that it does not interfere with the smoking process and yet prevents anything from getting away. The important thing is to make sure that this net is secure: there is nothing quite so exasperating as to have it fall down and envelop you in its folds just as the creatures inside the tree are starting to come out. With all your nets in position you have to deal with the problem of the fire: this, contrary to all proverbial expectations, has to be all smoke and no fire, unless you want your specimens roasted. A small pile of dry twigs is laid in the opening, soaked with kerosene, and set alight. As soon as it is ablaze, you lay a handful of green leaves on top, and keep replenishing them. The burning of these green leaves produces scarcely any flame but vast quantities of pungent smoke, which is immediately sucked up into the hollow interior of the tree. Your next problem is to make sure that there is not too much smoke, for, if you are not careful, you can quite easily asphyxiate your specimens before they can rush out of the tree. The idea is to strike the happy medium between roasting and suffocation. Once the fire has been lit and piled with green leaves, it generally takes about three minutes (depending on the size of the tree) before the smoke percolates to every part and the animals start to break cover.

STUDY QUESTIONS

Organization and Content

1. In this paragraph the author, a zoological collector who has made several expeditions to Africa, analyzes the process of smoking animals out of

a tree. Into how many steps does he divide the process? Are any of the steps subdivided into smaller operations?
2. Make an outline of the paragraph with the usual indications of divisions: I, A, B, 1, 2; II, and so forth.
3. What is the function of the first and last sentences?
4. To what extent does Durrell use enumeration?

Sentence Structure

1. By what means does Durrell provide transitions (connections) between the steps of the process he is analyzing?
2. Are Durrell's sentences generally formal or colloquial in style? Consider how complicated they are and whether the elements are mainly coordinate or subordinate.
3. What functions do the colons have in sentences 4 and 5?
4. Which sentences begin with subordinate elements? Are there enough of them to provide variety of sentence structure, or does the construction pattern of the sentences seem monotonous?

Diction

1. Look up *replenishing, pungent, suffocation, percolate.*
2. What is the relation between *replenish* and *plenty, pungent* and *point, percolate* and *colander?* Is there any difference between *asphyxiation* and *suffocation?*
3. Is Durrell's diction suitable to a formal style or a colloquial style?

Assignment

Write one analytical paragraph showing the steps in a simple process. Some suggestions: changing a tire, setting lines to catch fish, barbecuing a steak, making a dress, tuning up an engine.

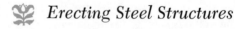 *Erecting Steel Structures*

JOSEPH MITCHELL

In the erection of steel structures, whether bridge or building, there are three main divisions of workers—raising gangs, fitting-up gangs, and riveting gangs. The steel comes to a job already cut and built up into various kinds of columns and beams and girders; the columns are the perpendicular pieces and the beams and girders are the horizontal ones. Each piece has two or more groups of holes bored through it to receive bolts and rivets, and each piece has a code mark chalked or painted on it, indicating where it should go in the structure. Using a crane or a derrick, the men in the raising gang hoist the pieces up and set them in position and join them by running bolts through a few of the holes in them; these bolts are temporary. Then the men in the fitting-up gang come along; they are divided into plumbers and bolters. The plumbers tighten up the pieces with guy wires and turnbuckles and make sure that they are in plumb. The bolters put in some more temporary bolts. Then the riveting gangs come along; one raising gang and one fitting-up gang will keep several riveting gangs busy. There are four men in a riveting gang—a heater, a sticker-in, a bucker-up, and a riveter. The heater lays some wooden planks across a couple of beams, making a platform for the portable, coal-burning forge in which he heats the rivets. The three other men hang a plank scaffold by ropes from the steel on which they are going to work. There are usually six two-by-ten planks in a scaffold, three on each side of the steel, affording just room enough to work; one false step and it's goodbye Charlie. The three men climb down with their tools and take their positions on the scaffold; most often the sticker-in and the bucker-up stand on one side and the riveter stands or kneels on the other. The heater, on his platform, picks a red-hot rivet off the coals in his forge with tongs and tosses it to the sticker-in, who catches it in a metal can. At this stage, the rivet is shaped like a mushroom; it has a buttonhead and a stem. Meanwhile, the bucker-up has unscrewed and pulled out one of the temporary bolts joining two pieces of steel, leaving the hole empty. The sticker-in picks the rivet out of his can with tongs and sticks it in the hole and pushes it in until the buttonhead is flush with the steel on his side and the stem protrudes from the other side, the riveter's side. The sticker-in steps out of the way. The bucker-up fits a tool called a dolly bar over the buttonhead and holds it there, bracing the rivet. Then the riveter presses the cupped head of his pneumatic hammer against the protruding stem end of the rivet, which is still red-hot and malleable, and turns on the power and forms a buttonhead on it. This operation is repeated until every hole that can be got at from the scaffold is riveted up. Then the scaffold is moved. The heater's platform stays in one place until all the work within a rivet-tossing radius of thirty to forty feet is completed. The men on the scaffold know each other's jobs and are interchangeable; the riveter's job is bone-shaking and nerve-racking, and every so often one of the others swaps with him for a while.

In the days before pneumatic hammers, the riveter used two tools, a cupped die and an iron maul; he placed the die over the stem end of the red-hot rivet and beat on it with the maul until he squashed the stem end into a buttonhead.

STUDY QUESTIONS

Organization and Content

1. In this piece of exposition analysis is applied to the workers, the material, and the process. Explain how the workers and the material are divided into parts.
2. Why does the author have to speak about the workers and the material before he explains the process?
3. The author does not number the steps in the process. How does he make clear the passing from one step to another?
4. How are the classes of workers fitted into the sequence of operations? Which class receives the most attention?
5. Make an outline indicating the divisions and subdivisions of the workers.
6. What is the purpose of the last three sentences?

Sentence Structure

1. Is this a substantial paragraph? How many sentences does it contain?
2. How long are the sentences? Which is the shortest sentence? The longest? What is the average length?
3. How many of the sentences begin with the subject instead of with a subordinate element?
4. How many sentences have a straightforward subject-verb-complement construction?
5. Is the sentence construction suitable for the topic which is being explained?
6. What grammatical constructions has the author used for introducing the divisions and subdivisions of things analyzed?

Diction

1. Make a list of the active verbs used in this paragraph. How many sentences contain such verbs?
2. What is the difference between a *crane* and a *derrick?* What are the sources of these words?
3. Explain the relationships among *maul, malleable,* and *mallet.*
4. Explain what gives *pneumatic, pneumatology,* and *pneumonia* a common element.
5. How can words so different as *scaffold* and *catafalque* have a common origin?
6. Is the author's style either too formal or too informal? Does he use chiefly a formal or a colloquial vocabulary?

Assignment

Analyze a process and explain the steps required. Some suggestions are:

1. The operation of an office, indicating what workers are needed and their duties
2. The production of a newspaper
3. The construction or the operation of a chicken house
4. The organizing of an efficiently managed picnic or other outing for a considerable group of people
5. Spraying fruit
6. Preparing a flower bed, from the first step to the blooming of the flowers
7. Making a pond
8. Raising dogs, pigs, or cattle from birth to maturity

 Robinson Crusoe's Dwelling

Daniel Defoe

1   My thoughts were now wholly employed about securing myself against either savages, if any should appear, or wild beasts, if any were in the island; and I had many thoughts of the method how to do this and what kind of dwelling to make, whether I should make me a cave in the earth or a tent upon the earth. And, in short, I resolved upon both, the manner and description of which it may not be improper to give an account of.

2   I consulted several things in my situation, which I found would be proper for me: first, health and fresh water; secondly, shelter from the heat of the sun; thirdly, security from ravenous creatures, whether men or beasts; fourthly, a view to the sea, that if God sent any ship in sight, I might not lose any advantage for my deliverance, of which I was not willing to banish all my expectation yet.

3   In search of a place proper for this I found a little plain on the side of a rising hill, whose front towards this little plain was steep as a house-side so that nothing could come down upon me from the top; on the side of this rock there was a hollow place worn

From Daniel Defoe, *The Life and Strange Surprizing Adventures of Robinson Crusoe, of York, Mariner* (1719).

a little way in like the entrance or door of a cave, but there was not really any cave, or way into the rock at all.

4   On the flat of the green, just before this hollow place, I resolved to pitch my tent. This plain was not above a hundred yards broad and about twice as long, and lay like a green before my door and at the end of it descended irregularly every way down into the low grounds by the seaside. It was on the north-northwest side of the hill, so that I was sheltered from the heat every day, till it came to a west and by south sun, or thereabouts, which in those countries is near the setting.

5   Before I set up my tent, I drew a half circle before the hollow place, which took in about ten yards in its semi-diameter from the rock and twenty yards in its diameter, from its beginning and ending.

6   In this half circle I pitched two rows of strong stakes, driving them into the ground till they stood very firm like piles, the biggest end being out of the ground about five foot and a half and sharpened on the top. The two rows did not stand above six inches from one another.

7   Then I took the pieces of cable which I had cut in the ship, and laid them in rows one upon another, within the circle, between these two rows of stakes, up to the top, placing other stakes in the inside, leaning against them, about two foot and a half high, like a spur to a post; and this fence was so strong that neither man nor beast could get into it or over it. This cost me a great deal of time and labor, especially to cut the piles in the woods, bring them to the place, and drive them into the earth.

8   The entrance into this place I made to be not by a door, but by a short ladder to go over the top, which ladder, when I was in, I lifted over after me, and so I was completely fenced in, and fortified, as I thought, from all the world, and consequently slept secure in the night, which otherwise I could not have done.

STUDY QUESTIONS

Organization and Content

1. Defoe's famous character Robinson Crusoe explains in eight short paragraphs the constructing of his dwelling on his island. What does he accomplish in paragraph 1? In paragraph 2?
2. After reading paragraph 2, what would you expect in the rest of the explanation?
3. How does this piece of exposition resemble the paragraph by Mitchell?
4. The paragraphing here might be called journalistic; that is, several of Defoe's paragraphs are extremely short, like those in a modern newspaper. Which paragraphs consist of only one sentence each?

5. Explain which of Defoe's paragraphs might logically be combined into longer paragraphs.
6. What topic sentences would you have to invent for new, longer paragraphs?
7. Where, in this selection, are you aware of the act of analysis?

Sentence Structure

1. How has Defoe used balanced phrasing and balanced grammatical constructions in sentence 1?
2. Where does grammatical balance appear in paragraph 2?
3. Which are the three longest of Defoe's sentences? Does their length make them hard to understand? Explain why it does or does not.

Diction

1. Defoe's language is quite simple. Are there any words that you need to look up?
2. Does Defoe use simpler, commoner, less technical words than Alberti and Mitchell?
3. List the conjunctions that Defoe uses. Which ones does he use most?
4. What is the effect, in terms of sentence length and complexity, of these conjunctions?

Assignment

Write three or four paragraphs explaining why some place in which you have lived was very pleasant or very unpleasant. You will have to analyze such things as its situation, arrangement, and particular facilities. Or, if you have ever built a camp, explain, after the manner of Robinson Crusoe, how you did it. Or write three or four paragraphs that tell what your plan would be for an ideal home. Underline the topic sentences of your paragraphs.

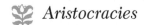 *Aristocracies*

THOMAS JEFFERSON
(FROM A LETTER TO JOHN ADAMS, 1813)

I agree with you that there is a natural aristocracy among men. The grounds of this are virtue and talents. Formerly, bodily powers gave place among the *aristoi*. But since the invention of gunpowder

From *The Writings of Thomas Jefferson,* The Thomas Jefferson Memorial Association (Washington, 1903).

has armed the weak as well as the strong with missile death, bodily strength like beauty, good humor, politeness, and other accomplishments has become but an auxiliary ground of distinction. There is also an artificial aristocracy, formed on wealth and birth, without either virtue or talents; for with these it would belong to the first class. The natural aristocracy I consider as the most precious gift of nature for the instruction, the trusts, and government of society. And, indeed, it would have been inconsistent in creation to have formed man for the social state and not to have provided virtue and wisdom enough to manage the concerns of society. May we not even say that that form of government is the best which provides the most effectually for a pure selection of these natural *aristoi* into the offices of government. The artificial aristocracy is a mischievous ingredient in government, and provision should be made to prevent its ascendancy. On the question what is the best provision, you and I differ, but we differ as rational friends, using the free exercise of our own reason and mutually indulging its errors. You think it best to put the pseudo-*aristoi* into a separate chamber of legislation, where they may be hindered from doing mischief by their co-ordinate branches and where, also, they may be a protection to wealth against the agrarian and plundering enterprises of the majority of the people. I think that to give them power in order to prevent them from doing mischief is arming them for it and increasing instead of remedying the evil.

STUDY QUESTIONS

Organization and Content

1. Jefferson has divided aristocrats into what main kinds?
2. What are the bases of each category?
3. Set down Jefferson's pattern of division using Roman numerals and capital letters.
4. What do sentences 2 and 3 contribute to the discussion?
5. At what point does Jefferson begin to discuss the functions of aristocrats in government?
6. Explain in your own words why he differed with John Adams on this point.

Sentence Structure

1. What methods of transition has Jefferson used in his sentences—repetition of important words, pronouns, special transitional terms?

2. In how many of the sentences do the key terms of the discussion appear?
3. Has Jefferson placed these key terms in his sentences so as to give them emphasis?
4. What contrast is indicated by the phrasing of the last two sentences?

Diction

1. Look up *aristocracy,* "aristoi," *auxiliary, pseudo, agrarian.*
2. From what languages have these words been taken?

Assignment

Write a paragraph like Jefferson's in which you analyze:

1. Your college class in terms of its qualities or its backgrounds
2. Student organizations in terms of the students' experience or environment
3. Teachers in terms of their classroom behavior
4. Classes in terms of their attitudes toward learning

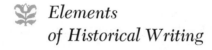 *Elements of Historical Writing*

ALLAN NEVINS

. . . Historical writing involves three elements. One is the element of factual inquiry and sifting—that is, research. This should be strictly scientific in its use of highly exact principles to accumulate, observe, and weigh data; it is scientific, that is, in method. The second element is that of interpretation. Having accumulated his facts, the historian must discover their logical connection with each other, the laws which rule them and their significance for the period studied and for our own time. In this second element lie broad possibilities for the establishment of a scientific set of deductions. But here the word science is used in a different sense; a scientific generalization from a large number of historical facts has the same quality as a generalization from a large number of zoological facts. It is an attempt to set up a general law resting on the weight of evidence. Darwin

From Allan Nevins, *The Gateway to History* (Boston: D. C. Heath and Company, 1938).

not merely accumulated a mass of data bearing on the differences among species; he tried to establish a law explaining the differences. A scientific historian who studied revolutions would not merely accumulate a vast mass of data on these human upheavals; he would try to formulate some laws common to all. Finally, the third element in historical writing is presentation—the narration, description, and exposition required to set forth the results of research and interpretation.

STUDY QUESTIONS

Organization and Content

1. Identify the elements of historical writing.
2. What do the first two elements have in common? How is the third element different from them?
3. What is the historian's purpose in "sifting" and "weighing" data?
4. Would *inductions* be a better word than *deductions* in sentence 5?
5. Explain the logical relations among sentences 6, 7, 8, and 9.
6. Darwin was not a historical writer. Why does Nevins mention him?
7. Make an outline of the paragraph, showing the main divisions and subdivisions by using Roman numerals and capital letters.

Sentence Structure

1. What means of connection (transitions) relate sentences 2 and 3; 4, 5, and 6; 7 and 8?
2. Why does Nevins use parallel structure in sentence 7?
3. Why should sentences 9 and 10 have the same structural pattern?
4. What is the function of the semicolon in sentences 3, 7, 9, and 10?

Diction

1. Is the diction of this paragraph mainly concrete or abstract? Why?
2. What is the singular of *data?* Do not confuse the singular and plural of words like this, such as *bacterium, criterion, media, phenomena,* and *strata.*

Assignment

Write one analytical paragraph, explaining the elements of a successful political campaign, successful gardening or flower growing, music appreciation, or proficiency in swimming, archery, golf, tennis, bowling, or in some other sport.

🌺 An Analysis
of American Society

DAVID RIESMAN

1   . . . One way of looking at American society at present is to divide it into two groups of people: one, a relatively small white-collar and professional group who work long hours and bear disproportionate responsibilities; and the other, a relatively large group who work short hours (even if one does not include coffee breaks) and bear few taxing responsibilities. This latter group includes the millions of forty-hour-per-week workers, of thirty-hour-per-week school children, and of retired people.

2   American life is, of course, unevenly mechanized and systematized, and the first-named group must fill in for America's deficiencies—and rise to its challenges—out of their personal energies and at the frequent expense of their own budget of leisure and ease. Some in this group of people are industrial managers, well-paid in money and prestige for worrying about productivity, the meaning of which has been extended to include employee morale, health, psychological security, and general happiness; and for worrying about selling a product, a transaction which now embraces many novel private and public services (budgeted for under "good will"). Some in this group of people are high civil servants, paid neither in money nor in unambiguous prestige for worrying about the resentments of the rest of the world. Some of these people are doctors, paid with very great prestige and moderately great fees for working sixty- and seventy-hour weeks to repair the health of a nation which can increasingly afford health, and which redefines it to extend from the somatic to the psychosomatic to the psychosocial, and from the cure of acute illness to the prevention of debility and the extension and beatitude of the life span. And some of the people in this first group of overtime worriers are professors, perhaps increasingly bitter about pay and prestige, and more harassed in trying to make sense of their data (too much of it, and too equivocal), of each other (more conferences, committees, and projects than ever), and of their students (more of whom can now afford college and fewer of whom, for reasons

From David Riesman, "Thoughts on Teachers and Schools," *The Anchor Review,* Vol. I (New York: Doubleday & Co., Inc., 1955).

we shall examine, come with elementary literacy). Even so, these professors' pay and prestige, if it appears low to them, is worlds above that of most public school teachers, and the latter also have many more compulsory classroom hours (though there are a few, in the best city and suburban systems, who will fare better financially than, for instance, a classics professor at a small non-ivy campus). Indeed many members of this first group are "paid" for their long hours by the variety and freedom their work permits: they prefer accepting even wearisome responsibilities to enduring meaningless routines under others' supervision.

3   Public school teachers are, in all probability, the largest aggregation of those who, themselves left behind by industrial advance and the general shortening and lightening of hours, must supply much of the energy for that advance and much of the training for the work-free future of their pupils. Teachers are in fact the archetype of these white-collar functionaries, who, in helping bring about a society of greater abundance, have their own official and unofficial lives torn and complicated in the process. The teaching function, since it does involve the training or "guidance" of children for an era of abundance, has been extended to include training in group co-operation, manners, the arts, and self-understanding, as well as in large residues of the traditional curriculum. Teachers, therefore, are under growing pressure to provide a "happy and rounded atmosphere" in the classroom, while they themselves lead lives of harried desperation, not only because of the multiplying demands of the classroom, but because of the many "voluntary" activities expected of them: advising the dramatics or journalism club, consulting with parents, participating in civic and church groups. Many feel they must use their "vacations" attending summer school to acquire needed credits, or earning extra money with summer camps.

STUDY QUESTIONS

Organization and Content

1. What preliminary division of American society does Riesman perform in paragraph 1?
2. What act of subdivision is performed in paragraph 2?
3. Show the division and subdivisions by making an outline of paragraphs 1 and 2.

4. How is paragraph 3 related to paragraph 2?
5. What are the bases of the division made in paragraph 1?
6. In what terms is "pay" represented in paragraph 2? Are these terms used consistently with each subgroup?
7. Does the author mean in paragraph 2, sentence 1, that American life should be "evenly mechanized and systematized"? If it were, what changes would be required?
8. Look up *irony* and *paradox*. Then explain what is ironical or paradoxical in paragraph 3.

Sentence Structure

1. Explain the functions of the three parts of sentence 1: the part before the colon, the one between the colon and the semicolon, and the one after the semicolon.
2. What is the grammatical relation of *workers, children,* and *people* in sentence 2?
3. What repetitions does the author use to provide good transitions in all three paragraphs?
4. Parallel grammatical constructions represent an important element of sentence style in paragraph 2. Show exactly where and how they are used.
5. The second half of paragraph 2 has four parentheses, the first three in one sentence. Do these parentheses clog the sentence, or do they perform a significant function?

Diction

1. Look up *prestige, novel* (adj.), *unambiguous, somatic, psychosomatic, debility, beatitude, equivocal, literacy, aggregation, archetype, functionaries, residues.*
2. The roots of all these words are important. Learn their meanings. From what languages do they come?
3. Explain the difference between *morale* (paragraph 2) and *moral.*
4. What is the meaning of "disproportionate responsibilities" in paragraph 1?
5. The author has placed quotation marks around a number of words: "good will" and "paid" in paragraph 2; "guidance," "happy and rounded atmosphere," "voluntary" and "vacations" in paragraph 3. Why?
6. David Riesman is a famous sociologist. Is his vocabulary highly technical? Is it difficult?

Assignment

Write an analysis of a group similar to Riesman's: you might divide a college student body on the basis of curricular efforts and extracurricular activities, and the honors or "pay" that go with them; or citizens of any community on the basis of civic activities. Or you might make a division of stores, dogs, sports, or types of clothing in terms of function or prestige.

❧ *Types of Coral Reefs*

F. D. OMMANNEY

1   There are three main types of coral reef. The first is the fringing reef which lies just off the main shore, separated from it by a narrow and shallow lagoon. It is this kind of reef which encircles Mauritius like a girdle, leaving between itself and the coast of the island a shallow stretch of water, in places only a few hundred yards wide but in others, as at Grand Port, expanding to a width of two miles or more. Fringing reefs, too, encircle many of the islands that we visited such as Coëtivy and Agalega and, though irregular and broken in places, lie off parts of the coasts of Mahé and Praslin in the Seychelles. Down the east coast of Africa from Cape Guardafui to the coast of Portuguese East there runs an almost continuous coral reef which is mostly of the fringing type.

2   The second type is the barrier reef, which lies at a much greater distance from the coast than the fringing reef and may be several miles wide with many channels through it, and is separated from the mainland by a wide lagoon. The most famous example of this type is the Great Barrier Reef off the eastern coast of Australia. It is over a thousand miles long. In its northern half the barrier may not be more than 20 or 30 miles from the Queensland coast, but in its southern half it is as much as 50 or 100 miles from the coast and consists of several parallel reefs with channels between them.

3   The third type of reef is the atoll, a ring of growing corals crowned with palm trees, often hundreds of miles from any true land and rising abruptly in the ocean from a depth of thousands of fathoms. In the Chagos Islands we found true atolls at Diego Garcia and Peros Banhos, irregular rings of coral rock and sand on which a lush vegetation has taken root, and on which plantations have long been cultivated by man. In the Aldabra group also, 700 miles south-west of the Seychelles, we found coral reefs of varying degrees of perfection.

STUDY QUESTIONS

Organization and Content

1. What is the purpose of the first sentence in each of the three paragraphs?
2. Explain by what principle Ommanney has classified coral reefs.
3. Besides telling the reader the characteristics of each kind of coral reef, what does Ommanney do in his paragraphs?

Sentence Structure

1. In paragraph 1, sentences 2, 3, and 5 have relative clauses introduced by *which,* and in paragraph 2, sentence 1 has a similar clause. Some of these are restrictive clauses. Are they punctuated correctly? Should some of them really be nonrestrictive?
2. How are participial phrases balanced in sentence 3?
3. In sentence 4 *reefs* is the subject of what verbs?
4. Note how *too* is tucked away after *reefs* in sentence 4; in the latter part of the sentence this adverb is balanced by what adverbial element similarly placed?

Diction

1. Why does Ommanney mention so many far-away place names?
2. Point out terms used for transition in these paragraphs.
3. To what extent has the author used a technical vocabulary?

Assignment

Analyze, as Ommanney does, some type of thing with which you are familiar—banks, grocery stores, games, vocations, or moving pictures would offer good possibilities. Classify according to a single principle, and give several examples of each type that you mention.

 The Work of the Manager

Peter F. Drucker

1   Every manager does many things that are not managing. He may spend most of his time on them. A sales manager makes a statistical analysis or placates an important customer. A foreman repairs

a tool or fills in a production report. A manufacturing manager designs a new plant layout or tests new materials. A company president works through the details of a bank loan or negotiates a big contract—or spends dreary hours presiding at a dinner in honor of long-service employees. All these things pertain to a particular function. All are necessary, and have to be done well.

2   But they are apart from that work which every manager does whatever his function or activity, whatever his rank and position, work which is common to all managers and peculiar to them. The best proof is that we can apply to the job of the manager the systematic analysis of Scientific Management. We can isolate that which a man does because he is a manager. We can divide it into the basic constituent operations. And a man can improve his performance as a manager by improving his performance of these constituent motions.

3   There are five such basic operations in the work of the manager. Together they result in the integration of resources into a living and growing organism.

4   A manager, in the first place, *sets objectives*. He determines what the objectives should be. He determines what the goals in each area of objectives should be. He decides what has to be done to reach these objectives. He makes the objectives effective by communicating them to the people whose performance is needed to attain them.

5   Secondly, a manager *organizes*. He analyzes the activities, decisions and relations needed. He classifies the work. He divides it into manageable activities. He further divides the activities into manageable jobs. He groups these units and jobs into an organization structure. He selects people for the management of these units and for the jobs to be done.

6   Next a manager *motivates and communicates*. He makes a team out of the people that are responsible for various jobs. He does that through the practices with which he manages. He does it in his own relation to the men he manages. He does it through incentives and rewards for successful work. He does it through his promotion policy. And he does it through constant communication, both from the manager to his subordinate, and from the subordinate to the manager.

7   The fourth basic element in the work of the manager is *the job of measurement*. The manager establishes measuring yardsticks— and there are few factors as important to the performance of the organization and of every man in it. He sees to it that each man in the organization has measurements available to him which are focused on the performance of the whole organization and which at the same time focus on the work of the individual and help him

do it. He analyzes performance, appraises it and interprets it. And again, as in every other area of his work, he communicates both the meaning of the measurements and their findings to his subordinates as well as to his superiors.

8   Finally, a manager *develops people*. Through the way he manages he makes it easy or difficult for them to develop themselves. He directs people or misdirects them. He brings out what is in them or he stifles them. He strengthens their integrity or he corrupts them. He trains them to stand upright and strong or he deforms them.

9   Every manager does these things when he manages—whether he knows it or not. He may do them well, or he may do them wretchedly. But he always does them.

STUDY QUESTIONS

Organization and Content

1. What is the purpose of paragraph 1? What is its topic sentence? How many examples support the topic idea? Why does Drucker begin the last two sentences with the emphatic *all*?
2. What signal tells us that paragraph 2 contrasts with paragraph 1? What is the basis of the contrast? How does Drucker define "analysis of Scientific Management"?
3. Why is paragraph 3 so short? What do paragraphs 4–8 have in common? What purpose does paragraph 9 serve, and why is it so short?
4. Explain in one sentence the pattern of Drucker's discussion of the work of the manager.
5. With what terms has Drucker enumerated the parts of his analysis? How has he emphasized the key terms of his explanation?
6. Paragraph 8 introduces an aspect of the manager's work not mentioned in the other paragraphs. What is it? Why include it in paragraph 8?

Sentence Structure

1. A large majority of Drucker's sentences belong to one of three types. Are most of his sentences simple, compound, or complex?
2. How many sentences belong to the subject-verb-complement type?
3. What do the answers to these two questions indicate about Drucker's style of writing?
4. By what method of transition does Drucker link most of his sentences?
5. Would you call Drucker's style of writing formal or colloquial? Compare it with the style of Hersey, Abbey, Maraini, and Nevins.

Diction

1. Look up *constituent, integration, organism, determines, incentives, integrity.*

2. What is the relation between *constituent* and *constitution, integration* and *integrity, determines* and *terminal?*
3. Is there a difference between *incentives* and *rewards?*
4. Is Drucker's vocabulary difficult to understand? Is it mainly abstract or concrete? Is there any relation between the vocabulary and the sentence style?

Assignment

Write a short theme in which you analyze the "basic constituent operations" of—for example—a teacher, a student, a housewife, a soldier, a policeman, a cook, a bus driver, a minister, or a priest.

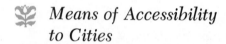 *Means of Accessibility to Cities*

VICTOR GRUEN

1   Now, let us assume that we have been able to create a city heart possessing all these criteria of good health. It would still not function if it were not within easy reach of those who wish to become activity participants. It must therefore have good *accessibility*—a term denoting ease of travel to and from the core, for people as well as for goods, from all land areas that make up the metropolitan region, and beyond that, from other cities and from the countryside, from the state, the nation and, in fact, the world. There must be a variety of *instruments of accessibility,* some effecting primarily the transportation of goods, others of people. One such instrument is *individualized transportation,* a term referring to comparatively small travel containers utilized by single individuals or by a small number of people (automobiles, taxicabs, motorcycles, bicycles) or for carrying a comparatively small quantity of goods (trucks of various sizes and types). Another instrument of accessibility is *mass transportation,* referring to transportation in much larger travel containers used by a considerable number of people at the same time, such as planes, railroad trains, rapid-transit trains, busses, conveyor systems and, for the transportation of goods, freight trains, trucks, etc. A healthy urban heart,

then, is also one that offers easy accessibility through a composite of instruments balanced to work most beneficially. A significant part of easy accessibility is good *core terminal facilities,* well placed. These are the starting or terminal points for travel in and out of the core, and they match in diversity the variety of instruments of accessibility. There will be commuter train and other railroad terminals, bus terminals, terminals for individualized transportation (automobile storage facilities), freight terminals.

2   The surfaces on which the various instruments of accessibility move in order to reach the core terminal facilities we will term *accessibility media.* As far as individualized transportation is concerned, these media are the *core-bound roads,* those which in the main are arranged radially, leading from the outlying areas toward the heart; and *distributary roads,* those which follow the basic pattern of concentric rings around the heart at various distances from it (often referred to, also, as ring roads or loop roads). To some extent mass transportation, as in the case of buses, uses the same media, but for the most part it utilizes media specifically reserved for it, like rail lines for trains, for rapid transit, and so on. Here, too, we find core-bound transportation media radially approaching the core from the outside, and distributary media following the pattern of concentric circles. A well-designed system of transportation media, balanced in quantity and quality to ensure the easiest accessibility, is another symptom of a healthy heart.

3   A large metropolitan area will have a core of proportionate size and will therefore require an adequate *core transportation system.* Transportation facilities within the core are: movement on foot, mass transportation specifically designed for suitability to short distances, possibly taxicabs, etc. A sign of good health in a large core area is a transportation system specifically adjusted to the needs of a compact area of great vitality—rather than a carbon copy, in reduced scale, of transportation systems designed to achieve easy accessibility to and from the outside.

STUDY QUESTIONS

Organization and Content

1. Sentence 1, paragraph 1, indicates that Gruen uses the metaphor of a "city heart" to illustrate his discussion. Explain how this metaphor functions in the analysis.

2. What problem is Gruen using this analysis to try to solve?
3. What is the reason behind the *therefore* of sentence 3?
4. How does the main idea of paragraph 3 differ from that of paragraphs 1 and 2?
5. How does Gruen define *accessibility?* What other terms are briefly defined? Why does Gruen use these definitions?
6. Of what importance in the discussion is the concept of balance?
7. Into how many main parts does Gruen divide means of accessibility? What names does he give to these parts?
8. Which part of the analysis is supported by the most examples?
9. Make an outline of this selection.

Sentence Structure

1. What transitional links does Gruen use between sentences 1–4? 4–6? 6–10?
2. Point out examples of grammatical parallelism in sentence 3. What is their function?
3. In several sentences Gruen has to arrange his material so as to include lists of examples. What different methods of introducing and setting off the examples does he use?
4. Why is the semicolon necessary in sentence 2, paragraph 2?
5. Could the dash in the last sentence be omitted or replaced by another mark of punctuation? What is the probable reason that Gruen used it?

Diction

1. Are abstract terms or concrete terms predominant in the author's vocabulary?
2. Look up *criteria, metropolitan, composite* (noun), *diversity, radially, transit.*
3. What is the etymological connection between *criteria* and *critic, metropolitan* and *cosmopolitan, composite* and *opposite, diversity* and *convert, radially* and *radiantly, transit* and *exit?* Do the roots of all these words come from Latin?

Assignment

1. In one, two, or three paragraphs explain the idea that there are different types of automobiles, houses, communities, or comic strips.
2. Analyze the needs of your home community.
3. Analyze the different means of gaining knowledge that a student can use or different types of recreation that are available to people in various places.
4. Analyze the various things that are used in any business office, on a farm, in a garage, or in a kitchen.

❧ The Marks of an Educated Man

ALAN SIMPSON

1   Any education that matters is *liberal*. All the saving truths and healing graces that distinguish a good education from a bad one or a full education from a half-empty one are contained in that word. Whatever ups and downs the term "liberal" suffers in the political vocabulary, it soars above all controversy in the educational world. In the blackest pits of pedagogy the squirming victim has only to ask, "What's liberal about this?" to shame his persecutors. In times past a liberal education set off a free man from a slave or a gentleman from laborers and artisans. It now distinguishes whatever nourishes the mind and spirit from the training which is merely practical or professional or from the trivialities which are no training at all. Such an education involves a combination of knowledge, skills, and standards.

2   So far as knowledge is concerned, the record is ambiguous. It is sufficiently confused for the fact-filled freak who excels in quiz shows to have passed himself off in some company as an educated man. More respectable is the notion that there are some things which every educated man ought to know; but many highly educated men would cheerfully admit to a vast ignorance, and the framers of curriculums have differed greatly in the knowledge they prescribe. If there have been times when all the students at school or college studied the same things, as if it were obvious that without exposure to a common body of knowledge they would not be educated at all, there have been other times when specialization ran so wild that it might almost seem as if educated men had abandoned the thought of ever talking to each other once their education was completed.

3   If knowledge is one of our marks, we can hardly be dogmatic about the kind or the amount. A single fertile field tilled with care and imagination can probably develop all the instincts of an educated man. However, if the framer of a curriculum wants to minimize his risks, he can invoke an ancient doctrine which holds that an educated man ought to know a little about everything and a lot about something.

4   The "little about everything" is best interpreted these days by

those who have given most thought to the sort of general education an informed individual ought to have. More is required than a sampling of the introductory courses which specialists offer in their own disciplines. Courses are needed in each of the major divisions of knowledge—the humanities, the natural sciences, and social sciences—which are organized with the breadth of view and the imaginative power of competent staffs who understand the needs of interested amateurs. But, over and above this exciting smattering of knowledge, students should bite deeply into at least one subject and taste its full flavor. It is not enough to be dilettantes in everything without striving also to be craftsmen in something.

5   If there is some ambiguity about the knowledge an educated man should have, there is none at all about the skills. The first is simply the training of the mind in the capacity to think clearly. This has always been the business of education, but the way it is done varies enormously. Marshalling the notes of a lecture is one experience; the opportunity to argue with a teacher is another. Thinking within an accepted tradition is one thing; to challenge the tradition itself is another. The best results are achieved when the idea of the examined life is held firmly before the mind and when the examination is conducted with the zest, rigor, and freedom which really stretches everyone's capacities.

6   The vital aid to clear thought is the habit of approaching everything we hear and everything we are taught to believe with a certain skepticism. The method of using doubt as an examiner is a familiar one among scholars and scientists, but it is also the best protection which a citizen has against the cant and humbug that surround us.

7   To be able to listen to a phony argument and to see its dishonesty is surely one of the marks of an educated man. We may not need to be educated to possess some of this quality. A shrewd peasant was always well enough protected against impostors in the market place, and we have all sorts of businessmen who have made themselves excellent judges of phoniness without the benefit of a high-school diploma; but this kind of shrewdness goes along with a great deal of credulity. Outside the limited field within which experience has taught the peasant or the illiterate businessman his lessons, he is often hopelessly gullible. The educated man, by contrast, has tried to develop a critical faculty for general use, and he likes to think that he is fortified against imposture in all its forms.

8   It does not matter for our purposes whether the impostor is a deliberate liar or not. Some are, but the commonest enemies of mankind are the unconscious frauds. Most salesmen under the intoxication of their own exuberance seem to believe in what they say.

Most experts whose *expertise* is only a pretentious sham behave as if they had been solemnly inducted into some kind of priesthood. Very few demagogues are so cynical as to remain undeceived by their own rhetoric, and some of the worst tyrants in history have been fatally sincere. We can leave the disentanglement of motives to the students of fraud and error, but we cannot afford to be taken in by the shams.

9   We are, of course, surrounded by shams. Until recently the schools were full of them—the notion that education can be had without tears, that puffed rice is a better intellectual diet than oatmeal, that adjustment to the group is more important than knowing where the group is going, and that democracy has made it a sin to separate the sheep from the goats. Mercifully, these are much less evident now than they were before Sputnik startled us into our wits.

10   In front of the professor are the shams of the learned fraternity. There is the sham science of the social scientist who first invented a speech for fuddling thought and then proceeded to tell us in his lockjawed way what we already knew. There is the sham humanism of the humanist who wonders why civilization that once feasted at his table is repelled by the shredded and desiccated dishes that often lie on it today. There is the sham message of the physical scientist who feels that his mastery of nature has made him an expert in politics and morals, and there are all the other brands of hokum which have furnished material for satire since the first quacks established themselves in the first cloisters.

11   If this is true of universities with their solemn vows and limited temptations, how much truer is it of the naughty world outside, where the prizes are far more dazzling and the only protection against humbug is the skepticism of the ordinary voter, customer, reader, listener, and viewer? Of course, the follies of human nature are not going to be exorcised by anything that the educator can do, and I am not sure that he would want to exorcise them if he could. There is something irresistibly funny about the old Adam, and life would be duller without his antics. But they ought to be kept within bounds. We are none the better for not recognizing a clown when we see one.

12   The other basic skill is simply the art of self-expression in speech and on paper. A man is uneducated who has not mastered the elements of clean forcible prose and picked up some relish for style.

13   It is a curious fact that we style everything in this country—our cars, our homes, our clothes—except our minds. They still chug along like a Model T—rugged, persevering, but far from graceful.

14   No doubt this appeal for style, like the appeal for clear thinking,

can be carried too far. There was once an American who said that the only important thing in life was "to set a chime of words ringing in a few fastidious minds." As far as can be learned, he left this country in a huff to tinkle his little bell in a foreign land. Most of us would think that he lacked a sense of proportion. After all, the political history of this country is full of good judgment expressed in bad prose, and the business history has smashed through to some of its grandest triumphs across acres of broken syntax. But we can discard some of these frontier manners without becoming absurdly precious.

15   The road ahead bristles with obstacles. There is the reluctance of many people to use one word where they can get away with a half-dozen or a word of one syllable if they can find a longer one. No one has ever told them about the first rule in English composition: every slaughtered syllable is a good deed. The most persuasive teachers of this maxim are undoubtedly the commercial firms that offer a thousand dollars for the completion of a slogan in twenty-five words. They are the only people who are putting a handsome premium on economy of statement.

16   There is the decay of the habit of memorizing good prose and good poetry in the years when tastes are being formed. It is very difficult to write a bad sentence if the Bible has been a steady companion and very easy to imagine a well-turned phrase if the ear has been tuned on enough poetry.

17   There is the monstrous proliferation of gobbledy-gook in government, business, and the professions. Take this horrible example of verbal smog.

> It is inherent to motivational phenomena that there is a drive for more gratification than is realistically possible, on any level or in any type of personality organization. Likewise it is inherent to the world of objects that not all potentially desirable opportunities can be realized within a human life span. Therefore, any personality must involve an organization that allocates opportunities for gratifications, that systematizes precedence relative to the limited possibilities. The possibilities of gratification, simultaneously or sequentially, of all need-dispositions are severely limited by the structure of the object system and by the intra-systemic incompatibility of the consequences of gratifying them all.

What this smothered soul is trying to say is simply, "We must pick and choose, because we cannot have everything we want."

18   Finally, there is the universal employment of the objective test as part of the price which has to be paid for mass education. Nothing but the difficulty of finding enough readers to mark essays can con-

done a system which reduces a literate student to the ignoble necessity of "blackening the answer space" when he might be giving his mind and pen free play. Though we have managed to get some benefits from these examinations, the simple fact remains that the shapely prose of the Declaration of Independence or the "Gettysburg Address" was never learned under an educational system which employed objective tests. It was mastered by people who took writing seriously, who had good models in front of them, good critics to judge them, and an endless capacity for taking pains. Without that sort of discipline, the arts of self-expression will remain as mutilated as they are now.

19   The standards which mark an educated man can be expressed in terms of three tests.

20   The first is a matter of sophistication. Emerson put it nicely when he talked about getting rid of "the nonsense of our wigwams." The wigwam may be an uncultivated home, a suburban conformity, a crass patriotism, or a cramped dogma. Some of this nonsense withers in the classroom. More of it rubs off by simply mixing with people, provided they are drawn from a wide range of backgrounds and exposed within a good college to a civilized tradition. An educated man can be judged by the quality of his prejudices. There is a refined nonsense which survives the raw nonsense which Emerson was talking about.

21   The second test is a matter of moral values. Though we all know individuals who have contrived to be both highly educated and highly immoral, and though we have all heard of periods in history when the subtlest resources of wit and sophistication were employed to make a mockery of simple values, we do not really believe that a college is doing its job when it is simply multiplying the number of educated scoundrels, hucksters, and triflers.

22   The health of society depends on simple virtues like honesty, decency, courage, and public spirit. There are forces in human nature which constantly tend to corrupt them, and every age has its own vices. The worst feature of ours is probably the obsession with violence. Up to some such time as 1914, it was possible to believe in a kind of moral progress. The quality which distinguished the Victorian from the Elizabethan was a sensitivity to suffering and a revulsion from cruelty which greatly enlarged the idea of human dignity. Since 1914 we have steadily brutalized ourselves. The horrors of modern war, the bestialities of modern political creeds, the uncontrollable vices of modern cities, the favorite themes of modern novelists—all have conspired to degrade us. Some of the corruption is blatant. The authors of the best sellers, after exhausting all the possibilities

of sex in its normal and abnormal forms and all the variations of alcoholism and drug addiction, are about to invade the recesses of the hospitals. A clinical study of a hero undergoing the irrigation of his colon is about all there is left to gratify a morbid appetite.

23   Some of the corruption is insidious. A national columnist recently wrote an article in praise of cockfighting. He had visited a cockfight in the company of Ernest Hemingway. After pointing out that Hemingway had made bull fighting respectable, he proceeded to describe the terrible beauty of fierce indomitable birds trained to kill each other for the excitement of the spectators. Needless to say, there used to be a terrible beauty about Christians defending themselves against lions or about heretics being burned at the stake, and there are still parts of the world where a public execution is regarded as a richly satisfying feast. But for three or four centuries the West taught itself to resist these excitements in the interest of a moral idea.

24   Educators are needlessly squeamish about their duty to uphold moral values and needlessly perplexed about how to implant them. The corruptions of our times are a sufficient warning that we cannot afford to abandon the duty to the homes and the churches, and the capacity which many institutions have shown to do their duty in a liberal spirit is a sufficient guaranty against bigotry.

25   Finally, there is the test imposed by the unique challenge of our own times. We are not unique in suffering from moral confusion—these crises are a familiar story—but we are unique in the tremendous acceleration of the rate of social change and in the tremendous risk of a catastrophic end to all our hopes. We cannot afford educated men who have every grace except the gift for survival. An indispensable mark of the modern educated man is the kind of versatile, flexible mind that can deal with new and explosive conditions.

26   With this reserve, there is little in this profile which has not been familiar for centuries. Unfortunately, the description which once sufficed to suggest its personality has been debased in journalistic currency. The "well-rounded man" has become the organization man, or the man who is so well rounded that he rolls wherever he is pushed. The humanists who invented the idea and preached it for centuries would recoil in contempt from any such notion. They understood the possibilities of the whole man and wanted an educational system which would give the many sides of his nature some chance to develop in harmony. They thought it a good idea to mix the wisdom of the world with the learning of the cloister, to develop the body as well as the mind, to pay a great deal of attention to character,

and to neglect no art which could add to the enjoyment of living. It was a spacious idea which offered every hospitality to creative energy. Anyone who is seriously interested in a liberal education must begin by rediscovering it.

STUDY QUESTIONS

Organization and Content

1. What is the function of paragraph 1? What purpose does sentence 7, paragraph 1, serve?
2. What brief definition of liberal education does Simpson provide?
3. What are the main elements into which he analyzes liberal education?
4. In which paragraphs does he discuss the first element?
5. At what point does he take up the second element, and what are his subdivisions of the second element? Where does he move from the first subdivision to the second subdivision?
6. List the obstacles on the road to style in speaking and writing. In which paragraphs are they enumerated?
7. Where does Simpson move from the second main element to the third? Into how many subdivisions does he analyze the third element?
8. Make an outline of the discussion of the third element.
9. In what respects are our ideas ambiguous, or even confused, about the knowledge that a liberally educated person should have?
10. What are the requirements for good general education?
11. How are educated men different from shrewd men of business?
12. How does paragraph 14 function in the discussion? What do sentences 2 and 6, paragraph 14, accomplish?
13. Explain the transitional function of paragraph 19.
14. What is the advantage of getting to know people of many different backgrounds?
15. Why does Simpson believe that the health of our society is endangered? What examples of degrading contemporary influences does he give?
16. Why does he mention Christians and heretics in sentence 5, paragraph 23? What "moral idea" is he speaking of at the end of that paragraph?
17. Why does he think a "guaranty against bigotry" is necessary (paragraph 24)?
18. Whose "profile" (paragraph 26) has Simpson been drawing?
19. Complete this statement: A person who meets the standards of an educated man is . . . .

Sentence Structure

1. In paragraph 1, Simpson brings out several contrasts. What methods of expressing contrasts does he use in sentences 2, 3, 5, and 6?
2. What different methods of contrast does he employ in sentences 3 and 4, paragraph 2? What is the advantage of the inverted sentence order in sentence 3?

3. Explain why it is effective to use balanced sentences, semicolons, and some repetition of words in sentences 4 and 5, paragraph 5.
4. What happens in the opening sentences of paragraphs 4, 9, and 10 that provides transition from the preceding paragraphs?
5. Explain the effectiveness of the two sentences of paragraph 13. What happens at the end of each one?
6. Simpson repeats a pattern of phrasing in paragraphs 15–18. Why is it good to do this in these paragraphs?
7. Explain the principle of organization that governs sentence 7, paragraph 22.
8. Explain the organization of sentence 5, paragraph 23, in terms of the pattern $A(a + b) + B(c)$.
9. What are the main parts of sentence 6, paragraph 26? In what sense might it be called a beautifully organized sentence?

Diction

1. Look up the following words (numerals represent paragraphs): *ambiguous* (2); *dogmatic, amateurs* (3); *cant, humbug* (6); *shrewdness, credulity, gullible* (7); *demagogues* (8); *humanism* (10); *precious* (14); *proliferation* (17); *condone* (18); *sophistication* (20); *blatant* (22); *squeamish* (24); *unique, versatile* (25); *cloister* (26).
2. What effect does Simpson get with *fact-filled freak?* How does he get that effect?
3. Simpson uses several metaphors: sheep and goats (paragraph 9), feast and dishes (paragraph 10), smashed through across acres of syntax (paragraph 14), road bristling with obstacles (paragraph 15), verbal smog (paragraph 17), journalistic currency (paragraph 26). How useful are these metaphors? Just what do they communicate? What sort of effect do they produce—poetic, ironic, amusing, contemptuous, ornamental, dignified, jolly, or some other?

Assignment.

1. Analyze the curriculum you are studying in terms of its chief educational values; or in terms of its shortcomings as you see them.
2. Analyze the qualities of a person who you feel sure is well educated, and show which of them he owes to his education.
3. Analyze a different person who lacks education.

Definition

If someone is asked to "define" a word, he knows that he is expected to explain the meaning of that word, and he may be able to give a satisfactory explanation of the meaning—that is, a definition. On the other hand, he may flounder; his attempt at a definition may be inefficient. There is an efficient way to make a definition, and one should always have it in mind when setting forth meanings of terms.

In the first place, the word *define* has as its root the Latin word *finis*, which means *limit*. If a limit is placed on something, a line is drawn, either physical or mental, beyond which no one can go. To put a limit to a term is to draw a line around it, to mark a line between the meaning of that term and the meanings of all other terms. By doing so, one is saying, "This is the territory which properly belongs to this term; over there beyond the line is the territory which properly belongs to that other term."

When any word is defined in an efficient way, it is necessary to take two steps. One must: (1) put the word in the right class; (2) explain what different qualities the word has from every other word that also belongs in that class. This is rather like making a map. The people of the United States are spoken of as Americans; yet there is a line between New York and Pennsylvania and another line between Pennsylvania and Ohio. The Americans of New York do not vote, pay taxes, or buy licenses in Pennsylvania, and though in some communities two Americans live only a block apart, one will vote for a governor of New York and the other for a governor of Pennsylvania because there is a map line drawn between these two men's houses.

If someone asks for a definition of *marble*, one would tell him first that it is a kind of rock. Thus the first step would be taken; the term would be put in the right *class*. It has now been established that marble is not a bird or a plant or a liquid; it is a rock. Of course, there are many other kinds of rocks. How is one to know marble from granite, for example? He will know by understanding the differences between marble and granite. If the class called *rock* is compared to the map of the United States, then the territory within that class called *marble* is like the state territory called New York, and the territory within that class called *granite* is like the state territory called Pennsylvania. What the definer has done is draw mental lines on the class-map between marble and granite.

Every correct definition has as its basis the two-step operation: placing in class—showing differences.

The class in which a term is placed should not be too large. If one is asked to define a *cabin* and he states, "A cabin is a thing," he has made a poor start. He might also say, "A fork is a thing." As a class, *thing* is much too general. Somewhere between the most *particular* term and the most *general* term there will be a term that will most efficiently classify the word being defined. A cabin is something like a hut, shack, mansion, or house. All of these are *dwellings*. *Dwelling* is a more general term than *cabin*. A dwelling could be classified as a *building*. A building would be placed in the class of *structures*. A *structure* is "something constructed." Thus, a structure is a *thing*.

So from the most general term to the least general term one goes through the series—thing-structure-building-dwelling-cabin. When defining *cabin,* a more efficient definition will be made if *cabin* is included in the class of *dwelling* rather than in some more general class.

In the same way one might go through another series of gradually narrowing classes, from thing to living thing to animal to mammal to human being to man to hero. If an attempt is being made to define *hero,* it will clearly be better to place the term in the class of *man* rather than in *animal* or even in *mammal.* Thus, having classified a hero as a man, one must show how he is different from all other men. A hero is a man acting in a certain way; the second step is explaining how the ways in which a hero acts are different from the ways of other men.

A word that is a name for a particular object can sometimes be explained most easily by simply pointing to the object—thus if one points at a tree or shovel or table, a quick definition without words is given. Such words stand for concrete things; they are called *concrete* terms. But what if it is necessary to define a term that does not stand for a concrete thing? How can *honesty* or *generosity* be defined? These are *abstract* words, which express a quality or characteristic. It is possible to say, "The man gave back to its owner a purse containing $100." The sentence tells of a concrete action. It would be an example to support such a statement as "He has often shown his honesty." "The owner of the purse showed his generosity by rewarding the man for his honesty." This sentence contains two abstract words, or *abstractions*—words representing qualities, words without a material basis such as *tree* or *shovel* has. But both of these abstractions, *generosity* and *honesty,* can be illustrated. "The owner showed his generosity by giving him a ten-dollar bill." When defining abstractions, one is constantly impelled to illustrate their meanings by using concrete examples. In general, whenever one uses abstract words, he will "come down" from the mental area of ideas (honesty, sweetness, condition) to the physical area of concrete objects and actions. Suppose a storekeeper says, "Economic conditions are bad." Just what does he mean? Furthermore, is he right? What evidence does he have about those abstract "conditions"? Suppose he gives evidence: "Ten of my customers, young married men who work for the steel company, have been laid off." From such concrete evidence his idea at once becomes clearer. The concrete and the specific are of much value in the process of definition.

Very often people know fairly well what the meaning of a word is. However, they have not considered it carefully; they do not know its meaning as well as does an expert or a careful thinker who has taken the trouble to consider it. Therefore, the type of exposition known as definition encountered in books and articles is somewhat more extensive than the definitions found in dictionaries. Such "extended definitions" are likely to be written to answer one or more of the following questions: In precisely what sense is the word being used? Just how much does this term take in? What new sense does the word now include? Regardless of other uses, or the general use, of the word, just what is its basic meaning?

Some writers may write pages or whole chapters that can be called definition. But even though their work is far more extensive than the definitions of a dictionary maker, these writers will always take the two essential steps of classification and differentiation. Then they may discuss the problem of classification—why one class is better than some other one that people have previously used—or they may discuss differences at length. They may go to some trouble to show what the word does *not* include—what is outside of the limit that should mark the meaning; they may give illustrations and make comparisons that are helpful; they may analyze the term, showing what its different parts are and explaining each part and its relation to the other parts; they may tell the reader something of the history of the word and why certain meanings developed as they did. Whatever methods they use, they are always using their minds to try to communicate a sharper and clearer idea or a broader and more stimulating idea of the meaning of the word.

Both analysis and definition are much used and highly important types of writing. The apprentice writer needs to practice them until he is efficient, for in life today he will never be able to avoid them.

❧ *A Cove*

MAURICE BROOKS

It is appropriate, I suppose, to define the term "cove." In hilly or mountainous country, rainfall and melted snow pour down the slopes in torrents, these carrying soil, gravel, and other products of erosion. As slopes become more gentle and water is slowed in its course, some of this debris is deposited, the larger elements first and then finally smaller soil particles. The result of such deposition is a fan delta, a common land form in the Southwest at the mouths of arroyos. In older mountain areas these fan deltas become stabilized by vegetation, and time softens their outlines. Each year there is an accretion of eroded material from above, and each year growing plants and animals contribute to soil formation. After enough millennia have passed the result is a cove, a naturally terraced valley near the foot of a mountain slope. Such areas are likely to be well watered, and to have deep and fertile soils. They are protected by heights to the rear and by flanking ridges on either side. They are good places for human habitation.

STUDY QUESTIONS

Organization and Content

1. Professor Brooks is an ecologist at West Virginia University. He decided that his discussion in a book about the Appalachians would be more meaningful if he defined the word *cove*. Is his first sentence a topic sentence?
2. What principle of organization has Brooks followed in sentences 2–7? Why do sentences 2–4 have the order they appear in? Sentences 5–7?
3. Is it correct to say that sentences 2–4 constitute one unit and sentences 5–7 another unit?
4. At what point does Brooks tell us what class *cove* belongs in?
5. What are the chief differences that set a cove apart from other members of the same class?
6. What do sentences 8–10 contribute to the paragraph?

Sentence Structure

1. Sentences 2 and 3 have three parts each. Explain how the parts operate in the sentences.

From Maurice Brooks, *The Appalachians.* Reprinted by permission of the publisher, Houghton Mifflin Company.

2. What similarity of structure do sentences 4 and 7 have?
3. In sentences 2–7, how is transition achieved by terms referring to place, time, or result?
4. What sort of transitional links connect sentences 7–10?
5. Point out how repetition and parallel structures help toward clarity in sentences 6, 8, and 9.

Diction

1. Look up *torrents, erosion, debris, arroyos, secretion, millennia.*
2. Explain the etymological connections among *torrents, toast, thirst,* and *torrid.* How is *erosion* related to *rodent?*
3. From what languages were *debris, delta,* and *arroyos* borrowed?
4. What other words are based on the same roots as *deposition* and *accretion?*
5. What is the singular of *millennia?* What are the meanings of its roots?

Assignment

Following Professor Brooks's method of definition, define (1) *river, mountain,* or *mesa;* or (2) a man-made object such as *book, library,* or *automobile.*

❧ *The Quipu*

VICTOR WOLFGANG VON HAGEN

1   The *quipu* (pronounced "kee-poo"), which means simply "knot," and which the couriers passed from hand to hand, was as close to writing as man got in South America; still no matter how much writers have strained their imagination, the *quipu is not writing,* and, moreover, the device is not even an Inca invention. It is simply a mnemonic device to aid the memory and its knotted strings are based on a decimal count. Too, all *quipus* had to be *accompanied by a verbal comment,* without which the meaning would have been unintelligible.
2   The *quipus* have been thoroughly studied and described. The *quipu* was a simple and ingenious device; it consisted of a main cord (ranging from a foot to many feet in length) and from this cord dangled smaller colored strings which had at intervals knots (*quipus*) tied into them. It has been shown most conclusively by

From pp. 561–562, Victor Wolfgang von Hagen, *The Ancient Sun Kingdoms of the Americas* (Cleveland: The World Publishing Company, 1961).

those who have studied them that the strings were used to record numbers in a decimal system, and that there was a symbol for zero, that is, a string with an "empty space"; this allowed them to count over ten thousand. Knots were tied into the string to represent numbers; if a governor was visiting a newly conquered tribe and the Inca wanted to know how many able-bodied Indians there were, these were counted and the number tied into the *quipu*. It may be that there was a certain symbol or heraldic device for "men," but if there was one it is not known. There was attached to the governor an official knot-string-record interpreter known as a *quipu-camayoc*, whose duty it was to tie in the records. He then had to remember which *quipu* recorded what; numbers of men, women, llamas, etc., in the newly conquered lands. When a governor had an audience with the Inca he could, with this knot-string record plus the "rememberer," recite the facts as gathered. It was a surprisingly efficacious method of counting and one that their Spanish conquerors much admired.

STUDY QUESTIONS

Organization and Content

1. What misuse or misunderstanding of the term *quipu* does Von Hagen wish to guard against? How far has he proceeded in his definition in paragraph 1?
2. In what class does the term *quipu* belong?
3. Where does Von Hagen explain what made a *quipu* different from all other members of the same class?
4. Explain why a *quipu* "had to be accompanied by a verbal comment."
5. How does the material of sentences 4–7, paragraph 2, differ in function from that of sentences 1–3?
6. What is the purpose of sentence 8, paragraph 2?

Sentence Structure

1. Explain how the structure of sentence 1 provides a pattern of contrast.
2. How is the function of the material after the semicolon in sentences 3 and 4, paragraph 2, different from that after the semicolon in sentence 2, paragraph 2?

Diction

1. Look up *couriers, mnemonic, heraldic, efficacious.*
2. What words are used for transition and emphasis in paragraph 1?

Assignment

Write a definition of an object with which people in our society are perfectly familiar, so that its components and its mode of operation will be clear to a person in another society who has never seen that object—for example, an egg beater, corkscrew, clothes pin, mousetrap, double boiler, pair of shears, crochet hook, dress pattern, vacuum cleaner, safety razor, typewriter, cash register, or newspaper.

 *A Gentleman*

JAMES FENIMORE COOPER

The word "gentleman" has a positive and limited signification. It means one elevated above the mass of society by his birth, manners, attainments, character and social condition. "Gentleman" is derived from the French *gentilhomme*, which originally signified one of noble birth. This was at a time when the characteristics of the condition were never found beyond a caste. As society advanced, ordinary men attained the qualifications of nobility, without that of birth, and the meaning of the word was extended. It is now possible to be a gentleman without birth, though, even in America, where such distinctions are purely conditional, they who have birth, except in extraordinary instances, are classed with gentlemen. To call a laborer, one who has neither education, manners, accomplishments, tastes, associations, nor any one of the ordinary requisites, a gentleman, is just as absurd as to call one who is thus qualified, a fellow. The word must have some especial significance, or it would be synonymous with man. One may have gentlemanlike feelings, principles and appearance, without possessing the liberal attainments that distinguish the gentleman. Least of all does money alone make a gentleman, though, as it becomes a means of obtaining the other requisites, it is usual to give it a place in the claims of the class. Men may be, and often are, very rich, without having the smallest title to be deemed gentlemen. A man may be a distinguished gentleman and not possess as much money as his own footman.

From James Fenimore Cooper, *The American Democrat* (1838).

STUDY QUESTIONS

Organization and Content

1. What misuse or misunderstanding of the word *gentleman* would cause Cooper to write sentence 1?
2. According to sentence 2, in what class does the word *gentleman* belong? What are the differences between a *gentleman* and all other members of the area in which *gentleman* has been classified?
3. How does sentence 3 relate to sentence 2? How does sentence 5 relate to sentence 2?
4. In sentence 5 Cooper says that "society advanced." What sort of "advancement" does he presumably mean?
5. In sentence 5 Cooper says that "the meaning of the word was extended." According to his explanation, why was it extended? What example in sentence 6 provides evidence that the meaning was extended?
6. What is the point of Cooper's mentioning the laborer in sentence 7? What connection does sentence 7 have with sentence 1?
7. In sentences 7, 9, and 10 Cooper shows what a gentleman is *not* (that is, he denies that certain supposed differences between a gentleman and other members of the class really *are* differences). What are the three false differences that Cooper eliminates?
8. Both sentence 11 and sentence 12 are related to sentence 10. Explain what different functions sentence 11 and sentence 12 have in the definition.

Sentence Structure

1. Sentences 3, 4, 5, and 6 indicate differences in time. In which part of the sentences is the time element indicated?
2. Why are the sentences constructed thus?
3. In how many of the sentences does the word *gentleman* or its equivalent appear to provide transition?
4. Explain how sentences 10, 11, and 12 are arranged so as to give strong emphasis to the idea that Cooper is expressing.

Diction

1. Look up the following words and show from what roots in what languages they were originally derived: *positive, limited signification, caste, synonymous, distinguished.*
2. In what special sense does Cooper use the word *birth?*
3. *Attainments* is a very general term. What specific examples of attainments do you think Cooper might have mentioned if he had gone into more detail?
4. In sentence 9 Cooper mentions *liberal attainments.* He contrasts these with what other qualifications? Look up *liberal.* Apparently it is an important term. What do you think is the difference between *liberal* attainments and any other attainments?

Assignment

1. The phrase "ladies and gentlemen" is used a good deal in English. Write a one-paragraph definition of *lady* like Cooper's definition of *gentleman*. Obtain some of your information by studying dictionaries. Tell a little about the origin and history of the word. But, having classified the word, use most of your space to show what makes a lady different from all other members of the same class. You may wish, as Cooper did, to rule out some falsely supposed differences.
2. Cooper says in sentence 7 that it would be absurd to call a man who has the qualifications of a gentleman, a *fellow*. After some dictionary study, write a definition of the word *fellow*, following the directions above.

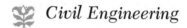 *Civil Engineering*

PAUL J. BRENNAN

1   Civil Engineering is a profession responsible for providing major physical needs of man. The principal activities of this profession include the planning, design, analysis, and construction of major structures, transportation routes and terminals, water and waste water systems; the use and control of the forces of nature, the control of the environment, and the development of land areas. Public health and natural resources conservation are areas of special import to the civil engineer.

2   Historically, the civil engineer is concerned with such facilities as bridges, buildings, highways, railways, airports, harbors, canals, tunnels, dams, reservoirs, water supply systems, water purification plants, waste water treatment plants, flood control, and many other similarly diverse activities.

3   The planning, design, analysis, research, management, and construction of these facilities are usually done by the civil engineer as a member of the consulting engineering office, industrial firm, construction firm, governmental agency, research laboratory, university, or private business firm. It is also of interest to note that many civil engineers are integral members of engineering groups that are devel-

From Paul J. Brennan, "Liberal Education through Civil Engineering," *Syracuse University Alumni News*, Vol. 42 (Spring 1961).

oping and designing aircraft structures, space vehicle structures, and space navigational methods. They are among those planning facilities for space travel and the habitation of other planets and are active in phases of the use and control of nuclear power.

4   Many of these activities benefit large numbers of people in a community, a region, or an entire nation, and civil engineering activities are thus closely allied with the economics, sociology, law, public administration, political science, climatology, geology, and geography of the environ. Although the civil engineer is not proficient in these disciplines he needs some knowledge of them and limited ability in them in order to evaluate and recognize problems beyond the scope of engineering and to consult with persons who are competent in these areas. This then is the broad field the University graduate in civil engineering enters.

STUDY QUESTIONS

Organization and Content

1. In what class does the author place the term *civil engineering?* What are some other terms that would also be placed in that same class?
2. What differences does the author point out between *civil engineering* and other terms of the same classification?
3. What is the relation of paragraph 2 to paragraph 1? The relation of paragraph 3 to paragraph 2?
4. What term used in the first sentence of paragraph 3 makes the transition from paragraph 2, and what term in the first sentence of paragraph 4 makes the transition from paragraph 3?
5. In sentence 2 of paragraph 1 there is a list of items, and paragraph 2 consists largely of a list of items. Which items are the more general, which the more specific?
6. What is the function of sentences 2 and 3 of paragraph 3? The function of the last sentence of paragraph 4?
7. This material defining *civil engineering* was published in the Syracuse University *Alumni News* as part of a discussion of the education of the civil engineer, and particularly the civil engineering curriculum in college. Point out how paragraph 4 is related to the topic of engineering education.

Sentence Structure

1. The sentences contain several lists of items. Explain by what grammatical means the different lists are introduced into sentence 2 of paragraph 1, the single sentence of paragraph 2, sentences 1 and 2 of paragraph 3, and sentence 1 of paragraph 4.
2. Why did the author use a semicolon in sentence 2?

3. In which sentences do the words *civil engineering* or *civil engineer* occur? In what grammatical situations do they occur?
4. Does this selection have good sentence variety or not?

Diction

1. Look up the following words and show from what roots in what langauges they were originally derived: *economics, sociology, climatology, geology, geography, proficient, disciplines.*
2. What is the difference between *climate* and *climatology?*
3. Is there a difference between *discipline* and *a discipline?*
4. How is the *environ* (noun) related to *environ* (verb)?

Assignment

Just as Brennan explained the work of a civil engineer, and beginning in exactly the same manner as he did, explain what work is done by a nurse, librarian, carpenter, salesman, artist, physician, farmer, teacher, chemist, policeman, minister, electrician, undertaker, or jeweler.

❧ The Engineer
Who Designs Railways

ARTHUR MELLEN WELLINGTON

1   It would be well if engineering were less generally thought of, and even defined, as the art of constructing. In a certain important sense it is rather the art of not constructing; or, to define it rudely but not inaptly, it is the art of doing that well with one dollar, which any bungler can do with two after a fashion.

2   There are, indeed, certain great triumphs of engineering genius—the locomotive, the truss bridge, the steel rail—which so rude a definition does not cover, for the bungler cannot attempt them at all; but such are rather invention than engineering proper. There is also in some branches of engineering, as in bridge-building, a certain other side to it, not covered by such a definition, which consists in doing that safely, at some cost or other which the bungler is likely to try to do and fail. He, therefore, in such branches, who is simply able to design a structure which will not fall down, may doubtless

From Arthur Mellen Wellington, *The Economic Theory of the Location of Railways* (1887).

in some measure be called an engineer, although certainly not one
of a very high type.

3   But to such engineering as is needed for laying out railways,
at least, the definition given is literally applicable, for the economic
problem is all there is to it. The ill-designed bridge breaks down;
the ill-designed dam gives way; the ill-designed boiler explodes; the
badly built tunnel caves in, and the bungler's bungling is betrayed.
But a little practice and a little study of field geometry will enable
any one of ordinary intelligence, without any engineering knowledge
whatever in the larger sense, to lay out a railway from almost anywhere to anywhere, which will carry the locomotive with perfect
safety, and perhaps show no obtrusive defects under what is too often
the only test—inspection after construction from the rear end of a
palace-car. Thus, for such work, the healthful checks which reveal the
bungler's errors to the world and to himself do not exist. Nature, unhappily, has provided no way for the locomotive . . . to refuse to
pass over an ill-designed railway as it refuses to pass over an ill-de-
fined bridge.

4   Therefore, since there is no natural line between safety and
danger to mark even so rude a distinction as that between the utterly
bad and the barely tolerable, in the kind of engineering work we
are to study, one may fairly say that the locating engineer has but
the one end before him to justify his existence as such—to get the
most value for a dollar which nature permits; and but one failure
to fear—that he will not do so. Except as his work necessarily involves
the preliminary design of constructive details, he has no lives to save
or imperil; and the young engineer cannot too early nor too forcibly
have it impressed upon his mind that it takes no skill worth speaking
of to do such work after a fashion, unless in the comparatively few
localities (rare indeed in the United States) where to get a reasonable
line of any kind is something of a feat. His true function and excuse
for being an engineer, as distinguished from a skilled workman,
begins and ends in comprehending and striking a just balance between
topographical possibilities, first cost, and future revenues and operating expenses.

STUDY QUESTIONS

Organization and Content

1. Wellington's book, *The Economic Theory of the Location of Railways*
   (New York, 1887), was the first major American engineering work

with literary quality. For what reason might we say that the first paragraph is intended to stimulate the reader's interest, or ideas?

2. Note that in both paragraphs 1 and 2 the author emphasizes the negative. What two aspects of engineering are ruled out of the definition in paragraph 2?
3. By what transition does the author take the reader to the positive aspect of his definition in paragraph 3? To what extent is the negative aspect still being expressed in paragraph 3?
4. What does the author mean by "healthful checks" in sentence 4, paragraph 3?
5. Judging by paragraph 4, how should you complete the following definition? "Railway engineering is . . ."
6. In what respects does Wellington's definition of railway engineering agree with Dr. Brennan's definition of civil engineering? What factor of engineering does Wellington introduce and emphasize that Dr. Brennan does not mention?

Sentence Structure

1. Explain why the pattern of sentence 2, paragraph 3, is especially good for giving vigorous emphasis to the author's ideas.
2. The author uses several transitional words; point out four and explain how they function.
3. In paragraph 4, sentence 1, the author mentions "one end" and "one failure," and explains what they are. For what grammatical purpose does the author use the semicolon and the two dashes in the sentence?
4. The last clause of sentence 1, paragraph 2, begins with *but;* two sentences of paragraph 3 also begin with *but.* Why does the author begin them thus?

Diction

1. Look up *literally, obtrusive, tolerable, topographical.*
2. What are their roots, and from what languages do they come?
3. What is the difference between *obtrude, intrude,* and *extrude?*

Assignment

Begin exactly as Wellington does: "It would be well if _____ were less generally thought of as . . ." and put in the blank one of the following terms: (1) cooking, (2) attending college, (3) writing themes, (4) dancing, (5) business, (6) painting, (7) pharmacy, (8) literature, (9) sewing, (10) farming. Write a definition of the term in which you first stress the negative: that is, show how a certain concept is false or inadequate—and then, in a second paragraph, explain what a more accurate or more significant concept is.

🌱 *A Fairy Story*

W. H. Auden

1   A fairy story, as distinct from a merry tale, or an animal story, is a serious tale with a human hero and a happy ending. The progression of its hero is the reverse of the tragic hero's: at the beginning he is either socially obscure or despised as being stupid or untalented, lacking in the heroic virtues, but at the end, he has surprised everyone by demonstrating his heroism and winning fame, riches, and love. Though ultimately he succeeds, he does not do so without a struggle in which his success is in doubt, for opposed to him are not only natural difficulties like glass mountains, or barriers of flame, but also hostile wicked powers, stepmothers, jealous brothers, and witches. In many cases, indeed, he would fail were he not assisted by friendly powers who give him instructions or perform tasks for him which he cannot do himself; that is, in addition to his own powers, he needs luck, but this luck is not fortuitous but dependent upon his character and his actions. The tale ends with the establishment of justice; not only are the good rewarded but also the evil are punished.

2   Take, for example, "The Water of Life." Three brothers set out in turn on a difficult quest, to find the water of life to restore the King, their sick father, to health. Each one meets a dwarf who asks him where he is going. The two elder give rude answers and are punished by being imprisoned in ravines. The third brother gives a courteous answer and is rewarded by being told where the water of life is and how to appease the lions who guard it, but is warned to leave before the clock strikes twelve. He reaches the enchanted castle, where he finds a Princess who tells him to return in a year and marry her. At this point he almost fails because he falls asleep and only just manages to escape as the clock strikes twelve and the iron door shuts, carrying away a piece of his heel. On the way home he again meets the dwarf and begs him to release his brothers, which he does with a warning that they have bad hearts. The brothers steal the water of life from him and substitute salt water so that his father condemns him to be secretly shot. The huntsman entrusted with the task has not the heart to do it, and lets the young Prince go away into the forest. Now begins a second quest for the Princess. She has built a golden road to test her suitors. Whoever rides straight

up it is to be admitted, whoever rides to the side is not. When the two elder brothers come to it they think "It would be a sin and a shame to ride over that" and so fail the test. At the end of the year, the exiled brother rides thither but is so preoccupied with thinking of the Princess that he never notices the golden road and rides straight up. They are married, the King learns how the elder brothers had betrayed the Prince, and they, to escape punishment, put to sea and never come back.

3   The hero is in the third or inferior position. (The youngest son inherits least.) There are two quests, each involving a test which the hero passes and his brothers fail.

4   The first test is the encounter with the dwarf. The elder brothers disregard him (a) because he looks like the last person on earth who could help them, (b) they are impatient and thinking only of their success, and (c) what is wrong with their concentration on their task is, firstly, over-confidence in their own powers and, secondly, the selfishness of their motive. They do not really love their father but want him to reward them.

5   The hero, on the other hand, is (a) humble enough, (b) cares enough for his father's recovery, and (c) has a loving disposition toward all men, so that he asks the dwarf for assistance and gets it.

6   The second test of the golden road is a reversal of the first: the right thing to do this time is to take no notice of it. The brothers who dismissed the dwarf notice the road because of its worldly value, which is more to them than any Princess, while the hero, who paid attention to the dwarf, ignores the road because he is truly in love.

7   The Water of Life and the Princess are guarded by lions; these, in this tale, are not malevolent but ensure that no one shall succeed who has not learned the true way. The hero almost fails here by forgetting the dwarf's warning and falling asleep; further it is through falling asleep and not watching his brothers that they almost succeed in destroying him. The readiness to fall asleep is a sign of the trustfulness and lack of fear which are the qualities which bring about his success; at the same time it is pointed out that, carried too far, they are a danger to him.

STUDY QUESTIONS

Organization and Content

1. In what class of things does the author place the term *fairy story?*
2. According to sentence 1, what differences exist between a fairy story and other kinds of stories?

3. We can hardly take sentence 1 as a sufficient definition. What other main differences should be added from the rest of paragraph 1? What contrasting situation of a tragic hero is implied in sentence 2?
4. What is the relation of paragraph 2 to paragraph 1?
5. Does "The Water of Life" meet all the requirements laid down for the fairy story in paragraph 1?
6. What is the main problem in organizing the material of paragraph 2?
7. To what extent does the interpretation in paragraphs 3–7 help in defining the term?
8. Point out how the author has used analysis in paragraphs 3, 4, 5, and 6.

Sentence Structure

1. What is the function of the colon in sentence 2, paragraph 1? In what other sentence is a colon used? Why? Does paragraph 1 or paragraph 2 have the longer sentences?
2. What is the likely reason why the average sentence length of the one paragraph is so much less than that of the other?
3. In the sentences of paragraphs 1, 4, 5, and 6 the author uses much parallel structure. Point it out, and explain why it is especially suitable in these paragraphs.
4. In sentence 2 of paragraph 6 which words receive chief emphasis?
5. Explain how sentence structure functions in terms of contrasts which are important in paragraph 7.

Diction

1. Look up the meanings of the following words and learn what roots they come from: *demonstrate, ultimately, fortuitous, quest, appease, encounter, malevolent.*
2. Is there a difference between *ultimately* and *lastly, fortuitous* and *accidental, malevolent* and *malicious?*
3. Explain how the words *appease* and *pacify* can come from the same root.
4. What are the differences among *quest, question, query, inquest, inquiry, inquisition?*

Assignment

Write a definition in three paragraphs of a fable or a joke. In the first paragraph, classify the term and show how it differs from other things in the same class. In the second paragraph, summarize a fable or tell a good joke to illustrate the basic definition. In the third paragraph, interpret your example in terms of the requirements you laid down in paragraph 1.

❧ New Orleans Jazz

WILLIAM L. GROSSMAN AND JACK W. FARRELL

1 New Orleans jazz is in common (four-quarter) time, with off-beat accents that in some performances are sufficiently pronounced to create a sort of duple rhythm. There is abundant use of syncopation. Also, an effect similar to that of syncopation is provided by the playing of a note slightly offbeat. It is sometimes hard to draw a definite distinction between such playing and clear-cut syncopation in the music.

2 In New Orleans jazz the major mode or scale is used almost exclusively. Sometimes, however, a note is played intentionally a little below the customary pitch. On the conventional piano, because the notes are fixed in pitch, an approximation of such off-pitch playing is sometimes achieved by the use of a note one half-tone below the note from which a deviation is intended; the two notes may even be played together. The third note in the scale is subjected to off-pitch flatting with especial frequency, but no note in the scale is wholly immune.

3 The chief reason for this practice is expressiveness. Unhampered by academic concepts of inviolable pitch, the New Orleans jazzmen found that by playing a note slightly below conventional pitch they could achieve an ironic, quasi-melancholy effect. Indeed, the off-pitch notes are sometimes referred to as "blue" (i.e., melancholy) notes and are especially common in the performance of blues. It should be noted also that the disregard of exact pitch is a logical corollary of the effort of New Orleans jazzmen to make their music "talk." . . .

4 With respect to tone or timbre, it should be noted that the speechlike quality of many jazz instrumental performances necessitates a tone far from the pure tone that a performer in the European tradition generally seeks to achieve. New Orleans jazzmen vary considerably in the degree to which their training and aesthetic ideals lead them to adhere to the European concept of acceptable tone and, accordingly, vary considerably in their degree of departure from it. . . .

From William L. Grossman and Jack W. Farrell, *The Heart of Jazz* (New York: New York University Press, 1956).

5   In the ensemble or *tutti* parts of the performance (they may constitute the entire performance), the trumpet or cornet generally plays an approximation of the basic melody, while the clarinet and trombone follow their own respective lines in what often amounts to a sort of counterpoint. This counterpoint is not usually imitative; in other words, one instrument does not usually repeat a phrase just rendered by another. Rather, the trombone plays a free sort of bass, which often assumes distinct melodic significance, with occasional use of *glissandi* (slides from one note to another), and the clarinet combines runs, arpeggios, and genuinely melodic phrases into a line of its own.

6   The rhythm section supplies both the basic rhythm and the harmony, which is generally simple. In some cases, as in the traditional twelve-bar blues form, it consists wholly of three or four elementary chords. As a rule, the harmonic progressions are not changed from variation to variation, nor is the tempo or the basic rhythm. Variation is, therefore, wholly a matter of melody and internal rhythm . . . .

7   In addition to the ensembles, a performance may include one or more solo variations, generally by one of the wind instruments. During the solo, the rhythm section continues to supply the harmony and basic rhythm. The other wind instruments are sometimes silent during a solo, but in many cases one or both of them play softly and polyphonically behind it. Indeed, it is sometimes difficult to distinguish a trombone or clarinet solo from a shift of the melody lead from the cornet to such instrument. In New Orleans jazz, as distinguished from some of its progeny, ensemble choruses, rather than solos, usually predominate.

8   A formal device characteristic of New Orleans jazz is the *break*. This is a passage interpolated during a rest at the end of a phrase. It is generally played by one instrument alone and serves as a sort of reminder of the vitality and independence of the individual in what is essentially a group performance. Jelly Roll Morton was insistent upon its indispensability to good jazz. Characterizing a break as "a musical surprise," he maintained that "without breaks and without clean breaks and without beautiful ideas in breaks, you don't even need to think about doing anything else, you haven't got a jazz band and you can't play jazz. Even if a tune haven't got a break in it, it's always necessary to arrange some kind of a spot to make a break." In many jazz tunes, such "spots" are readily available. . . .

STUDY QUESTIONS

Organization and Content

1. In a previous part of their discussion the authors placed the term *New Orleans jazz* in a particular musical tradition. In what tradition, or class, would they presumably have placed it?
2. Of the following terms, which ones clearly represent differences that set New Orleans jazz off from other members of the same class: blues, break, counterpoint, effect, ensemble choruses, flatting, harmony, instruments, offbeat accents, pitch, rhythm, scale, syncopation, tempo, tone, variations, vitality? Which differences are the most significant?
3. Some readers might find the technical terms used in this explanation too difficult. By what means (as in sentence 1) have the authors tried to lessen this difficulty?
4. What logical connection is there between paragraph 3 and paragraph 2? Paragraph 4 and paragraph 3?
5. In paragraph 8 the break is called a "formal device." What, then, should the other characteristics of New Orleans jazz be called?
6. Does the discussion of the break have to wait till paragraph 8? What principle, if any, do you think the authors used in deciding upon the order of their material?
7. Why do the authors quote an authority in paragraph 8 and in no other paragraph?

Sentence Structure

1. Note the position of *sometimes* (sentence 4, paragraph 1; sentences 2 and 3, paragraph 2) and *with especial frequency* (sentence 4, paragraph 2). What do you learn about the placement of adverbial modifiers?
2. The authors use other adverbial modifiers, such as *indeed, rather, therefore*. For what purpose? What emphasis do they gain by using *indeed* (sentence 3, paragraph 3; sentence 3, paragraph 7)?
3. Pick out the sentence in which the authors use verbs in the passive voice. Do the sentences lack vigor? Do they have less or more awkwardness than they would if they were written in the active voice?
4. How have the authors secured variety of beginning and of length for their sentences?

Diction

1. Look up *duple, syncopation, deviation, inviolable, ironic, quasi, corollary, aesthetic, counterpoint, polyphonically, progeny, interpolated.*
2. What rather surprising root-meanings do you find in *syncopation, deviation, interpolate?*
3. Why are *tutti* and *glissandi* italicized, whereas *arpeggios* is not (paragraph 5)?
4. Look up *jargon*. Have the authors used too much musical jargon in this discussion?

Assignment

Write a definition of a folk song or of folk-rock music. If you have enough technical information, define blues, barrelhouse, Chicago jazz, symphony, or anthem. Handel's *Messiah* is an oratorio; define oratorio.

❦ *History*

JULIAN HUXLEY

1   The word *History* is one of those general semantic omnibuses which convey a number of different meanings to a number of different destinations. It may simply be used as a term for the objective sequence of events in time. Within this limitation, it can be used for any and every such sequence, as "the history of life" or "the history of the solar system"; or it can be restricted to the sequence of human events; or still further restricted to the historian's sense, of recorded history. . . .

2   But, strictly speaking, *history* should not be used in a purely objective sense, any more than *colour,* for instance, should be used to denote the objective physical radiations on which it depends. Scientific laws would perhaps be a better comparison, for they are not automatically presented to our minds by outer events, as are colours, but come into being as the result of intellectual effort. They do not exist objectively in nature. In nature, events happen; and scientific laws are one of the ways in which we formulate our understanding of how they happen.

3   History is in similar case. Only by a convenient form of shorthand—convenient, but sometimes misleading—can it be used to denote the objective sequence of human events. It is properly only our knowledge of that sequence, our formulation of how they happened. The accumulation of brute facts is a prerequisite for history as it is for science; but the raw historical data are not history, any more than the raw scientific data are science. The same old facts, when combined with others and harmonized in a new point of view,

may produce something quite new in science, as the facts of geology and biology have ceased to support the idea of special creation, and became part of an Einsteinian instead of a Newtonian universe. So too history is constantly developing into something novel: new kinds of history are constantly being born. This is partly due to the collection of new historical data, new facts about past events; but partly— since human history includes the present, and since it is subjective as well as objective—to the discovery by each succeeding present of new ways of looking at life, new questions to ask of the facts, new formulations by which they may be ordered.

4   History, in other words, is not merely a set of facts: it is also the building up of the facts into a comprehensible whole, a coherent picture of the world of human development.

STUDY QUESTIONS

Organization and Content

1. What alternative meanings of *history* does Huxley present in paragraph 1?
2. What is ruled out, following the *but* of sentence 1, paragraph 2?
3. Why does Huxley discuss color and scientific laws in paragraph 2?
4. How is paragraph 3 related to paragraph 2?
5. Explain the contrast of objective events and subjective responses in paragraphs 2 and 3.
6. Would Nevins agree with Huxley's explanation of history in paragraph 3?
7. Are Huxley's metaphors—omnibus, shorthand, birth—appropriate to the ideas they are intended to illustrate?
8. What important comparison does Huxley make in sentences 5 and 6, paragraph 3?
9. How is it possible that new kinds of history can be created?
10. What is the function of the very brief paragraph 4?
11. How does Huxley handle the negative and the positive aspects of his topic?

Sentence Structure

1. Sentence 3, paragraph 1, has four main parts. What does each part do? Why are semicolons used here?
2. How does Huxley provide transitional links within his paragraphs?
3. Explain the meaning of the colons in sentence 6, paragraph 3, and in paragraph 4.
4. Sentence 7, paragraph 3, is long. Explain the function in this sentence of interrupters, parallel structure, appositives, and repetition of words.

Diction

1. Look up *semantic, objective, strictly, formulate, subjective.*
2. What does the term *strictly speaking* signal in sentence 1, paragraph 2? What is an antonym of *strictly?*
3. Are *brute* and *raw* appropriate adjectives in sentence 4, paragraph 3? What are their connotations?
4. To whom do the adjectives *Einsteinian* and *Newtonian* refer? Why does Huxley use these allusions here?

Assignment

Select some term, and in your first paragraph explain how a certain concept of it is false or inadequate; then in a second paragraph explain what a more accurate or more significant concept is. Some suggestions: a college education; athletics, psychology, art, popular music; a tolerant person, a good sport, a religious man, a professor; prejudice.

 *Civilization*

Winston S. Churchill

1   There are few words which are used more loosely than the word "Civilization." What does it mean? It means a society based upon the opinion of civilians. It means that violence, the rule of warriors and despotic chiefs, the conditions of camps and warfare, of riot and tyranny, give place to parliaments where laws are made, and independent courts of justice in which over long periods those laws are maintained. That is Civilization—and in its soil grow continually freedom, comfort and culture. When Civilization reigns in any country, a wider and less harassed life is afforded to the masses of the people. The traditions of the past are cherished, and the inheritance bequeathed to us by former wise or valiant men becomes a rich estate to be enjoyed and used by all.

2   The central principle of Civilization is the subordination of the ruling authority to the settled customs of the people and to their will as expressed through the Constitution. In this Island we have today achieved in a high degree the blessings of Civilization. There

is freedom; there is law; there is love of country; there is a great measure of good will between classes; there is a widening prosperity. There are unmeasured opportunities of correcting abuses and making further progress.

STUDY QUESTIONS

Organization and Content

1. Into what class does the author put the term *civilization?*
2. What does he say about the differences that set this term off from other members of the same class?
3. What term in sentence 4 contrasts with *civilians* in sentence 3?
4. What is the subject of *give* in sentence 4?
5. What is the relation of sentence 6 to sentence 5? Of sentence 7 to sentence 6?
6. Explain the usefulness, in the explanation, of the metaphor of the "rich estate" in sentence 7.
7. How is the first sentence of paragraph 2 related to ideas in paragraph 1?
8. Sentence 3 of paragraph 2 is related particularly to what word of sentence 2?
9. Why is the idea of sentence 4 of paragraph 2 not included in sentence 3, and what does sentence 4 contribute to the definition?

Sentence Structure

1. In paragraph 1 what words are repeated in sentences 2, 3, and 4 to provide links of transition?
2. By what means does the author expand the idea of "violence" in sentence 4?
3. In the second half of sentence 4 what terms balance terms in the first half?
4. What effect is gained by the unusual order of words in sentence 5?
5. Why does sentence 3 of paragraph 2 require four semicolons? Would the sentence be improved if it were shortened?

Diction

1. Look up *civic, civil, civilian.* What root appears in all three words?
2. Look up the origins of *despotic, tyranny, parliament.*
3. Is the vocabulary of the definition mostly abstract or mostly concrete? Point out examples of both kinds of terms.

Assignment

Write a one-paragraph definition of tyranny, comfort, prosperity, or progress. Try to show both positive and negative aspects of the term.

🌼 *Civilization*

CLIVE BELL

1   I have not yet defined civilization; but perhaps I have made definition superfluous. Any one, I fancy, who has done me the honour of reading so far will by now understand pretty well what I mean. Civilization is a characteristic of societies. In its crudest form it is the characteristic which differentiates what anthropologists call "advanced" from what they call "low" or "backward" societies. So soon as savages begin to apply reason to instinct, so soon as they acquire a rudimentary sense of values—so soon, that is, as they begin to distinguish between ends and means, or between direct means to good and remote—they have taken the first step upward. The first step towards civilization is the correcting of instinct by reason: the second, the deliberate rejection of immediate satisfactions with a view to obtaining subtler. The hungry savage, when he catches a rabbit, eats it there and then, or instinctively takes it home, as a fox might, to be eaten raw by his cubs; the first who, all hungry though he was, took it home and cooked it was on the road to Athens. He was a pioneer, who with equal justice may be described as the first decadent. The fact is significant. Civilization is something artificial and unnatural. Progress and Decadence are interchangeable terms. All who have added to human knowledge and sensibility, and most of those even who have merely increased material comfort, have been hailed by contemporaries capable of profiting by their discoveries as benefactors, and denounced by all whom age, stupidity, or jealousy rendered incapable, as degenerates. It is silly to quarrel about words: let us agree that the habit of cooking one's victuals may with equal propriety be considered a step towards civilization or a falling away from the primitive perfection of the upstanding ape.

2   From these primary qualities, Reasonableness and a Sense of Values, may spring a host of secondaries: a taste for truth and beauty, tolerance, intellectual honesty, fastidiousness, a sense of humour, good manners, curiosity, a dislike of vulgarity, brutality, and over-emphasis, freedom from superstition and prudery, a fearless acceptance of the good things of life, a desire for complete self-expression and for a liberal education, a contempt for utilitarianism and philistinism; in two words—sweetness and light. Not all societies that struggle out of barbarism grasp all or even most of these, and fewer still grasp

From Clive Bell, *Civilization* (London: Chatto and Windus, 1928).

any of them firmly. That is why we find a considerable number of civilized societies and very few highly civilized, for only by grasping a good handful of civilized qualities and holding them tight does a society become that.

STUDY QUESTIONS

Organization and Content

1. The definition of civilization by Winston Churchill is part of a short speech entitled "Civilization"; that by Clive Bell is from a book entitled *Civilization*. These facts somewhat account for the different approaches that the two men take toward their topic. Does Bell place the term in the same class that Churchill used?
2. Using Bell's ideas, formulate a simple, one-sentence definition of civilization, showing precisely both class and differences.
3. Explain how the statements about the hungry savage help to explain the author's ideas about ends and means.
4. How can decadence possibly be a synonym for progress? Is this a paradox? How is paragraph 2 related to paragraph 1?
5. How has the author used analysis in making his definition?
6. Bell uses at least three terms that were used also by Churchill: *progress, comfort,* and *freedom.* Does he give them any different emphasis?

Sentence Structure

1. A few of Bell's sentences have only four or six words. Is there any reason why they should be so much shorter than the rest?
2. Explain the parallelism of sentence 5; of sentence 6.
3. Point out the contrasting elements of sentence 12.
4. What is the function of the colon in sentence 13? In paragraph 2, sentence 1?
5. What balanced ideas control the structure of the last two sentences?

Diction

1. Look up *superfluous, anthropologists, rudimentary, decadent, sensibility, denounce, degenerates, fastidiousness, vulgarity, prudery, utilitarianism, philistinism, barbarism.*
2. In paragraph 1, sentence 7, the author uses a historical allusion. What does he mean by saying that the savage who cooked the rabbit was "on the road to Athens"?
3. Sentence 1 of paragraph 2 ends with "sweetness and light." It is another allusion; "Sweetness and Light" is the title of a chapter of Matthew Arnold's *Culture and Anarchy.* "Sweetness" means beauty, "light" means intelligence. Arnold also used the term *philistinism;* he called middle-

class people Philistines—"enemies of the children of light." Why should he?
4. Is the vocabulary of this definition more concrete than that of the definition by Churchill?

Assignment

1. Write a definition of *reasonableness*. Be sure to take both steps essential to good definition. Use at least two concrete examples to illustrate this abstraction.
2. How great a difference is there between *customs* and *traditions?* In one or two paragraphs explain how you would "draw the line" between them.
3. Do you or do you not believe that it is good to follow custom? Explain your position, largely by making use of a definition of custom.
4. Do you think that fastidiousness is good and vulgarity bad? Explain your position, making particular use of definition.

An American

J. HECTOR ST. JOHN DE CRÈVECOEUR

What then is the American, this new man? He is either an European, or the descendant of an European, hence that strange mixture of blood, which you will find in no other country. I could point out to you a family whose grandfather was an Englishman, whose wife was Dutch, whose son married a French woman, and whose present four sons have now four wives of different nations. He is an American, who, leaving behind him all his ancient prejudices and manners, receives new ones from the new mode of life he has embraced, the new government he obeys, and the new rank he holds. He becomes an American by being received in the broad lap of our great *Alma Mater*. Here individuals of all nations are melted into a new race of men, whose labours and posterity will one day cause great changes in the world. Americans are the western pilgrims, who are carrying along with them that great mass of arts, sciences, vigour, and industry which began long since in the east; they will finish

From J. Hector St. John de Crèvecoeur, *Letters from an American Farmer* (1782).

the great circle. The Americans were once scattered all over Europe; here they are incorporated into one of the finest systems of population which has ever appeared, and which will hereafter become distinct by the power of the different climates they inhabit. The American ought therefore to love this country much better than that wherein either he or his forefathers were born. Here the rewards of his industry follow with equal steps the progress of his labour; his labour is founded on the basis of nature, *self-interest;* can it want a stronger allurement? Wives and children, who before in vain demanded of him a morsel of bread, now, fat and frolicsome, gladly help their father to clear those fields whence exuberant crops are to arise to feed and to clothe them all; without any part being claimed, either by a despotic prince, a rich abbot, or a mighty lord. Here religion demands but little of him; a small voluntary salary to the minister, and gratitude to God; can he refuse these? The American is a new man, who acts upon new principles; he must therefore entertain new ideas, and form new opinions. From involuntary idleness, servile dependence, penury, and useful labour, he has passed to toils of a very different nature, rewarded by ample subsistence.—This is an American.

STUDY QUESTIONS

Organization and Content

1. Crèvecoeur (1735–1813) the author of the definition of an American, belonged by birth to the lesser nobility of Normandy. He served in the French forces under Montcalm from about 1755 to 1760, came to the British Colonies, and was naturalized in New York in 1764. His *Letters from an American Farmer* (1782) were based on his travels and on his experiences as the owner of farms in New York and New Jersey in pre-Revolutionary days. The American, then, of whom he writes, "this new man," is the American of the eighteenth century before there was a nation called the United States of America. What evidence does the author give that the American is a "new man"?
2. What is the function of sentence 3 in the explanation?
3. If Americans are pilgrims, what sort of pilgrimage are they making?
4. How has the American become different from his European brothers or grandfathers?
5. What is the particularly American attitude regarding labor, agriculture, marriage, religion?
6. Explain how the last three sentences are related to the discussion which precedes them.

7. Put the essential idea of Crèvecoeur into a one-sentence definition of an American.

Sentence Structure

1. Sentence 4 has both parallel structure and repetition of words. Point them out.
2. Why are parallel structure and repetition effective in sentence 4?
3. At least half the sentences of this paragraph contain the word *American* or *Americans*. Consider why these words are so often repeated and the emphasis they receive in their positions in the sentences where they appear.
4. Several clauses begin with *here*. Explain what particular emphasis *here* has in those clauses.

Diction

1. Look up *prejudices, manners, Alma Mater, posterity, incorporate, allurement, exuberant, servile, penury.*
2. What other words are based on the same roots as *prejudices, incorporate, servile?*
3. Crèvecoeur says that the American works because the basis of nature is self-interest. *Nature* is an important and difficult term; it has been used in many different senses. What meaning does the author intend it to have?

Assignment

An American is a man who acts in a certain way. Similarly, as was stated earlier, a hero is a man acting in a certain way. Write a definition of a hero, showing how the way in which a hero acts is different from the way of all other persons. In writing your definitions, take into account the following questions:

1. Must a hero undergo some kind of test?
2. Must he be involved in a struggle and incur some risk?
3. Must he do something out of the ordinary?
4. Must he show courage?
5. Must he do something for the good of others?
6. Can a person be a hero if he merely does what he is ordered to do or if he himself feels no danger?
7. Must he succeed in his undertakings, or is it permissible for him to fail?
8. Can he be a hero if no one knows about his acts?

You will no doubt find that specific examples will help you to communicate your ideas.

❧ *The Spirit of Liberty*

LEARNED HAND

1   We have gathered here to affirm a faith, a faith in a common purpose, a common conviction, a common devotion. Some of us have chosen America as the land of our adoption; the rest have come from those who did the same. For this reason we have some right to consider ourselves a picked group, a group of those who had the courage to break from the past and brave the dangers and the loneliness of a strange land.

2   What was the object that nerved us, or those who went before us, to this choice? We sought liberty: freedom from oppression, freedom from want, freedom to be ourselves. This we then sought. This we now believe that we are by way of winning.

3   What do we mean when we say that first of all we seek liberty? I often wonder whether we do not rest our hopes too much upon constitutions, upon laws and upon courts. These are false hopes; believe me, these are false hopes. Liberty lives in the hearts of men and women. When it dies there, no constitution, no law, no court can save it. No constitution, no law, no court can even do much to help it. While it lives there, it needs no constitution, no law, no court to save it.

4   And what is this liberty which must live in the hearts of men and women? It is not the ruthless, the unbridled will. It is not freedom to do as one likes. That is the denial of liberty, and leads straight to its overthrow. A society in which men recognize no check upon their freedom, soon becomes a society where freedom is the possession of only a savage few; as we have learned to our sorrow.

5   What then is the spirit of liberty? I cannot define it; I can only tell you my own faith. The spirit of liberty is the spirit which is not too sure that it is right. The spirit of liberty is the spirit which seeks to understand the minds of other men and women. The spirit of liberty is the spirit which weighs their interests alongside its own without bias. The spirit of liberty remembers that not even a sparrow falls to earth unheeded. The spirit of liberty is the spirit of Him, who, near 2000 years ago, taught mankind that lesson it has never learned, but has never quite forgotten; that there may be a kingdom where the least shall be heard and considered side by side with the greatest.

Reprinted by permission of *The New York Times*. Published July 2, 1944.

6   And now in that spirit, that spirit of America which has never been, and which may never be; nay, which never will be, except as the conscience and the courage of Americans create it; yet in the spirit of that America which lies hidden in some form in the aspirations of us all; in the spirit of that America for which our young men are at this moment fighting and dying; in that spirit of liberty and of America I ask you to rise and with me to pledge our faith in the glorious destiny of our beloved country: "I pledge allegiance to the flag of the United States of America and to the Republic for which it stands—one nation indivisible, with liberty and justice for all."

STUDY QUESTIONS

Organization and Content

On May 21, 1944, Justice Hand of the United States Circuit Court of Appeals made this speech in Central Park, New York City, when American citizenship was being awarded to 150,000 newly naturalized citizens. The United States at that time was at war. The speaker was addressing an audience of more than one million persons. His main purpose was not to give a definition but to speak in an inspiring way on a patriotic occasion. But the speech is a good example of how definition may be used in connection with other purposes.

It is worth while to pay some attention to the problem that the speaker faced. (1) The speech had to end with the pledge to the flag. (2) It could not be very long. (3) It must have some connection with the pledge. (4) It must interest both citizens of long standing, who had often heard the pledge and perhaps thought it trite, and the newly naturalized ones, to many of whom the pledge was a new thing; somehow the pledge to the flag must be made to seem significant to both groups.

1. The speech is divided into three parts: I. paragraphs 1 and 2; II. paragraphs 3, 4, and 5; III. paragraph 6. After answering the other questions on organization and content, explain how this pattern of organization is related to the problem of the speaker.
2. In paragraphs 1 and 2 *we* and *us* appear nine times. What noun (or nouns) do these pronouns represent?
3. The speaker insists that "we" have things in "common." To which part of the pledge to the flag does this idea refer?
4. First of all, the speaker says, "we sought liberty." To what questions of definition is he then led?
5. In paragraph 3 liberty is treated mostly in a negative way. Instead of living in the political structure of a nation, liberty lives where?
6. In paragraph 4 the speaker also tells us where liberty *is not*. If liberty

is not freedom to do as one likes, what instruments must society then use to help preserve liberty?

7. In its treatment of liberty paragraph 5 sets up a kind of golden mean between extremes of individualism and of dependence upon political machinery. What relation then does paragraph 5 have with paragraphs 3 and 4?

8. In his definition of the spirit of liberty the author says that it weighs the interests of others alongside its own without bias. What aspect of the pledge to the flag does this idea represent?

9. Judging by paragraph 5, what ethical tradition has especially influenced the thoughts and feelings of the author?

10. The author says that he cannot define the spirit of liberty; yet he gives a kind of definition of it. How does his definition differ from some of the other definitions you have studied?

11. In paragraph 6 the speaker asks the audience to pledge allegiance in "that spirit of an America which has never been." What does *America* then represent, as the speaker uses the term?

Sentence Structure

1. In each paragraph of the speech several words and phrases are repeated. Point them out.
2. Explain how grammatical parallelism is related to the repetition.
3. What is the effect of the repetition? What is the probable reason for it?
4. Which sentences are so constructed that they have a strong and fairly regular rhythm?

Diction

1. Are there any words that you do not know?
2. Is the vocabulary of the speech mainly abstract and general or mainly concrete and particular?
3. Which portion is the most abstract; which portion is the most concrete?
4. Look up *alliteration*. Point out two examples where the author may have chosen a word because of its alliteration.
5. The value of this speech may lie more in its emotional force than in its intellectual keenness. Does its emotional force come from the connotations of the words more than from the rhythm of the sentences? (Consider, for example, the connotations of *sparrow* and *kingdom* in paragraph 5.) Do any other factors increase the emotional quality of the speech?

Assignment

In one or two paragraphs write a definition of the American Cause or the American Dream or American Democracy or the American Educational Ideal or something ennobling like the Spirit of Beauty or the Spirit of Science. Imitate Justice Hand's method by repeating some of the key terms so as to achieve an emotional effect. However, do not become overemotional; keep the writing dignified.

❧ *American Liberalism*

D. JOY HUMES

1   Any attempt at such an analysis [an analysis of American liberalism] would need to recognize first and foremost that liberalism is rooted in humanism, a philosophy which sets up as the chief end of human endeavor the happiness, freedom, and progress of all mankind. But American liberalism is highly individualistic. It places the human personality (existence as a self-conscious being) at the center of its system of values. It is devoted to the supreme worth and dignity of the individual man and stands for his fullest and freest development. It insists that the individual maintain his personal freedom, obey his own conscience, and not be content to be a mere item in the multitude. It is this individualistic factor in American liberalism which is responsible for the belief that the most important criterion for measuring the success or failure of social organization and institutions is their effect on the destiny of the individual. The function of the liberal becomes that of translating into political reality those opportunities without which men cannot attain their fullest potential. Individualism in turn embraces several related doctrines, namely rationalism, libertarianism, and humanitarianism.

2   In its appeal to reason, American liberalism has been an appeal to the reason of the common man rather than to that of a select few. It recognizes that men must live together in organized society and that the society itself helps to shape their destiny. It assumes that men are sufficiently reasonable to meet the necessity of modifying those social institutions which they feel do not operate to the best interests of human welfare. It assumes further that they are reasonable enough to do so without resort to violence, through deliberation rather than reliance on the arbitrary force of governmental authority. Recognizing that political power necessarily exists in any organized society, the American liberal is concerned with both its use and its abuse. Assuming that each individual is rational enough to share in the governmental process, the liberal is concerned with enlarging his opportunity to do so, thus enlarging his opportunity to direct the use to which government is put. His emphasis on the rationality of human beings and human institutions imposes upon

the liberal the categorical opposition to the exercise of unlimited power.

3   In its more strictly libertarian aspect, American liberalism has become identified with the defense of individual civil liberties. The American liberal still believes that certain rights are inviolable, not only as means for the realization of other values but as values in themselves. Man is entitled to certain rights by virtue of his capacity for independent thought and action. Thus rights become the legal recognition of the worth of human personality. The American liberal, however, is not content with the mere legal form of individual rights. He has been so insistent on the living substance of such rights that he has been accused of becoming professional in his search for their violation. He recognizes that self-government is meaningless and individualism and rationalism are prostrate without freedom of thought and expression, a free press, and free assembly. It follows naturally that the liberal has been insistent on tolerance and tenacious in his defense of minorities. An ever-present concern is that minorities shall be enabled to become majorities.

4   The American liberal has extended his concern over civil rights to include protection against abuse by private individuals as well as protection against the encroachment of government. The American liberal would increase the scope of governmental activity in this area. President Truman expressed this point of view when he said that "the extension of civil rights today means not protection of the people against the Government but the protection of the people by the Government" [*New York Times*, June 30, 1947].

5   The doctrine of individual rights has undergone for American liberals another extension—one which has created new rights for the individual, new rights which tend to re-enforce the traditional. Historically, humanitarianism and libertarianism have been closely related doctrines. The American liberal would seriously question the value of the individual's right to freedom of thought and expression if that individual were denied, overtly or otherwise, a fair opportunity to a minimum of education. Freedom of the press, the liberal would hold, is meaningless to those unable to read. The liberal contends that those social measures which tend to ameliorate poverty and ignorance operate to enlarge the individual's freedom. The individual becomes free to do and enjoy things unavailable to him if the attainment of certain social conditions is left to his own or private initiative. Thus the liberal concept of liberty is one that embraces every aspect and phase of human life—liberty of thought, of expression, and of cultural opportunity and the belief that such liberty is not to be had without a degree of economic security. The American concept

of liberty then has been expanded to include positive as well as negative freedoms—freedom "to" as well as freedom "from." It has been extended to include such new rights as that of security from economic hazards over which the individual has no control, and the right to organize and bargain collectively.

6   Based on the individualistic premise that a person is entitled to respect simply because he is a living human being, and recognizing that the individual is subject to conditions beyond his control which are the responsibility of society, American liberalism committed itself to the use of governmental power to remedy those evils, environmental and economic, from which the less fortunate classes suffer. To this extent, it is indeed humanitarian.

7   This, then, is the philosophic content of American liberalism. From a fundamentally humanistic base, it has embodied individualism, rationalism, libertarianism, and humanitarianism. In its practical application of these precepts, American liberalism has appealed, through the government, for collective social action. It has demanded a positive program of governmental action to provide the conditions—economic, political, and other—which would give the common man the opportunity to realize the essential dignity to which he is by nature entitled. It is in its philosophic content and in its method of social engineering that the consistency and continuity of American liberalism is to be found.

STUDY QUESTIONS

Organization and Content

1. The author uses analysis in formulating her definition. What is the most important "factor" in American liberalism? What three other factors are significant? Where are they announced?
2. Which factor is discussed in paragraph 2? In paragraph 3? How are paragraphs 4–6 related? What function does paragraph 7 serve?
3. What brief subsidiary definitions does the author furnish?
4. What contrast does the *but* of sentence 2 introduce?
5. The definition contains few concrete examples. What examples can you supply for the statement of sentence 3, paragraph 2; sentences 1 and 6, paragraph 5; the *otherwise* of sentence 3, paragraph 5?
6. How does paragraph 3 reflect the leading idea of paragraph 1? What concept is contrasted with "mere legal form" of sentence 5, paragraph 3?
7. Why might some people say that sentence 2, paragraph 4, expresses a paradox?
8. What examples of "a positive program of governmental action" favored by American liberals can you name?

Sentence Structure

1. What similar sentence structures providing good transition do you find in paragraph 1; paragraph 2; paragraph 3? What repeated terms provide transition in paragraph 4; paragraph 5?
2. What is the function of the dashes in sentences 7–8, paragraph 5?
3. Explain how parallel grammatical elements and balance are utilized in the structure of sentence 1, paragraph 6.
4. Point out the variety of sentence structure in paragraph 7.

Diction

1. Look up *humanism, rationalism, libertarianism, humanitarianism.* What would a representative of each of these "isms" be called?
2. Look up *categorical, prostrate, tolerance, tenacious, encroachment, overtly, ameliorate, hazards, premise, embodied.*
3. What pictures do *rooted* (paragraph 1) and *embodied* (paragraph 7) metaphorically suggest?
4. What does *social engineering* (last sentence) mean? Is it a metaphor?
5. Can you find as many as three concrete terms in this definition? Which one is most concrete? Does the nature of the subject compel the author to use abstract words?

Assignment

Write a definition in which you analyze some abstract term such as friendship, justice, love, or science; or some, "ism," such as anarchism, determinism, Protestantism, capitalism, Populism, or Puritanism.

 Conservatism

CLINTON ROSSITER

1 The Conservative holds definite opinions about man's nature, his capacity for self-government, his relations with other men, the kind of life he should lead, and the rights he may properly claim. On these opinions rests the whole Conservative tradition.

2 Man, says the Conservative, is a composite of good and evil, a blend of ennobling excellencies and degrading imperfections. He

is not perfect; he is not perfectible. If educated properly, placed in a favorable environment, and held in restraint by tradition and authority, he may display innate qualities of rationality, sociability, industry, decency, and love of liberty. Never, no matter how he is educated or situated or restrained, will he throw off completely his other innate qualities of irrationality, selfishness, laziness, depravity, and corruptibility. Man's nature is essentially immutable, and the immutable strain is one of deep-seated wickedness. Although some Conservatives find support for their skeptical view of man in recent experiments in psychology, most continue to rely on religious teachings and the study of history. Those who are Christians, and most Conservatives are, prefer to call the motivation for iniquitous and irrational behavior by its proper name: Original Sin.

3   No truth about human nature and capabilities is more important than this: man can govern himself, but there is no certainty that he will; free government is possible but far from inevitable. Man will need all the help he can get from education, religion, tradition, and institutions if he is to enjoy even a limited success in his experiments in self-government. He must be counseled, encouraged, informed, and checked. Above all, he must realize that the collective wisdom of the community, itself the union of countless partial and imperfect wisdoms like his own, is alone equal to this mightiest of social tasks. A clear recognition of man's conditional capacity for ruling himself and others is the first requisite of constitution-making.

4   Conservatism holds out obstinately against two popular beliefs about human relations in modern society: individualism and equality. . . .

5   Each man is equal to every other man in only one meaningful sense: he is a man, a physical and spiritual entity, and is thus entitled by God and nature to be treated as end rather than means. From the basic fact of moral equality come several secondary equalities that the modern Conservative recognizes, more eloquently in public than in private: equality of opportunity, the right of each individual to exploit his own talents up to their natural limits; equality before the law, the right to justice on the same terms as other men; and political equality, which takes the form of universal suffrage. Beyond this the Conservative is unwilling to go. Recognizing the infinite variety among men in talent, taste, appearance, intelligence, and virtue, he is candid enough to assert that this variety extends vertically as well as horizontally. Men are grossly unequal—and, what is more, can never be made equal—in all qualities of mind, body, and spirit.

6   The good society rests solidly on this great truth. The social

order is organized in such a way as to take advantage of ineradicable natural distinctions among men. It exhibits a class structure in which there are several quite distinct levels, most men find their level early and stay in it without rancor, and equality of opportunity keeps the way at least partially open to ascent and decline. At the same time the social order aims to temper those distinctions that are not natural. It recognizes the inevitability and indeed the necessity of orders and classes, but it insists that all privileges, ranks, and other visible signs of inequality be as natural and functional as possible. The Conservative, of course—and this point is of decisive importance—is much more inclined than other men to consider artificial distinctions as natural. Equity rather than equality is the mark of his society; the reconciliation rather than the abolition of classes is his constant aim. When he is forced to choose between liberty and equality, he throws his support unhesitatingly to liberty. Indeed, the preference for liberty over equality lies at the root of the Conservative tradition.

7   What virtues must the individual cultivate? [Conservatives] . . . all agree to this catalogue of primary virtues: wisdom, justice, temperance, and courage; industry, frugality, piety, and honesty; contentment, obedience, compassion, and good manners. The good man is peaceful but not resigned and is conservative through habit and choice rather than sloth and cowardice. He assumes that duty comes before pleasure, self-sacrifice before self-indulgence. Believing that the test of life is accomplishment rather than enjoyment, he takes pride in doing a good job in the station to which he has been called. He is alert to the identity and malignity of the vices he must shun: ignorance, injustice, intemperance, and cowardice; laziness, luxury, selfishness, and dishonesty; envy, disobedience, violence, and bad manners. And he is aware, too, of the larger implications of his own life of virtue: self-government is for moral men; those who would be free must be virtuous.

8   The Conservative's theory of government displays an unusual degree of symmetry, and he is rarely stumped by practical questions about its nature, pattern, and purpose. In discussing the nature of government, he likes to point out to radicals that it is good rather than evil, and to collectivists that it is limited rather than unlimited in potentialities and scope.

9   Man, he insists, is a political as well as social animal; government is necessary to his existence as man. . . . Natural in origin, it is also natural in development. Like society, it is a tree rather than a machine. Laws and institutions are the result of centuries of imperceptible growth, not the fiat of one generation of constitu-

tion-makers. A new constitution will not last long unless it incorporates a good part of the old, and most successful reforms in the pattern of government are recognitions of prescriptive changes that have already taken place.

10   Government is a positive blessing for which men can thank wise Providence, not a necessary evil for which they can blame their own moral insufficiencies. Even if men were angels, some political organization would be necessary to adjust the complexity of angelic relations and to do for the citizens of heaven-on-earth what they could not do as individuals or families. Government serves genuine purposes that cannot be fulfilled by any other means. Any time-honored instrument that is so essential to man's liberty and security cannot be considered inherently evil.

11   Government, in the Conservative view, is something like fire. Under control, it is the most useful of servants; out of control, it is a ravaging tyrant. The danger of its getting out of control is no argument against its extended and generous use. Held within proper limits, government answers all these purposes:

12   It defends the community against external assault.

13   It is the symbol of unity, the focus of that patriotic fervor which turns a lumpy mass of men and groups into a living unity.

14   It establishes and administers an equitable system of justice, which alone makes it possible for men to live and do business with one another.

15   It protects men against the violence they can do one another. By the judicious use of force, it ensures "domestic tranquillity."

16   It secures the rights of men, including the right of property, against the assaults of license, anarchy, and jealousy.

17   It adjusts conflicts among groups and regulates their activities, thus acting as the major equilibrating force in the balance of social forces.

18   It promotes public and private morality, without which freedom cannot long exist. In league with church and family, it strives to separate men's virtues from their vices and to keep the latter under tight rein. It does all this by encouraging or at least protecting organized religion, by supporting the means of education, by enacting laws against vice, and by offering a high example of justice and rectitude.

19   It aids men in their pursuit of happiness, chiefly by removing obstacles in the path of individual development.

20   Finally, government acts as a humanitarian agency in cases of clear necessity. It relieves human suffering by acts of care and charity, and in more developed communities it may guarantee each

citizen the minimum material requirements of a decent existence. In discharging this function, government operates under two clear restrictions. First, it can achieve only limited success as a welfare agency. Many of man's ills, especially those that are spiritual in nature, are not curable by legislation. Second, there is, as Peter Viereck insists, a "line of diminishing returns for humanitarianism. Beyond it, the increase in security is less than the loss in liberty." The humanitarian function of government will always remain secondary to its great duties to ensure tranquillity, establish justice, secure rights and property, and raise the level of morality.

21   Man's place in society, especially his relations to government, presents a continuing problem on which the Conservative refuses to take a doctrinaire stand. In general, he tries to strike a workable compromise between the needs of the community and the rights of the individual, both of which he champions eloquently.

22   In the world as it is, the world in which men live, it is often necessary to make a hard choice between individual and community. In such instances, the Conservative says, the interests of the community come first. This does not mean that every instance of friction will be resolved in favor of society, nor does it mean disrespect for the dignity of man's person or the inviolability of his soul. It does mean that society, the individual's fellow men considered as a collective entity, must get first consideration. If the community is visibly decayed or arbitrary, the margin of doubt may swing to the individual. As a general principle, however, it must never be forgotten that man is no better than a lonely beast outside the educating, protecting, civilizing pale of society, and that he must therefore pay a stiff price for its blessings. Many philosophers have denied that man has natural rights; none has denied that he has natural needs, which can be filled only through communal association with other men. Society, the total community, which is a great deal more than the government, is historically, ethically, and logically superior to the individual. Government, family, church, and countrymen past, present, and future—how can it ever be asserted with candor that any one man is more valuable than these? Conservative doctrine speaks of the primacy of society.

23   Yet it speaks, too, of the rights of man. If man has needs that force him to submit to the community, he also has rights that the community must honor. In every man there is a sphere of personality and activity into which other men, whether private citizens or public officials, have no logical or moral claim to intrude. This area is labeled "the rights of man."

24   These rights are both natural and social—natural because they

belong to man as man, are part of the great scheme of nature, and are thus properly considered the gift of God; social because man can in fact enjoy them only in an organized community. Moreover, if society is the environment in which abstract rights come to life, government, the political arm of society, is the agency that protects and defines them. Only under government will a man's rights be honored by other men; only under government will they be kept within bounds.

25   . . . The Conservative is not an extreme individualist. He may be willing to concede numerous arguments of the unqualified individualists, for his own respect for the dignity of the individual is not surpassed by that of any man. Yet he cannot agree to the full implications of individualism, which is based, so he thinks, on an incorrect appraisal of man, society, history, and government. In his own way, the individualist is as much a perfectionist as the Socialist, and with perfectionism the Conservative can have no truck.

26   In particular, the Conservative refuses to go all the way with economic individualism. His distrust of unfettered man, his devotion to groups, his sense of the complexity of the social process, his recognition of the real services that government can perform—all these sentiments make it impossible for him to subscribe to the dogmas and shibboleths of economic individualism: laissez-faire, the negative state, enlightened self-interest, the law of supply and demand, the profit motive. The Conservative may occasionally have kind words for each of these notions, but he is careful to qualify his support by stating other, more important social truths. For example, he does not for a moment deny the prominence of the profit motive, but he insists that it be recognized for the selfish thing it is and be kept within reasonable, socially imposed limits.

STUDY QUESTIONS

Organization and Content

1. What five opinions regarding man does Rossiter announce in paragraph 1? What does the reader expect after such a paragraph? Does Rossiter fulfill the reader's expectations?
2. In which paragraphs does Rossiter discuss each of the five opinions?
3. According to conservative belief is man's nature innately good or bad?
4. What do education and authority have to do with his nature?
5. According to the conservative view, what part do rationality and Original Sin play in man's nature?
6. Rossiter states in paragraph 4 that the Conservative is against a belief

in equality. To what extent is he willing to grant that citizens are equal? What does he think he gains by a "preference for liberty over equality"?

7. How can "artificial distinctions" be "natural" (paragraph 6)? What examples of artificial distinctions and of natural distinctions can you list?

8. In a case involving academic freedom, how do you think a professor and others involved should resolve the claims of courage, justice, obedience, and good manners (paragraph 7)?

9. What does being "called" to a station mean? Where does the call come from?

10. Are the vices listed in paragraph 7 the exact opposites of the "catalogue of primary virtues"?

11. How does the Conservative's view of government differ from that of radicals and collectivists? What specific people would be examples of the radicals and collectivists?

12. Give examples of agencies through which government answers the purposes listed in paragraphs 12–20.

13. In what two ways does Rossiter believe that governmental humanitarianism is restricted?

14. Can the Conservative logically be the champion of both community needs and individual rights? Why does he think the community must generally come before the individual?

15. In sentence 6, paragraph 22, Rossiter says that man "must *therefore* pay a *stiff* price" for the blessings of society. Explain his logic.

16. In what sense, if any, can one say that society is "ethically" superior to the individual?

17. What does "the great scheme of nature" have to do with the rights of man?

18. According to Rossiter, should a government interfere in any way with a person's right to make profits?

19. What part does analysis play in this extended definition?

20. What are the main points on which Rossiter and Humes agree and disagree?

Sentence Structure

1. Explain the contrast in structure and effect between sentence 1, paragraph 1 (loose), and sentence 2 (periodic).

2. How is the balance of sentence 2, paragraph 2, achieved? Why is the second half more emphatically significant than the first half?

3. How is the beginning of sentence 4, paragraph 2, made emphatic?

4. Rossiter uses colons in some sentences. What functions do they perform in, for example, sentence 7, paragraph 2; sentence 1, paragraph 3; paragraph 4; sentences 1 and 2, paragraph 5; sentences 2 and 7, paragraph 7?

5. What terms are repeated to provide transition among sentences of paragraphs 3, 6, 11–20, 26?

6. What are the specific purposes of the varied transitional terms Rossiter uses at the beginnings of sentence 4, paragraph 3; sentence 4, paragraph 6; sentence 7, paragraph 7; sentence 2, paragraph 8; sentence 1, para-

graph 20; sentence 2, paragraph 22; sentence 1, paragraph 23; and sentence 1, paragraph 26?
7. Examine any paragraph with five to ten sentences, and show what means Rossiter has used to secure variety of sentence structure.

Diction

1. Look up the following words (numerals represent paragraphs): *innate, immutable* (1); *entity* (5); *temper* (6); *sloth, malignity* (7); *symmetry* (8); *fiat, prescriptive* (9); *rectitude* (18); *doctrinaire* (21); *shibbo-leths, laissez-faire* (26).
2. From what different languages did these words originally come?
3. Is there any etymological connection between *entity* and *entitled; symmetry* and *sympathy; doctrinaire* and *doctor?*
4. Does Rossiter's vocabulary have the same abstractness that Humes's has?

Assignment

1. According to your own views, define the good society; a good man; or a successful welfare agency.
2. How would you define a decayed or arbitrary community (according to the criteria implied in paragraph 22)?
3. How would you define a satisfactory community, judging it in terms of the qualities that you value most highly?

Comparison

and Contrast

It has already been shown to some extent how writers use the principles of comparison and contrast in explaining meanings. Since definition requires the showing of differences among terms, some element of contrast naturally appears in definition and is indeed almost inevitable.

Comparison and contrast are also used frequently in other types of expository writing. Indeed, the human mind turns naturally and with ease to the locating of likenesses and differences. It is convenient to try to explain something unfamiliar by indicating how it resembles something familiar. The *how* will be brought out by producing evidence for the resemblance in the form of specific details. The details are illustrations of the main idea, that likeness exists. Thus, comparison and contrast as methods of exposition gain their effectiveness and power from their force as examples. The examples, that is, the particular details, are brought into view no doubt through an act of analysis.

The mind is impressed by differences as well as by similarities. If a person travels abroad, he will often be thinking: This is *not* the way we do it at home. Or when he inspects his personality, he discovers: "This is *not* the way I felt last year, or when I was a freshman, or when I was a child." Constantly, too, he is watching to see whether things turn out as they were forecast. "No," he tells the politician, "this is *not* what you promised; the state of affairs is different from what it should be." Since he has noticed a difference, he complains because one condition is less good than another that he hoped for. Contrast is often the basis of criticism and complaint; yet both contrast and comparison may be also the basis of praise. Whenever anything is judged, a standard is used; that is, the thing in question is compared with the standard. Therefore, one is very likely to turn to comparison and contrast when discussing anything in terms of standards of excellence. The selections ahead on women before marriage and after marriage, on American and British students, and on two aspects of sport all involve judgments of worth or value. Comparison and contrast have a special usefulness, then, for the bringing out of values.

The technique of presenting material according to these methods of exposition presents certain possibilities. Suppose two things, A and B, are being compared. The author may write one whole paragraph on A and a second paragraph on B. He might, using shorter paragraphs perhaps, do this and then continue with a third paragraph on A, a fourth on B, and so on alternately to the end. On the other hand, the writer might switch from A to B when halfway through the first paragraph and follow that half-paragraph pattern until he was finished. Clearly also one might write first one sentence about A, the next about B, and so forth, following a pattern of more rapid alternation. As will be seen by studying the models, each of these techniques offers advantages and creates certain effects.

Educated Women Before Marriage and After Marriage

Adlai E. Stevenson

Now, as I have said, women, especially educated women such as you, have a unique opportunity to influence us, man and boy, and to play a direct part in the unfolding drama of our free society. But I am told that nowadays the young wife or mother is short of time for the subtle arts, that things are not what they used to be; that once immersed in the very pressing and particular problems of domesticity many women feel frustrated and far apart from the great issues and stirring debates for which their education has given them understanding and relish. Once they read Baudelaire. Now it is the *Consumers' Guide*. Once they wrote poetry. Now it's the laundry list. Once they discussed art and philosophy until late in the night.

From *What I Think* by Adlai E. Stevenson. Copyright 1956. Reprinted by permission of Harper & Row, Publishers.

Now they are so tired they fall asleep as soon as the dishes are finished. There is, often, a sense of contraction, of closing horizons and lost opportunities. They had hoped to play their part in the crisis of the age. But what they do is wash the diapers.

STUDY QUESTIONS

Organization and Content

1. This paragraph is a part of a commencement address that Adlai Stevenson gave at Smith College; therefore, the manner in which he speaks to his audience in sentence 1. *But,* a word of contrast, begins sentence 2. With what idea of sentence 1 does the idea of sentence 2 contrast?
2. What relation does sentence 9 have to the six preceding sentences?
3. What are the contrasting terms in sentences 10 and 11?
4. Would the paragraph be better if it closed with sentence 9? Or better if sentence 9 were placed at the end? Give reasons for your answer.

Sentence Structure

1. Note the variety of sentence length. How long is sentence 2? How long are the next half-dozen sentences?
2. In these sentences what repeated words provide the points of contrast?
3. Which of these half-dozen sentences sound more dignified? Which less dignified?
4. What is the effect of this contrast in tone?

Diction

1. Look up *subtle, immersed, frustrated, Baudelaire.*
2. Does the author use any colloquial words or expressions?
3. Point out two examples of alliteration in sentence 2.
4. If the words that alliterate were replaced by nonalliterating words, would there be any change in effect?

Assignment

Write a paragraph in which you contrast a hope and a reality; it might be in terms of anticipation and disappointment or of fear and delight. Such topics as dormitory life, a college course, a trip, a vacation, a friendship would be suitable. Use several short contrasting sentences like Stevenson's.

American Students and British Students

J. Frank Dobie

1   As far as quality of mind is concerned—and quality of mind is something that all the theories of democracy in the world cannot equalize—there is no detectable difference between top American students and top British students. The average student at the one English University I have acquaintance with is, however, better trained mentally, has the fibers in his mind better developed, enjoys the act of thinking more and has more intellectual curiosity than the average American student. He is more civilized, just as the average member of Parliament is more civilized than the average Congressman, less given to the puerile in thought, speech and conduct. He demonstrates how the charm of youthfulness may be added to by dignity and mental maturity. He gives a richer meaning to Wordsworth's "The child is father of the man."

2   Go back a few years before the war to any State University in America. The first class of the morning is over. Students make a rush for breakfast or for coffee or maybe only for some form of "pep" beverage at a drugstore near at hand. Those that are not talking are looking maybe at a newspaper. What are they looking at in the newspaper? Two things generally: sports or the funnies. Within the last fifteen years a much higher percentage of American students than formerly have come to take a serious interest in political, economic, social questions. But it is still a widespread idea among Americans who are not students, that amusement—entertainment—consists of something that will not require the constitutionally tired business man to exercise his brain. The tired businessman's brain is devoted to practical things, and it isn't fun to use it. Fun is something to be bought, through a nickelodeon, in a picture show, from the voices of radio wits, out of colored Sunday supplements and their weekday counterparts.

3   The English collegian, on the contrary, has no colored Sunday supplement. He follows sports, goes to cinemas, wouldn't stand for having the peace of his pub or his tea-house constantly violated by jazz music; he listens to ideas as well as opiates over the radio, and reads the editorials and reports on Parliamentary de-

bates in his newspaper. His intellectual activity is not modeled on that of the tired businessman.

STUDY QUESTIONS

Organization and Content

1. What class of college student is the author primarily discussing?
2. What is the function of sentence 1?
3. What "contrast-word" is significant in sentence 2?
4. Sentence 2 lists four ways in which certain British students are superior to certain American students. What are they?
5. In the rest of paragraph 1 the British student is praised for what other qualities?
6. What do the first six sentences of paragraph 2 accomplish?
7. What sort of objection is sentence 7 intended to meet?
8. According to paragraph 2, Americans largely expect to get "fun" by what means? And by what means do they *not* expect to get fun?
9. What is the relation of the second half of paragraph 2 to the first half?
10. According to paragraph 2, the American student is following what model? In the light of this discussion, is it fair to infer that his model is a bad one?
11. What contrast is brought out in paragraph 3?
12. What points of paragraph 1 is paragraph 3 intended to illustrate?
13. Though he is writing about college students, do you think that the author is actually contrasting British society and American society?
14. Do these three paragraphs have topic sentences? If so, what are they?

Sentence Structure

1. The beginning and the ending of a sentence are positions of emphasis. Contrast sentences 1 and 2 of paragraph 1 in terms of the material placed at the beginning and at the end.
2. Why do sentences 3, 4, and 5 all begin with *He?*
3. Does the material at the end of sentences 3, 4, and 5 have enough emphasis?
4. Contrast the structure of the first six sentences of paragraph 2 with that of the other four sentences in the remainder of that paragraph.

Diction

1. Look up *puerile, cinema, pub, violate, opiate.*
2. In paragraph 1 is "more civilized" to be equated with "less given to the puerile"?
3. Point out colloquial diction. Is this colloquialism pleasing or not?
4. Does the author's "more civilized" fit one of the definitions of "civilization" that you have studied? Explain.

Assignment

Write three similar paragraphs on one of the following topics, contrasting:

1. Men students and women students
2. Cultured people and "tired businessmen"
3. Admirable young people and juvenile delinquents
4. Typical students in two different curricula

Follow Mr. Dobie's pattern of organization: that is, A, then B, then back to A.

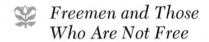 *Freemen and Those*
Who Are Not Free

EDMUND BURKE

You will, therefore, not listen to those who tell you that these matters are above you, and ought to be left entirely to those into whose hands the King has put them. The public interest is more your business than theirs; and it is from want of spirit, and not from want of ability, that you can become wholly unfit to argue or to judge upon it. For in this very thing lies the difference between freemen and those that are not free. In a free country every man thinks he has a concern in all public matters; that he has a right to form and a right to deliver an opinion upon them. They sift, examine, and discuss them. They are curious, eager, attentive, and jealous; and by making such matters the daily subjects of their thoughts and discoveries, vast numbers contract a very tolerable knowledge of them, and some a very considerable one. And this it is that fills free countries with men of ability in all stations. Whereas in other countries none but men whose office calls them to it having much care or thought about public affairs, and not daring to try the force of their opinions with one another, ability of this sort is extremely rare in any station of life. In free countries, there is often found more real public wisdom and sagacity in shops and manufactories than in the cabinets of princes in countries where none dares to have an opinion until he

From Edmund Burke, *Correspondence of Edmund Burke* (1844).

comes into them. Your whole importance, therefore, depends upon a constant, discreet use of your own reason; otherwise you and your country sink to nothing. If upon any particular occasion you should be roused, you will not know what to do. Your fire will be a fire in straw, fitter to waste and consume yourselves than to warm or enliven anything else. You will be only a giddy mob, upon whom no sort of reliance is to be had. You may disturb your country, but you never can reform your government. . . .

STUDY QUESTIONS

Organization and Content

1. This is a paragraph from a letter written by Edmund Burke, a famous British statesman, on October 13, 1777, to a political club. In order to encourage the members to be concerned with public affairs, Burke contrasts the opportunities and abilities of people in a country like England and those in a country with less freedom. Does he emphasize the positive elements of the contrast or the negative elements?
2. According to sentence 1, the voters of England have what choice? How is the answer to that question of choice made the basis of the contrast in sentence 3?
3. What is the main point of the sentences devoted to the activities of men in a free country?
4. In which sentences does Burke stress the shortcomings of people in nations without the tradition of freedom?
5. What idea does the *therefore* stand for in sentence 10? What does *otherwise* mean in the second half of sentence 10?
6. In sentences 11–14 Burke predicts things that *will* or *may* happen; they will or may happen if what takes place? On which sentence do all these predictions depend?
7. Sentences 11, 12, and 14 contain contrasts. What are they?
8. Why should Burke mention the idea of "reforming" a government in sentence 14?

Sentence Structure

1. Indicate how emphasis is gained through repetition in sentences 2, 3, and 4.
2. What is the effect of the lists of verbs and adjectives in sentences 5 and 6?
3. Does it seem reasonable that in sentence 9 Burke decided to balance the two different kinds of countries, one at the beginning and the other at the end of the sentence? To what extent does he secure effective emphasis? (Note the problem of handling the four *in*-phrases in sentence 9.)

4. What emphatic contrasts does sentence 9 contain?
5. Explain the principles of organization upon which sentences 11–14 are organized.

Diction

1. What does "want of spirit" mean (sentence 2)?
2. Explain the precise differences of meaning among the adjectives in sentence 6.
3. Look up *sagacity, discreet.*
4. What is the difference between a *factory* and a *manufactory?*

Assignment

Write a paragraph contrasting the advantages of one sort of person with the disadvantages of another sort:

1. A lover of reading with one who does not read
2. A nonfraternity member with a fraternity member, or vice versa
3. A college graduate with one who is not a college graduate
4. A person who has traveled with one who has not traveled
5. A person who loves nature with one who does not
6. A person reared in a city with one reared elsewhere

Develop the topic by emphasizing positive aspects and making only occasional reference to the contrasting negative ones. You might do well to assume that your paragraph is from a letter you are writing to a friend encouraging him to do something: for example, travel, attend college, and so on.

    Common Law and Civil Law

Max Radin

1   We began by saying that most civilized communities have a law and could not be without one, since being civilized means being organized, and organization implies a law. But civilization also implies history, and history gives law an individual national character.
2   It is quite true that in western civilized society certain common elements are derived from the common tradition of Christianity and from the institutions of Greece and Rome. Besides these common elements, an entire national system may be borrowed and trans-

From Max Radin, *The Law and You* (New York: The New American Library of World Literature, 1948). Reprinted by permission of Rhea Radin.

planted into another country, where it inevitably will create a new history of its own and develop in a new way.

3   Within this western civilization, two systems of law have grown up which have in the last century spread beyond their original boundaries. One of these two systems is based on the Roman law. It is misleadingly called the civil law, a term that is used also to describe the noncriminal law of all systems. It has suffered of course extensive changes, and in its modern form is generally found as a code in which the more general ideas of the law are carefully and systematically set forth. Most of these modern codes embodying the civil law are based on the French Civil Code of 1804, and a few on the German Civil Code of 1900 and the Swiss Civil Code of 1907–1911. Nearly all the codes of Latin America are derived from the French.

4   The other system is that of the common law of England, which is the basis of the law of England, Ireland, the United States (except Louisiana), all of Canada (except Quebec), Australia, New Zealand, to a less degree India, and to an even lesser degree South Africa. This common law has been codified quite imperfectly in a few American states, but in the main it has remained in the form of a judicial tradition and has not taken statutory form.

5   The civil law and the common law often have been contrasted, and the superiority of one to the other has been made much of by the panegyrist of each. They are much more alike in fundamentals than is generally admitted. The differences are rather matters of detail.

6   One of the most striking differences is in the treatment of property. The common law, in this respect true to its feudal origin, makes a sharp distinction between land and things built on it, or attached to it, and all other kinds of property. The former is called real property or real estate or realty, and the latter, personal property or personalty or sometimes chattels, although personalty and chattels are not quite synonymous. Some kinds of personal rights are associated so definitely with realty that the same rules cover them.

7   Personalty is transferred, leased, hired, mortgaged, lent in very simple ways. As a rule it can be done by word of mouth. It is very different with realty. Most of the transactions in regard to realty must be in writing, and it still is common, although no longer essential, to use exact and elaborate formulas in the deeds, leases, and mortgages by which these transactions are carried out.

8   At the civil law, no such distinction is made, at any rate no such sharp distinction. When property is spoken of, or sales or leases, either kind of property can be meant. But in practice it obviously is impossible to deal with immovables, like land, as though

they were exactly like movables. For one thing, the latter can be picked up and literally transferred, and the others cannot. It turns out that differences in legal treatment of movables and immovables, which are very much like personalty and realty, do exist at the civil law although the differences are not so thoroughgoing or extensive.

9   The jury system is one of the most famous institutions of the common law. It is used in both civil and criminal cases. Under the Constitution, the right to a trial by jury was declared to be fundamental in both civil and criminal trials. In many of the states, however, a jury may be waived in civil cases and may even be abolished altogether.

10   The English jury was regarded in England and in Europe generally as a symbol of civic liberty. After the French Revolution, most of the European countries adopted it with modifications but adopted it only for criminal cases. The modifications, however, give the civil law jury a substantially different aspect from that of the common law criminal jury. A majority vote is sufficient for conviction or acquittal. The judges, usually several, vote with the jury. It is usual in the same proceedings—although before the court alone, without a jury—to decide on the money compensation which a convicted criminal must give his victim if such compensation is demanded.

11   On the side of criminal law, there are many differences between the common law and the civil law. Many of the civil rights guaranteed by the Bill of Rights do not exist at the civil law. The right of habeas corpus does not exist there, but we must note that a number of Latin American countries have developed an institution which much resembles it. There is further no right against self-incrimination at the civil law.

12   But most of the other rules intended to safeguard the rights of an accused exist in both systems. Especially, it may be well to repeat here what was stated before—the common assertion that in the civil law countries there is a presumption of guilt as against the common law presumption of innocence is quite false. The presumption of innocence exists in both systems and, it must be confessed, is not so valuable a safeguard in either as it ought to be.

13   If we add to what has been said the fact that, in the modern civil law, statutes are given a much higher place than precedent among sources of law, we have almost exhausted the important differences between the two great modern systems. There are enough indications of mutual adaptation to render it quite possible that, in a federated world, a general law might come into existence which would be a fusion of the two, without destroying certain special institutions which individual nations may prefer to retain.

STUDY QUESTIONS

Organization and Content

1. What is the function of paragraphs 1 and 2?
2. What does sentence 1 of paragraph 3 lead the reader to expect?
3. To what extent does paragraph 3 satisfy the reader's expectation?
4. What relation does paragraph 4 have to paragraph 3?
5. To what new phase of the subject does paragraph 5 lead the reader?
6. What particular differences between the two systems of law are discussed?
7. How is the material of paragraphs 6–13 proportioned among the subtopics?
8. Make a two-level outline (using Roman numerals and capital letters) of the selection.

Sentence Structure

1. In length and structure do the sentences of this selection most nearly resemble the sentences of the preceding selection by Dobie or by Burke?
2. To clarify your ideas on this question, analyze the two sentences of paragraph 2 and compare them with sentences 4 and 5 of paragraph 3.
3. Then compare the two sentences of paragraph 4 with the three sentences of paragraph 5.
4. Also compare the sentences of paragraph 10 with those of paragraph 13.

Diction

1. Look up *codify, statutory, panegyrist, feudal, waive, habeas corpus, presumption, precedent.*
2. Explain the etymology of *realty* and *personalty.*
3. Explain how differences of meaning developed among *chattel, cattle,* and *capital.*
4. Is the diction of this selection more formal or more colloquial than that of the preceding selection by Dobie? By Burke?

Assignment

Following the same method that Radin used but using a smaller scale, explain similarities and differences between:

1. A junior high school and a senior high school
2. A college and a university
3. A folk song and a ballad
4. Popular music and swing music
5. A Northerner and a Southerner
6. An Easterner and a Westerner
7. Canadians and people of the United States
8. People from two different Latin American or European countries
9. Two Protestant church denominations

Ukrainians and Texans

JOHN FISCHER

1 The Ukrainians are the Texans of Russia. They believe they can fight, drink, ride, sing, and make love better than anybody else in the world, and if pressed will admit it. Their country, too, was a borderland—that's what "Ukraine" means—and like Texas it was originally settled by outlaws, horse thieves, land-hungry farmers, and people who hadn't made a go of it somewhere else. Some of these hard cases banded together, long ago, to raise hell and livestock. They called themselves Cossacks, and they would have felt right at home in any Western movie. Even today the Ukrainians cherish a wistful tradition of horsemanship, although most of them would feel as uncomfortable in a saddle as any Dallas banker. They still like to wear knee-high boots and big, furry hats, made of gray or black Persian lamb, which are the local equivalent of the Stetson.

2 Even the country looks a good deal like Texas—flat, dry prairie, shading off in the south to semidesert. Through the middle runs a strip of dark, rich soil, the Chernozom Belt, which is almost identical with the black waxy soil of central Texas. It grows the best wheat in the Soviet Union. The Ukraine is also famous for its cattle, sheep, and cotton, and—again like Texas—it has been in the throes of an industrial boom for the last twenty years. On all other people the Ukrainians look with a sort of kindly pity. They might have thought up for their own use the old Western rule of etiquette: "Never ask a man where he comes from. If he's a Texan, he'll tell you; if he's not, don't embarrass him."

STUDY QUESTIONS

Organization and Content

1. Can any sentences of the two paragraphs be taken as topic sentences?
2. A comparison might be presented paragraph by paragraph, half-para-

From pp. 22, 23, *Why They Behave Like Russians* by John Fischer. Copyright 1946 by John Fischer. Reprinted by permission of Harper & Row, Publishers.

graph by half-paragraph, sentence by sentence, and so forth. What is the pattern in which the comparison is presented here?

3. Similarities presented in a comparison might be geographical, historical, traditional, commercial, agricultural, educational, recreational, artistic, psychological, and so forth. What similarities has Fischer stressed in his discussion?

4. Are both parts of the comparison consistently represented?

5. To what extent is suggestion utilized?

6. In which sentences has Fischer referred to specific things or activities in order to make his comparison vivid?

Sentence Structure

1. What transitional links make it easy for the reader to go from sentence to sentence?

2. Just how is the comparison of Ukrainians with Texans brought out in sentences 3–7?

3. Fischer's sentences are fairly short. How many are simple, compound, complex?

4. Is the sentence style prevailingly formal or colloquial?

Diction

1. Look up *wistful, throes*.

2. What is the effect on the reader of using contractions?

3. Is this an example of dignified or undignified writing? Consider phrases like "people who hadn't made a go of it," "hard cases," "to raise hell," "felt right at home."

4. Is it the diction that is responsible for the humorous tone of the selection, or is it something else?

Assignment

Most of the selections in this section have shown differences, have developed contrasts; this selection emphasizes likenesses. Imitate it by writing one or two paragraphs showing how two things are alike. Some suggestions:

1. Scientists are like explorers.

2. Successful college life is like disciplined military life.

3. Twentieth-century American painting or architecture or music is like that of other contemporary Western countries.

4. A great man of the present day is like great men of the past.

5. The American of the present is like Americans of the past.

6. Those who live on the sea or in the mountains are like those of the same environment though in different countries.

7. An athlete is like a soldier.

🌿　*Winter and Summer*

Laurie Lee

1　The seasons of my childhood seemed (of course) so violent, so intense and true to their nature, that they have become for me ever since a reference of perfection whenever such names are mentioned. They possessed us so completely they seemed to change our nationality; and when I look back to the valley it cannot be one place I see, but village-winter or village-summer, both separate. It becomes increasingly easy in urban life to ignore their extreme humours, but in those days winter and summer dominated our every action, broke into our houses, conscripted our thoughts, ruled our games, and ordered our lives.

2　Winter was no more typical of our valley than summer, it was not even summer's opposite; it was merely that other place. And somehow one never remembered the journey towards it; one arrived, and winter was here. The day came suddenly when all details were different and the village had to be rediscovered. One's nose went dead so that it hurt to breathe, and there were jigsaws of frost on the window. The light filled the house with a green polar glow; while outside—in the invisible world—there was a strange hard silence, or a metallic creaking, a faint throbbing of twigs and wires.

3　The kitchen that morning would be full of steam, billowing from kettles and pots. The outside pump was frozen again, making a sound like broken crockery, so that the girls tore icicles from the eaves for water and we drank boiled ice in our tea.

4　"It's wicked," said Mother. "The poor, poor birds." And she flapped her arms with vigour. . . .

5　Now the winter's day was set in motion and we rode through its crystal kingdom. We examined the village for its freaks of frost, for anything we might use. We saw the frozen spring by the side of the road, huge like a swollen flower. Water wagtails hovered over it, nonplussed at its silent hardness, and again and again they dropped down to drink only to go sprawling in a tumble of feathers. We saw the stream in the valley, black and halted, a tarred path threading through the willows. We saw trees lopped off by their burdens of ice, cow tracks like pot-holes in rock, quiet lumps of sheep licking the spiky grass with their black and rotting tongues. The church clock had stopped and the weathercock was frozen, so that both time and the winds were stilled; and nothing, we thought, could be more exciting than this: interference by a hand unknown, the winter's No! to routine and laws—sinister, awesome, welcome. . . .

6   Summer, June summer, with the green back on earth and the whole world unlocked and seething—like winter, it came suddenly and one knew it in bed, almost before waking up; with cuckoos and pigeons hollowing the woods since daylight and the chipping of tits in the pear blossom. . . .

7   Summer was also the time of these: of sudden plenty, of slow hours and actions, of diamond haze and dust on the eyes, of the valley in post-vernal slumber; of burying birds saved from seething corruption; of Mother sleeping heavily at noon; of jazzing wasps and dragonflies, hay stooks and thistle seeds, snows of white butterflies, skylarks' eggs, bee orchids and frantic ants; of wolf-cub parades and boy-scout's bugles; of sweat running down the legs; of boiling potatoes on bramble fires, of flames glass-blue in the sun, of lying naked in the hill-cold stream; begging pennies for bottles of pop; of girls' bare arms; of unripe cherries, green apples and liquid walnuts; of fights and falls and new-scabbed knees, sobbing pursuits and flights; of picnics high up in the crumbling quarries, of butter running like oil, of sunstroke, fever, and cucumber peel stuck cool to one's burning brow. All this, and the feeling that it would never end, that such days had come for ever, with the pump drying up and the water-butt crawling, and the chalk ground hard as the moon. All sights twice-brilliant and smells twice-sharp, all game-days twice as long. Double charged as we were, like the meadow ants, with the frenzy of the sun, we used up the light to its last violet drop, and even then couldn't go to bed.

STUDY QUESTIONS

Organization and Content

1. In this description of the contrasting seasons of winter and summer, what feelings did both of them arouse? Where is this matter discussed?
2. Explain the *place*-idea expressed in sentence 2, paragraph 1, and sentence 1, paragraph 2.
3. What tactual, visual, and auditory details does Lee make the reader aware of?
4. What situation is implied by paragraph 4?

5. All the sentences of paragraph 5, after sentence 1, deal with what particular kind of details?
6. In sentence 7, paragraph 5, Lee asserts that "both time and the winds were stilled"—an occurrence literally impossible. How should this fanciful statement be interpreted? How is it related to "the winter's No!"?
7. What contrast is implied in paragraph 6 by "the whole world unlocked"? Yet what similarity of summer and winter is brought out in this paragraph?
8. What is the long catalog of details about summer in paragraph 7 intended to make us feel about the season?
9. What does Lee accomplish with the three sentences that follow the catalog?

Sentence Structure

1. What is the effect of the striking parallel verbs in sentence 3, paragraph 1?
2. In paragraph .5 after *we rode*, note the similarity of sentence pattern. What is the effect of so many sentences with subject-verb-complement pattern?
3. Paragraph 6 consists of one unusual sentence, with subject, appositive, modifiers, then a dash, an interrupter, and the pronoun *it* appearing as a subject. Consider the difference if the appositive *June summer* and the interrupter *like winter* were omitted.
4. Point out the parallelism in sentence 1, paragraph 7. What is its purpose?
5. Sentences 2 and 3, paragraph 7, lack independent clauses. What words do we "understand" to have been left out? Why is it appropriate to have these "fragments" here?

Diction

1. Comment on the choice of diction to express the ideas of paragraph 1. Consider particularly the adjectives of sentence 1 and the verbs in sentences 2 and 3.
2. Look up *humours, conscripted, freaks, nonplussed, pot-holes, seething, hollowing, vernal, stooks, charged.*
3. Lee writes in a vivid, poetic fashion. Analyze and explain the following metaphors: *jigsaws* of frost (paragraph 2); *rode* through its crystal *kingdom, a tarred path threading* through the willows (paragraph 5); *snows* of white butterflies, light to its last violet *drop* (paragraph 7).
4. What do Lee's similes contribute to the description? Which of the following does most to stimulate the imagination: "sound like broken crockery"; "huge like a swollen flower"; "like pot-holes in rock"; "hard as the moon"; "like the meadow ants"?
5. Consider their connotations, and comment on the choice of such terms as *seething* (paragraph 6); *diamond haze, flames glass-blue, hill-cold stream* (sentence 1, paragraph 7). What gives the hyphenated adjectives their power?
6. To appreciate fully the quality of paragraph 7, you ought to read it aloud. (Note the alliteration of "begging pennies for bottles of pop" and the alliteration and economy of "fights and falls and new-scabbed knees, sobbing pursuits and flights.")

Assignment

Write two paragraphs expressing the contrast of spring and fall as you have known them; of school life and vacation life; or of civilian life and military life.

 Two Aspects of Sport

ALDOUS HUXLEY

Like every other instrument that man has invented, sport can be used either for good or for evil purposes. Used well, it can teach endurance and courage, a sense of fair play and a respect for rules, co-ordinated effort and the subordination of personal interests to those of the group. Used badly, it can encourage personal vanity and group vanity, greedy desire for victory and hatred for rivals, an intolerant *esprit de corps* and contempt for people who are beyond a certain arbitrarily selected pale. In either case sport inculcates responsible co-operation; but when it is used badly the co-operation is for undesirable ends and the result upon the individual character is an increase of attachment; when it is used well, the character is modified in the direction of nonattachment. Sport can be either a preparation for war or, in some measure, a substitute for war; a trainer either of potential war-mongers or of potential peace-lovers; an educative influence forming either militarists or men who will be ready and able to apply the principles of pacifism in every activity of life. It is for us to choose which part the organized amusements of children and adults shall play. In the dictatorial countries the choice has been made, consciously and without compromise. Sport there is definitely a preparation for war—doubly a preparation. It is used, first of all, to prepare children for the term of military slavery which they will have to serve when they come of age—to train them in habits of endurance, courage and co-ordinated effort, and to cultivate that *esprit de corps,* that group-vanity and group-pride which are the very foundations of the character of a good soldier. In the second place, it is used as an instrument of nationalistic propaganda. Football matches with teams belonging to foreign countries are treated as matters of national prestige, victory is hailed as a triumph over an enemy, a sign of racial or national superiority; a defeat is put down to foul play and treated almost as a *casus belli*. Optimistic theorists count sport as a bond between nations. In the present state of nationalistic feeling it is only another cause of international misunderstanding. The battles waged on the football field and the race-track are merely preliminaries to, and even contributory causes of, more serious contests. In a world that has no common religion or philosophy of life, but where every national group practises its own private idolatry, international football matches and athletic contests can do almost nothing but harm.

STUDY QUESTIONS

Organization and Content

1. What is the relation of sentences 2 and 3 to sentence 1?
2. Note that sentences 2 and 3 each have a series of three items. How many parts does each item have? How are the items of sentence 3 related with those of sentence 2?
3. How does the early part of sentence 4 look back to preceding sentences? How do the two parts after semicolons relate to preceding sentences?
4. *Attachment* as Huxley uses it in sentence 4 suggests an attachment to what?
5. What is the function of the *either-or* in the three sections of sentence 5?
6. How does sentence 6 provide transition to the second half of the paragraph?
7. How does sentence 8 introduce sentences 9 and 10? Where does Huxley use enumeration?
8. What purpose does sentence 11 serve?
9. By "dictatorial countries," Huxley in 1937 would have meant Germany, Italy, and Russia. Are there any countries at present that use sport for nationalistic propaganda?
10. The word *bond* in sentence 12 is contrasted with what term in sentence 13? What is the implied contrast to *optimistic theorists?* What does "more serious contests" of sentence 14 mean?
11. Explain the sequence of topics by which Huxley arrived at the conclusion expressed in sentence 15.

Sentence Structure

1. Explain how the principles of balance and parallelism are exemplified in sentences 2 and 3; and within sentence 4.

2. Note the parallel *either-or* construction of sentence 5: *either* a preparation . . . *or* what?_____; a trainer *either* of . . . *or* of what?
_____; forming *either* militarists *or* what?_____.
3. What parallel elements occur after the dash in sentence 9?
4. Are balanced sentences with parallel construction appropriate in this
paragraph? Explain.

Diction

1. Look up *pale* (noun), *mongers, nationalistic, propaganda, idolatry.*
2. What is the relation of *pale* and *palisade? Idolatry* and *Mariolatry?*
What connotation does *monger* have? What is the source of *propaganda?*
3. Why should *esprit de corps* and *casus belli* be italicized? What do
these phrases mean?

Assignment

Huxley says that all the instruments man has invented can be used
for good or for evil purposes. In the same way that he contrasts the
good and evil results of sport, contrast in one paragraph the good and
evil aspects of business enterprise, the family, religion or a church, atomic
science, or military establishments.

 Two Kinds of Theaters

ROBERT BRUSTEIN

1   Let us begin with a pair of images.
2   First, imagine an open temple of classical proportions, surrounded by rising tiers. Gathered on separate levels are artisans, citizens, nobility—divided into classes but forming a unified congregation
of spectators. In front of the temple is an altar before which stands
a high priest in hieratic robes. Beyond the temple is a city; beyond
the city, the celestial spheres, moving steadily in their orbits. The
priest conducts a ritual ceremony by miming a myth of heroism and
violence. The congregation is startled by the growing frenzy of the
action; the atmosphere grows taut and strained. The high priest con-
cludes his service with a ritual sacrifice, and blood pours from the
altar. The congregation screams as if it were the victim. Some specta-

tors fall from their seats; the temple cracks; the city begins to crumble; the spheres start wildly from their course. At the point when total dissolution seems imminent, the scene freezes. The spectators file out, their anxiety mingled with an ethereal calm.

3   Now, imagine a perfectly level plain in a desolate land. In the foreground, an uneasy crowd of citizens huddle together on the ruins of an ancient temple. Beyond them, a broken altar, bristling with artifacts. Beyond that, empty space. An emaciated priest in disreputable garments stands before the ruined altar, level with the crowd, glancing into a distorting mirror. He cavorts grotesquely before it, inspecting his own image in several outlandish positions. The crowd mutters ominously and partially disperses. The priest turns the mirror on those who remain to reflect them sitting stupidly on rubble. They gaze at their images for a moment, painfully transfixed; then, horror-struck, they run away, hurling stones at the altar and angry imprecations at the priest. The priest, shaking with anger, futility, and irony, turns the mirror on the void. He is alone in the void.

4   The first is an image for the theater of communion; the second for the theater of revolt.

5   By theater of communion, I mean the theater of the past, dominated by Sophocles, Shakespeare, and Racine, where traditional myths were enacted before an audience of believers against the background of a shifting but still coherent universe. By theater of revolt, I mean the theater of the great insurgent modern dramatists, where myths of rebellion are enacted before a dwindling number of spectators in a flux of vacancy, bafflement, and accident. I have described these two theaters metaphorically in order to make two points rapidly: (1) that the traditional and the modern theaters are clearly distinguishable from each other in regard to the function of their dramatists, the engagement of their audiences, and the nature of the worlds they imply and evoke, and (2) that the playwrights of the modern theater form a movement just as distinctive as the various schools of the past. Ibsen, Strindberg, Chekhov, Shaw, Brecht, Pirandello, O'Neill, and Genet—to name the dramatists discussed at length in this book—are all highly individualistic artists. Yet they share one thing in common which separates them from their predecessors and links them to each other. This is their attitude of revolt, an attitude which is the product of an essentially Romantic inheritance. It is my purpose in this book to isolate the distinguishing characteristics of modern drama, to demonstrate its unity as a Romantic movement, and to trace the development of Romantic revolt in the works of its eight foremost playwrights.

STUDY QUESTIONS

Organization and Content

1. Most paragraphs are units of composition in which topics are developed; they have several sentences and are from 100 to 500 words long. Occasionally, however, paragraphs of only one sentence are used for special purposes. Brustein's paragraphs 1 and 4 are good examples of one-sentence paragraphs. What is the purpose of each? What special effect does Brustein get with these very short paragraphs?
2. How do paragraphs 2 and 3 function in terms of comparison and contrast?
3. What are the key terms used in paragraph 4? In what three ways are the theater of revolt and the theater of communion distinguished in paragraph 5?
4. What does Brustein do in paragraph 5, sentences 1 and 2? Sentences 3–6? Sentence 7?
5. Note details of paragraph 2: temple, rising tiers, unified congregation, altar, high priest, hieratic robes, a city, celestial spheres, ritual ceremony, spectators file out. Identify the contrasting details of paragraph 3.
6. Where does Brustein interpret the metaphors of paragraphs 2 and 3? The images of these paragraphs bring into contrast not only two types of theater but something else as well. What is it?
7. Why does Brustein list the names of eight dramatists? What do they have in common? Look up their dates and nationalities.

Sentence Structure

1. What is the difference between the way of beginning sentences 2–4, paragraph 2, and that of sentences 5–9?
2. What does inverted order have to do with emphasis in the latter part of sentence 3, paragraph 2?
3. Point out the grammatical pattern that Brustein uses in the four parts of sentence 9, paragraph 2.
4. Indicate the economy in the grammatically incomplete statements of sentences 3 and 4, paragraph 3.
5. Show how Brustein attains variety of sentence structure in sentences 5–11, paragraph 3.
6. Why does Brustein use parallel structure and phrasing in sentences 1 and 2, paragraph 5?
7. How is the enumeration handled in sentence 3, paragraph 5?
8. Why use parallel infinitives in the last sentence?

Diction

1. Look up *congregation, hieratic, celestial spheres, miming, dissolution, imminent, ethereal, artifacts, emaciated, insurgent, flux, engagement.*
2. What are the roots of *congregation, hieratic, dissolution, imminent?*
3. What are the connotations of an "altar bristling with *artifacts*"?

4. Point out connotations of the vocabulary used in sentences 1–6, paragraph 3. How do these connotations contrast with those of the equivalent terms in paragraph 2?

Assignment

Imitate Brustein (using contrasting symbols or figurative examples if you can), and contrast two types of things, such as college courses, teachers, communities, homes, stores, or churches. Or distinguish between two schools of painting, styles of music, or styles of dress.

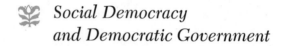

Social Democracy and Democratic Government

GEORGE SANTAYANA

1   The word democracy may stand for a natural social equality in the body politic or for a constitutional form of government in which power lies more or less directly in the people's hands. The former may be called social democracy and the latter democratic government. The two differ widely, both in origin and in moral principle. Genetically considered, social democracy is something primitive, unintended, proper to communities where there is general competence and no marked personal eminence. It is the democracy of Arcadia, Switzerland, and the American pioneers. Such a community might be said to have also a democratic government, for everything in it is naturally democratic. There will be no aristocracy, no prestige; but instead an intelligent readiness to lend a hand and to do in unison whatever is done, not so much under leaders as by a kind of conspiring instinct and contagious sympathy. In other words, there will be that most democratic of governments—no government at all. But when pressure of circumstances, danger, or inward strife makes recognised and prolonged guidance necessary to a social democracy, the form its government takes is that of a rudimentary monarchy, established by election or general consent. A natural leader presents himself and he is instinctively obeyed. He may indeed be freely criticised and will not be screened by any pomp or traditional mystery; he will

From George Santayana, *The Life of Reason* (1905).

be easy to replace and every citizen will feel himself radically his equal. Yet such a state is at the beginnings of monarchy and aristocracy, close to the stage depicted in Homer, where pre-eminences are still obviously natural, although already over-emphasised by the force of custom and wealth, and by the fission of society into divergent classes.

2   Political democracy, on the other hand, is a late and artificial product. It arises by a gradual extension of aristocratic privileges, through rebellion against abuses, and in answer to restlessness on the people's part. Its principle is not the absence of eminence, but the discovery that existing eminence is no longer genuine and representative. It is compatible with a very complex government, great empire, and an aristocratic society; it may retain, as notably in England and in all ancient republics, many vestiges of older and less democratic institutions. For under democratic governments the people have not created the state; they merely control it. Their suspicions and jealousies are quieted by assigning to them a voice, perhaps only a veto, in the administration; but the state administered is a prodigious self-created historical engine. Popular votes never established the family, private property, religious practices, or international frontiers. Institutions, ideals, and administrators may all be such as the popular classes could never have produced; but these products of natural aristocracy are suffered to subsist so long as no very urgent protest is raised against them. The people's liberty consists not in their original responsibility for what exists—for they are guiltless of it—but merely in the faculty they have acquired of abolishing any detail that may distress or wound them, and of imposing any new measure, which, seen against the background of existing laws, may commend itself from time to time to their instinct and mind.

3   If we turn from origins to ideals, the contrast between social and political democracy is no less marked. Social democracy is a general ethical ideal, looking to human equality and brotherhood, and inconsistent, in its radical form, with such institutions as the family and hereditary property. Democratic government, on the contrary, is merely a means to an end, an expedient for the better and smoother government of certain states at certain junctures. It involves no special ideals of life; it is a question of policy, namely, whether the general interest will be better served by granting all men (and perhaps all women) an equal voice in elections. For political democracy, arising in great and complex states, must necessarily be a government by deputy, and the questions actually submitted to the people can be only very large rough matters of general policy or of confidence in party leaders.

STUDY QUESTIONS

Organization and Content

1. What distinction does Santayana make in sentence 1, paragraph 1? In what way does sentence 2 advance his discussion? What two kinds of differences are mentioned in sentence 3? According to sentence 4, which kind of difference will be discussed first?
2. By what means of transition are sentences 1–4 linked?
3. What does Santayana mainly discuss in paragraph 1? In paragraph 2? In paragraph 3?
4. What contrast does *but* introduce in sentence 9, paragraph 1? The situations mentioned in sentence 9 force social democracy to take a first step toward what?
5. What transitional element links paragraph 2 to the preceding discussion? To paragraph 3? What term in paragraph 1 does *ideals* in sentence 1, paragraph 3, represent?
6. State in one sentence the main differences between social democracy and democratic government.
7. Explain to what extent Santayana's discussion is based on analysis.
8. In paragraph 1 Santayana applies the terms *primitive, unintended,* and *natural* to social democracy. What contrasting terms does he apply to democratic government?
9. According to paragraph 2, what are the causes of political democracy? In paragraph 3 democratic government is called an expedient. An expedient of whom?
10. Judging by the tone of his discussion, would you consider Santayana most sympathetic toward social democracy, democratic government, or aristocracy?

Sentence Structure

1. Santayana makes considerable use of the conjunctions *and, or, both,* and *both . . . and.* This use of conjunctions is related to his mentioning items in pairs or in trios. Point out which sentences emphasize pairs of items and which ones present items in groups of three.
2. In which sentences does Santayana use semicolons to assist in the expression of comparison and contrast?
3. Analyze the sentences of paragraph 3, and explain how parallel structures and interrupters have been used to achieve variety and elegance in these sentences.

Diction

1. Look up *democracy, genetically, Arcadia, aristocracy, rudimentary, pomp, radically, fission, divergent, eminence, vestiges, popular, subsist, expedient, policy.*
2. Relate *genetically* to *genesis, generate,* and *genus.*
3. Learn the roots and their meanings of *democracy, aristocracy, rudimentary, radically, divergent, popular,* and *policy.*

4. In the paragraphs where they appear, what is the influence of the connotations of *Arcadia* (paragraph 1), *distress or wound* (paragraph 2), and *large rough matters* (paragraph 3)?

Assignment

Imitating Santayana in a general way, write a contrast of two of the following forms of city government: mayor-council, city manager, commission. Contrast direct democracy and representative democracy, democracy and aristocracy, or democracy and dictatorship. If you are not able to discuss them in terms of origins, discuss them in terms of ideals, operations, and results.

The Distinction
of Civilization and Culture

ROBERT M. MACIVER

1   . . . Let us contrast, say, a factory and a monument, a machine and a picture, a camera and a movie film, a legal document and a play. On the one side we have placed utilitarian objects, means which we employ to satisfy our wants; on the other, things we want, so to speak, for themselves, for the direct satisfaction which they bring us. It is one form of the contrast between means and ends, between the apparatus of living and the expressions of our life. The former we call civilization, the latter culture. By civilization, then, we mean the whole mechanism and organization which man has devised in his endeavor to control the conditions of his life. It would include not only our systems of social organization but also our techniques and our material instruments. It would include alike the ballot-box and the telephone, the Interstate Commerce Commission and the railroads, our laws as well as our schools, and our banking systems as well as our banks. Culture on the other hand is the expression of our nature in our modes of living and of thinking, in our everyday intercourse, in art, in literature, in religion, in recreation and enjoy-

From Robert M. MacIver, *Society: Its Structure and Changes* (Long and Smith, 1931). Revised edition by Robert M. MacIver and Charles H. Page, *Society: An Introductory Analysis,* published by Holt, Rinehart and Winston, Inc. Copyright 1937 by Robert M. MacIver; copyright 1949 by Robert M. MacIver and Charles H. Page.

ment. While, as we shall see, many objects possess both a civilizational and a cultural element, we can often decide the question of their classification by asking: do we want these things themselves or do we merely use them in order to attain some other thing we want? Do they exist because of some outer necessity or because we seek them as such? Often we make a virtue of necessity and impress on utilitarian objects a cultural quality, as when we build banks to rival temples, but if these objects would not exist at all for the *direct* satisfaction they yield us we may classify them as within the category of civilization. On the other hand many objects combine both elements so inextricably, for example our clothing and our homes, that we must be content simply to distinguish the two aspects of the service they render.

2   The distinction between the two categories is seen in the way they respectively enter into the social heritage. An achievement of civilization is generally exploited and improved, going on from strength to strength, until it is superseded or rendered obsolete by some new invention. It is true that in past ages some achievements of civilization have again been lost. Men forgot the arts which raised the pyramids of Egypt and which constructed the roads and aqueducts of the Romans. But these losses occurred through catastrophic changes which blotted out the records of civilization. With the widening of the areas of civilization and with superior methods of recording discoveries any utilitarian or technical gain becomes a permanent possession within the social heritage and the condition of further gains. Civilization is thus a cumulative process, a "march." It is otherwise with cultural achievements. They do not lead assuredly to higher or improved ones. Since man first invented the automobile, it has continuously improved. Our means of transportation grow constantly more swift and more efficient. They are vastly superior to those which the ancient Greeks employed. But can we say the same of our dramas and our sculptures, our conversation and our recreation? Here certitude fails us. There are no automobiles to-day so comparatively inefficient as the first vehicles of Henry Ford—his work and that of other inventors inevitably prepared the way for better ones. But our plays are not necessarily better to-day because of the achievements of Shakespeare. There is no "march" of culture. It is subject to retrogression as well as to advance. Its past does not assure its future.

3   In a word, the social heritage does not ensure the future of culture with the same probability with which it provides the conditions of civilization. Culture, being the immediate expression of the human spirit, can advance only if that spirit is capable of finer efforts, has itself something more to express. Civilization is the vehicle of

culture: its improvement is no guarantee of finer quality in that which it conveys. The radio can carry our words to the ends of the earth, but the words need be no wiser on that account. The civilization around us can be enjoyed without any special effort, without any particular merit on our part. The culture we "inherit" is ours only if we are worthy of it. A new generation cannot enjoy the culture of the past unless they win it afresh for themselves. Culture is communicated only to the like-minded. No one without the quality of the artist can appreciate art, nor without the ear of the musician can one enjoy music. Civilization in general makes no such demand. We can enjoy its products without sharing the capacity which creates them. Moreover, the process of creation itself is different. Lesser minds improve the work of the great inventors, but lesser poets do not improve on Shakespeare. The product of the artist is more revelatory of his personality than is that of the technician, just as the quality of a people is peculiarly expressed in its culture rather than in its civilization.

4   This more intimate relation of culture and society is seen also in the fact that culture is not transferable in the simple mode characteristic of civilization. Given adequate means of communication, any improvement in the apparatus of life will quickly spread. In fact with the modern development of communications a single system of civilization is already encompassing nearly all the earth. Even the savage is ready to discard his bow and spear and to adopt the rifle. The power-machine displaces the hand tool wherever men have the means to acquire it. The corporate form of industry encroaches everywhere on older forms as irresistibly as the factory displaces the domestic system of production. We have pointed out that these techniques are readily comparable and the relative superiority of one over the other is easily adjudged. Civilization has its objective tests so that it is a simple matter to decide that one mode of hygiene or one method of road-building is preferable to another. The advance of civilization is seriously resisted only when the older form is closely associated with the culture of a people. For a people will not freely abandon its culture for another, since to do so would be to sacrifice its intrinsic quality. Even when one civilization covers the globe great cultural differences, modified as they become under such conditions, will endure, just as they endure to-day among the industrialized peoples. It is true that cultural "borrowing" occurs, but it is selective and seemingly wayward, dependent on a degree of affinity, of like-mindedness, in the borrowers and always colored or even distorted by their personality. The history of religious conversion and proselytism affords sufficient evidences of this selective process. The Geneva

of Calvin and the Scotland of Knox and the Massachusetts of Cotton Mather were receptive of certain strains in the multiform tradition of Christianity, selecting ascetic, authoritarian, patriarchal, eschatological elements within it and translating them into a system which they identified with Christianity itself, just as other peoples and other times selected and transmuted other elements to form their creeds. It may also be noted that this selective "borrowing" is not limited to recent or contemporaneous contributions to the stock of culture. In this also it differs from the process by which civilization spreads. Culture elements may be adopted as readily from the past as from the present, from any epoch of the past no less than from the present hour. Cultural affinity may revert to the legends of Greece or of the German forests, to the art of tenth-century China or of pre-Raphaelite Florence, to the meditations of Job or of Marcus Aurelius. Its range of selection runs from the newest culture-fashion to the myths that linger from the dawn of history.

5   In the light of these distinctions it is obvious that the expansion of a civilization follows different principles from those which determine cultural development. Where communications admit, the former tends to proceed more rapidly, more simply, less selectively, always spreading outwards from the foci of technological and economic advance. The products of civilization are conveyed over every trade route, and they prepare the way for the techniques and systems which created them. People trade with one another before they understand one another. The expansion of civilization has perils on that very account. For the interdependence of peoples within a common civilization outstrips the formation of those cultural attitudes necessary for its maintenance. This peril was glaringly exposed in the Great War. The spread of civilization makes certain cultural readjustments imperative.

STUDY QUESTIONS

Organization and Content

1. Explain the movement from the specific to the general which takes place in sentences 1–4.
2. What relation have sentences 5–7 with sentences 8–11?
3. Is there any reason why sentence 12 should be the last sentence of paragraph 1?
4. Can you identify topic sentences in paragraphs 2–5?
5. How does paragraph 3 differ in emphasis from paragraph 2?
6. What do "objective tests" of civilization have to do with the "simple

mode" of its transfer? What term relating to culture contrasts with "objective tests"?

7. What further differences between civilization and culture are pointed out in the latter part of paragraph 4?
8. What is the most important idea of paragraph 5?
9. How many specific examples does MacIver use in each paragraph? Is there any reason why there should be more of them in one paragraph than another?
10. Which examples are the most effective? The least easy to understand?
11. Contrasts may be organized paragraph by paragraph, sentence by sentence, and so on. What method of organizing the contrast has Mac-Iver employed? Has he been systematic? In this respect does the selection by MacIver most resemble, or most differ from, the selection by Santayana, Aldous Huxley, or Dobie?
12. This contrast contains elements of analysis and definition. Does the discussion of civilization and culture by a famous sociologist have any agreement with the definitions by Churchill (statesman) and Bell (art critic)?

Sentence Structure

1. By what sentence patterns has the author indicated contrasts in paragraph 1? Point out different specific patterns.
2. Indicate special terms and phrases used for transition in the contrasts of paragraphs 1–3.
3. Does the author use any different type of sentence for his examples from that which he uses in the rest?
4. On might expect that contrasts would be brought out especially by compound sentences. Has MacIver used a large proportion of compound sentences?
5. Has he used other patterns of grammatical parallelism?
6. Which paragraph contains the shortest sentences? Do they have an effect of choppiness, forceful emphasis, crisp summary, or what?

Diction

1. Look up *inextricably, heritage, exploited, peculiarly, encroaches, intrinsic, proselytism, ascetic, eschatological, pre-Raphaelite, imperative.*
2. From what language do the following words come: *utilitarian, supersede, aqueduct, retrogression, encompass, patriarchal, foci?* Learn the meanings of the roots as well as of the words.
3. How significant is MacIver's use of metaphor—for example, his calling civilization *apparatus* and *mechanism?*
4. What implications are suggested by other metaphors: the "march" of civilization, and civilization as the "vehicle" of culture?
5. Is the term *social heritage* a metaphor or not?

Assignment

Write one or two substantial paragraphs in which you:

1. Contrast the state of civilization and culture in your home town
2. Contrast an artist and a technician

3. Either contrast or compare a temple and a modern bank
4. Bring out the differing qualities of peoples with contrasting cultures
5. Show the differences between persons who "win culture afresh for themselves" and those who simply take advantage of the civilization about them "without any special effort"

(Elsewhere MacIver has written of the inventions of American civilization as "foolproof," that is, able to be used without effort by people who are completely ignorant of how they operate.)

Section Three

Argument

*A*n argument is not a quarrel. Originally to argue meant to make clear, and thus to show, to prove, to give evidence. An argument is a presenting of reasons for or reasons against something; it implies that the person who states an argument has tried to understand the matter in question and that he is using his powers of reason to show why evidence supports his position. The setting forth of a conviction or belief and the evidence for it does not need to imply any opposition. Perhaps everyone in the world would agree with the argument.

However, there is always potential disagreement with an argument; and on many matters people disagree. An argument for one side of a question calls forth an opposing argument from a person who disagrees. When two people engage in argument, they disagree. When two people quarrel, they also disagree. But a quarrel implies that they become angry; they may call each other names, make threats, shake their fists, break off friendly relations. When they are so filled with emotion, they are not likely to be very reasonable. It is hard to think of either person *winning* a quarrel.

In an argument, however, one person may win. If he wins, he wins because his *evidence* is greater in quantity or superior in importance to the evidence of the other person, or because he reasons better, shows more clearly the *logical conclusions* that must be drawn from the material. Even the opponent may be completely convinced by the winning argument—particularly if he has not thought very much or very deeply about the subject before. To win an argument properly, then, one should have both knowledge that provides evidence and good powers of reasoning. To become violently emotional, to become quarrelsome, unpleasant, or nasty, is not likely to help one to argue well.

Many people, when they find that someone else disagrees with them, tend to start a quarrel rather than an argument. They may make attacks on the other person's character, accuse him of selfish motives for his beliefs, treat his reasoning and evidence with scoffing and sarcasm. They may be tempted to repeat, more and more loudly, the thing that they believe. Then they may become exasperated when asked to give reasons for their belief. The apprentice writer is likely to need practice, therefore, in argument, so that he will not confuse an argument with a quarrel or mistake sarcasm for evidence.

The next step for the apprentice writer is to learn (it seems to be difficult for many people) that mere assertion has no value in argument. There are any number of assertions which people make, and their statements may represent very strong belief, yet such statements, without evidence, will not convince another person that they are true. People disagree on a great many questions, but often they disagree because they have not thought enough about these questions, because they have not gathered evidence or have not analyzed the evidence to discover what it really means.

Below are some examples of assertions that are often made (but other people may disagree and therefore argue):

> The team is better this year than last.
> This novel is well written (or dramatic, significant, and so on).
> Everyone should vote for Candidate X.
> Smoke PQR cigars for the best flavor.
> President X was right (or wrong).
> Senator X was wrong (or right).
> Take this course, not that one.
> Mr. ABC is a better teacher (singer, scientist) than XYZ.

Many assertions will immediately bring exactly opposite statements of belief from some listener or reader. For example:

> We should raise taxes—tax property owners more.
> We should lower taxes—exempt the property owners.
>
> We ought to have censorship of "comic" books.
> No, we ought to have complete freedom of the press.
>
> We ought to take Latin (a dead language) out of the curriculum!
> No, we ought to make *everybody* study Latin!
>
> Children need more discipline!
> No, more freedom!

Such assertions immediately raise questions in the minds of those who hear them. Listeners will say: "You have made a statement, you two have made opposing statements. But what *is* the truth of the matter? What *should* we do? What course *should* we follow?" In order to answer these questions, of course, evidence must be produced. "What is the truth?" is a question of fact. Often it can be satisfactorily answered, sometimes easily answered. If it is asserted that Mrs. A's living room is longer than Mrs. B's, the truth can be found just by taking a tape measure or a yardstick and measuring the two rooms. In such a situation there could properly be no argument. Often questions can be settled (and quarrels avoided) by the simple means of looking up the facts.

However, very frequently the facts are not so easily found; and sometimes, even when found, they do not automatically decide an argument. Suppose someone says, "Team X is better than Team Y." If arrangements could be made for the two teams to play several games, then very likely the evidence would be clear; people would say that the question of fact had been answered. If such arrangements could not be made, many facts about the teams, all sorts of records, may be listed; yet whether the assertion is true or not may still be a matter of doubt. Of course, the question of fact involved in the assertion "Our team this year is better than our team was last year" cannot be settled by playing. It is impossible for the two teams in question to play any games. It would be necessary to work on the question of fact entirely by statistics. Similarly, two teams of the same year may not have a chance to play against each other enough to show without doubt which is the better team, so that it is then necessary to gather statistical evidence to try to settle the question of fact. This sort of evidence will never be so convincing as the scores of actual games.

Without clear evidence of actual scores, the question of whether one team is "better" than the other cannot be measured like two living rooms; it is not a simple question of fact alone. Interpretation of facts is involved, and evaluation may enter in. Many people will be inclined to "weight" or "discount" some of the evidence. Will it not make a difference whether a team is excellent in defensive strength, or capacity to take advantage of opponents' mistakes, or speed, or deceptiveness, or plodding power?

Yet questions of fact and questions of fact-plus-interpretation are usually easier to deal with than questions of policy, questions in which *should* is the key word. "Everybody should study Latin. Children should have more freedom. The United States should enter the European Common Market." Such propositions involve judgment as well as fact; they involve the weighing of facts; they involve values; and they may involve experience as well as information. Judgments are based upon standards that people accept; that is, they are based upon certain assumptions regarding what is valuable. And when one is trying to look into the future (which one must always do when a question of policy is being argued), his argument may depend strongly upon his reasoning from what has happened in the past—and this is why the light that experience gives may play an important part in deciding arguments on questions of policy.

At any rate, in all arguments the evidence should have a bearing upon the question (it must be *relevant*), it should be presented *logically,* and it should have the power to convince (it should be *cogent*).

Here is an example of argument from ancient Greece. The men of Corcyra and the men of Corinth went to war over the city of Epidamnum, and those of Corcyra won. Then for two years the Corinthians built up their navy, and the men of Corcyra became alarmed. They decided in 433 B.C. that they would join the Athenian alliance and get help from Athens, if they could, against Corinth. According to the Greek historian Thucydides they presented their argument to the men of Athens as follows:

> Those who, like ourselves, come to others who are not their allies and to whom they have never rendered any considerable service and ask help of them, are bound to show, in the first place, that the granting of their request is expedient, or at any rate not inexpedient, and, secondly, that their gratitude will be lasting. If they fulfil neither requirement they have no right to complain of a refusal. . . .
>
> To you at this moment the request which we are making offers a glorious opportunity. In the first place, you will assist the oppressed and not the oppressors; secondly, you will admit us to your alliance at a time when our vital interests are at stake, and will lay up a treasure of gratitude in our memories which will have the most abiding of all records. Lastly, we have a navy greater than any but your own. Reflect; what good fortune can be more extraordinary, what more annoying to your enemies than the voluntary accession of a power for whose alliance you would have given any amount of money and could never have been too thankful. This power now places herself at your disposal.

In formal terms, the argument of the men of Corcyra is on the *proposition,* Athens *should* take Corcyra into alliance and give it help. They are bound to show, they say, two things, in order to convince the Athenians: (1) that granting the request is expedient; (2) that Corcyra will feel lasting gratitude.

These two things are the points upon which argument will center. They are the *issues* of the argument. It is important in an efficient argument that both the proposition and the issues be clearly brought out.

What evidence do the representatives of Corcyra use to support their side of the argument? Their first assertion is intended to support the issue of gratitude; it depends for effectiveness on the idea that those who are being oppressed will feel more gratitude for assistance than will the oppressors; their second assertion that Corcyra will feel gratitude rests on the idea that those who receive help when their vital interests are at stake will be especially grateful for assistance. It implies a sequence of reasoning—a syllogism of *deductive logic*. The syllogism is:

Major Premise: Those who are in great danger are very grateful for help.

Minor Premise: Corcyra is in great danger from Corinth.

Conclusion: Therefore Corcyra will be very grateful for help from Athens.

If a syllogism is true, the premises must be true. If a person believes in the truth of the major premise of this syllogism, he must have made an evaluation based on his judgment of human nature or upon cases that he has learned about from the past which support this interpretation of human nature. If one believes in the major premise because of cases observed in the past, he has used *inductive logic*. The process is as follows: (1) In Case A help was given in time of danger and gratitude was shown. (2) In Case B the same thing happened. (3) In Case C the same thing happened. . . . If there is a sufficiently large number of cases in which the same result is observed, then it will be thought that the probability is very high that the same result will always occur. Not a certainty but a probability. That is, if the series of cases were indefinitely extended, one would expect to learn that in Case N gratitude would also be shown. But the cases cannot actually be extended indefinitely. Therefore, one must make what is called an *inductive leap* to the conclusion; one must leap over all the other cases which may exist but which have not been examined, on to Case N representing the last in the possible series, expecting that on the basis of the cases already observed, the same thing will hold true. Thus the truth of the major premise would be arrived at: *All* who are in great danger are grateful for help.

If there were any exceptions among the cases examined, the probability of the inductive conclusion would, of course, be weakened. This idea is brought out in the old saying that "the exception proves the rule," which does not mean that an exception gives a proof of the rule but that an exception tests the rule, that is, the conclusion or generalization. If an example were found in which people were not grateful for help even when in great danger, the conclusion would have to be modified to something like "Nearly all people are grateful. . . ." or "All people except Persians are grateful. . . ."

At any rate inductive logic and deductive logic go together

and support each other. For example, it must have taken a good many observations to establish the rule that at sea level water freezes at 32 degrees Fahrenheit. But once this inductive conclusion had been established, it could be used to cover every individual case of water when the temperature was likely to go down to 32 degrees. In such a case one would know that to keep water from freezing he must plan to use antifreeze, make a fire, add hot water, or take some such measure. Such a universal proposition, well based in induction, gives the human mind an enormous amount of practical power.

The second issue of the argument by the men of Corcyra is supported by their pointing out to the Athenians that it would be expedient for Athens to add the strength of another large navy to that of the Athenian navy. Such a statement about national military forces would doubtless be regarded as self-evident. But it, too, rests upon conclusions of inductive logic and also an implied deductive syllogism. The student will not find it difficult to establish the logical bases of this part of the argument. Certainly in all that they say the men of Corcyra intend to convince the Athenians that to give them help would be completely reasonable.

Yet there are two modifications of the preceding ideas that should be kept in mind. In the first place, though it is bad to become overemotional to the point that reason, evidence, and logic are tossed aside, an argument does not have to be utterly cold and unemotional. Naturally, personal feeling enters into much argument, both spoken and written. And the presence of such feeling may help very much to make the argument seem convincing. A good example of personal feeling helping the effectiveness of an argument is the famous funeral oration of Marc Antony for Julius Caesar in Shakespeare's *Julius Caesar*. Brutus had spoken briefly and rather coldly: he said that he honored Caesar for many good qualities—"but, as he was ambitious, I slew him." (*Ambitious* here means aggressively determined to seize power.) Marc Antony's speech is, in terms of argument, largely a refutation of the idea that Caesar was "ambitious." He cites several pieces of evidence indicating that Caesar was not, after all, really "ambitious."

> He was my friend, faithful and just to me:
> But Brutus says he was ambitious;
> And Brutus is an honourable man.
> He hath brought many captives home to Rome,
> Whose ransoms did the general coffers fill:
> Did this in Caesar seem ambitious?
> When that the poor have cried, Caesar hath wept:
> Ambition should be made of sterner stuff:

Yet Brutus says he was ambitious;
And Brutus is an honourable man.
You all did see that on the Lupercal
I thrice presented him a kingly crown,
Which he did thrice refuse: was this ambition?
Yet Brutus says he was ambitious;
And sure he is an honourable man.
I speak not to disprove what Brutus spoke,
But here I am to speak what I do know.

Since Antony had been ordered by Brutus to say nothing against the conspirators who had killed Caesar, Antony kept the letter of the order; but he was trying to persuade the crowd that the conspirators were really murderers—"butchers"—and not saviors of Rome. So Antony mentions four pieces of evidence: faithful friendship, captives, sympathy with the poor, refusal of a crown, all of which contradict the idea of ruthless, aggressive "ambition." Furthermore, he uses two questions—"rhetorical" questions—which provide a personal contact with the audience, and he mentions himself and his own feeling—note the emphasis of "just to *me*" and "here I am to speak what *I do know*." Such sincerely felt emotion will impress the audience. But Antony does not allow the emotion to get out of control; he systematically cites four examples intended to refute the veracity of the motives Brutus had alleged. We should say, then, that although overemotional arguments are not good, emotion in argument is not ruled out. Some authorities give the name of persuasion to arguments that have emotional appeals.

In the second place, though arguments should be logical, considerable use is made in argument of analogy, and analogy does not force one to inescapable logical conclusions. Nevertheless, similarities between situations, when such similarities exist, cause people to tend to think that the situation being argued about should be treated in the same manner that a former situation was treated. The effect of analogy may be expressed in such a phrase as "the same treatment for the same disease"; or it may be regarded as a kind of extension of the mathematical axiom that things equal to the same thing are equal to each other.

John Locke, a seventeenth-century philosopher, believed that a young man should not be kept without any knowledge of worldly matters, even though there is evil in the world. Locke argued that it was especially important to have a tutor teach a knowledge of "men and their manners." The pupil should be "warned who are like to oppose, who to mislead, who to undermine him, and who to serve him. He should be instructed how to know and distinguish them."

Locke than uses an analogy in his argument.

> Therefore I think it of most value to be instilled into a young man upon all occasions which offer themselves that when he comes to launch into the deep himself he may not be like one at sea without a line, compass or sea-chart, but may have some notice beforehand of the rocks and shoals, the currents and quicksands, and know a little how to steer that he sink not before he get experience.

In Locke's analogy the world is like the ocean, and the young man is like a captain who has the responsibility of sailing a ship safely through the ocean. The dangers and evils of the world are like rocks, shoals, and quicksand. Knowledge of the world gained from a tutor is like a compass and a chart, which supply information regarding the ocean.

If it seems reasonable that a captain should have experience and knowledge of the ocean, then it should seem reasonable that a young man should have knowledge and experience of the world. Locke was certainly assuming that the likenesses between the two situations were significant ones. Unless they were, his analogy would be worthless. And though likenesses may exist, the analogy does not *prove* the point. Possibly worldly knowledge might damage the character of the young man in a way that knowledge of the sea would not harm the capabilities of a captain for handling a ship. One situation in the analogy concerns a physical matter or problem; but the other situation concerns a moral and psychological problem. Therefore, this analogy, and all analogies, must be viewed with some caution. They may be very effective illustrations, but they are not proofs.

Locke made the assumption that knowledge of evils is a significant requirement for success in managing one's life, just as knowledge of the location of rocks and quicksands is a significant requirement for success in sailing a ship. Yet he did not state clearly that he was making that assumption. Assumptions are often hidden in arguments. They are often taken for granted—that is, the speaker feels that the assumption he makes is so reasonable, so natural, so unquestionable, that he does not even realize that other people may regard it differently. Consequently, it is essential to be on guard for this tendency in all arguments; one ought to test his own arguments as well as those of opponents to find out what assumptions have actually been made.

In a sense, of course, all exposition is argument; that is, the writer wishes the reader to feel satisfied that what he has written is true. It was stated earlier that each paragraph should contain evidence to support the topic idea. The writer wants the reader to say to himself, "Yes, this paragraph is a solid one; I believe what the writer says"—perhaps that two things are similar, or that the meaning of a term has changed, or that a machine has four main sections, or that a certain man was both brilliant and responsible. . . . But, in the kind of writing properly called argument, the writer is presenting a *justification* of his belief, his opinion, his judgment, his preference; he is always trying to convince the reader that he is *right* and frequently he is trying to persuade the reader that the reader ought to do something: cast a ballot, purchase an article, give money, write a letter, use his influence. . . . And this is why arguers are tempted to use tricks—anything to get the reader to do the thing desired.

Honorable people ought not, however, to try to trick other people in argument. To use devices of "one-upmanship" or to use fallacies in argument is improper. *Fallacies* are falsities of argument—tricky, deceptive, *faulty* ways of persuasion. There are many of them. One book[1] on this subject lists 51 fallacies classified under "Material Fallacies," such as faulty generalization and faulty analogy; "Psychological Fallacies," such as abusing the emotional power of words, ridicule, or appealing to prejudice; and "Logical Fallacies," such as the undistributed middle term in a syllogism, circular definition, and begging the question. If the apprentice writer has the opportunity to take a course in logic or in argumentation, he will become more skillful in detecting fallacies. But, in the meantime, he as an apprentice writer can consistently try to be fair and logical in all his arguments.

In writing arguments, one will, of course, make use of all of the other forms of writing that have been set forth in this text. Definitions appear in arguments—in fact, defining terms is often necessary so that people can agree on exactly what the argument is about—as do analysis, enumeration, comparison and contrast; all of these types of writing have their function. There may even be examples of description, characterization, and narrative, as writers undertake to make people understand historical backgrounds, physical situations, and the attitudes of people involved in public questions.

The Committee for Cultural Freedom, which was established in 1939, set forth a Code of Ethics to be followed in political controversy. Mr. Sidney Hook was the main author of this Code.

> These are the ten points by which we think all political controversy ought to be guided:
> 1. Nothing and no one is immune from criticism.

[1] W. Ward Fearnside and William B. Holther, *Fallacy: The Counterfeit of Argument* (Englewood Cliffs, N.J.: Prentice-Hall, Inc., 1959).

2. Everyone involved in a controversy has an intellectual responsibility to inform himself of the available facts.
3. Criticism should be directed first to policies and against persons only when they are responsible for policies, and against their motives or purposes only when there is some independent evidence of their character.
4. Because certain words are legally permissible, they are not therefore morally permissible.
5. Before impugning an opponent's motives, even when they legitimately may be impugned, answer his arguments.
6. Do not treat an opponent of a policy as if he were therefore a personal enemy, or an enemy of the country, or a concealed enemy of democracy.
7. Since a good cause may be defended by bad arguments, after answering the bad arguments for another's position, present positive evidence for your own.
8. Do not hesitate to admit lack of knowledge or to suspend judgment if evidence is not decisive either way.
9. Because something is logically possible, it is not therefore probable. "It is not impossible" is a preface to an irrelevant statement about human affairs. The question is always one of the balance of probabilities.
10. The cardinal sin, when we are looking for truth of fact or wisdom of policy, is refusal to discuss, or action which blocks discussion.

These are wise rules to observe in all arguments. They apply especially to politics, but whether one is trying to convince scientists that something they had not known before is really true (like William Harvey presenting the case for the circulation of the blood), whether one is arguing for a particular business policy or defending a client in a law case or showing why a college curriculum needs changes or why art enriches life or why a Beethoven symphony has higher esthetic value than a popular song—no matter what the area of argument, one does best to argue honestly, with pertinent evidence, good reasoning, and good manners.

The readings that follow can be divided into two general groups. The first group—from Commager through Russell—could be conveniently classified as examples of Evidence for Proof; the second group—those from De Rougemont through Keeney—as More Complex Arguments.

Carelessness Is Evident throughout American Life

HENRY STEELE COMMAGER

1   Carelessness was perhaps the most pervasive and persistent quality in the American. He was careless about himself, his speech, his dress, his food, even his manners; those who did not know him thought him slovenly and rude. His attitude toward the English language pained the traditionalists but he brought to language and grammar something of the same vitality and ingenuity that he brought to his work or his religion, and they served his needs and reflected his character. He was careless about rank and class, about tradition and precedent, about the rights and prerogatives of others and about his own rights and prerogatives. He tolerated in others minor infractions of law or custom and expected to be similarly indulged in his own transgressions: hence his vast patience with noise, litter, the invasion of privacy, and sharp practices. Although he had, as it were, invented time, he did not, like his English cousins, make a fetish of punctuality, nor did he celebrate the hours with such ritual as tea or dressing for dinner. He was careless about his work and his trade, and, preferring to have machines work for him, he regarded with equanimity the decline of inherited traditions of craftsmanship. While the products of his machines could compete anywhere in the world market, the products of his handicraft could not.

2   The American took, in fact, little pride in a finished job, prizing versatility above thoroughness. He was the world's most successful farmer, but his cultivation was gargantuan rather than intensive, and scientific agriculture lagged a generation or more behind that of Europe while, after the eighteenth century, landscape gardening was regarded as a European rather than an American art. The construction of the transcontinentals was one of the greatest engineering feats of modern history, but the American's railway tracks, like his roads, had to be rebuilt every few years. Every town and city confessed the same characteristic—whole sections only half built, houses falling down a decade after they had been put up, ambitious plans unful-

From Henry Steele Commager, *The American Mind* (New Haven: Yale University Press, 1950).

filled. A ragged, unfinished quality characterized much of his culture. He undertook the most gigantic educational program in history, but it was the universal opinion that American education was eclectic rather than thorough. His speech revealed his impatience: he slurred over his words, left his sentences unfinished, and developed to the full the possibilities of slang. Neither transcendentalism nor pragmatism, the two ways of thinking that can properly be designated American, had a systematic quality, and it was suggestive that his most characteristic form of philosophy, pragmatism, should emphasize the unfinished nature of the universe. Many Americans preferred their preachers untrained, and most of them distrusted the professional soldier.

STUDY QUESTIONS

Organization and Content

1. Do these two paragraphs have topic sentences? If so, what are they?
2. What is the nature of the evidence Commager uses to convince the reader that Americans are careless?
3. Is there enough evidence to convince his audience?
4. In what different areas of life is American carelessness revealed?
5. Does it matter which pieces of Commager's evidence are presented first or presented last?
6. Sentence 5 of paragraph 2 is a general statement. What justifies such a general statement at this point?
7. Is Commager willing to grant that American life has anything noteworthy to compensate for carelessness?
8. Is there any reason why a philosophy of pragmatism should be developed in a culture which carelessness pervades?

Sentence Structure

1. Indicate transitional links among the author's sentences.
2. What is the effect of repetition of grammatical patterns here: for instance, "He was careless about"?
3. Indicate parallelism of structure in sentences 2–5.
4. In which sentences of both paragraphs does Commager bring out contrasts? By what means?
5. To what extent do the sentences have variety in the way they begin?
6. Do these sentences have too much similarity of pattern: too many *and's*, for example?

Diction

1. Look up *pervasive, ingenuity, precedent, infraction, transgressions, versatility*. What other words are based on the same roots as these?

2. Look up *prerogatives, fetish, ritual, equanimity, eclectic, slang, transcendentalism, pragmatism.*
3. What accounts for the form and meaning of *gargantuan?*

Assignment

Give a considerable amount of evidence to convince someone that a certain condition exists. For example:

1. _____ is the most pervasive quality of students at this college.
2. Generosity is a persistent quality in American life.
3. Americans tend to be suspicious of foreigners.
4. The life of people in North America is a wholesome one.
5. Americans are an extravagant people.

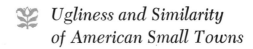 *Ugliness and Similarity of American Small Towns*

SINCLAIR LEWIS

1   She [Carol Kennicott] had sought to be definite in analyzing the surface ugliness of the Gopher Prairies. She asserted that it is a matter of universal similarity; of flimsiness of construction, so that the towns resemble frontier camps; of neglect of natural advantages, so that the hills are covered with brush, the lakes shut off by railroads, and the creeks lined with dumping-grounds; of depressing sobriety of color; rectangularity of buildings; and excessive breadth and straightness of the gashed streets so that there is no escape from gales and from sight of the grim sweep of land, nor any windings to coax the loiterer along, while the breadth which would be majestic in an avenue of palaces makes the low shabby shops creeping down the typical Main Street the more mean by comparison.

2   The universal similarity—that is the physical expression of the philosophy of dull safety. Nine-tenths of the American towns are so alike that it is the completest boredom to wander from one to another. Always, west of Pittsburg, and often east of it, there is the same lumber yard, the same railroad station, the same Ford garage, the same creamery, the same box-like houses and two-story shops.

The new, more conscious houses are alike in their very attempts at diversity: the same bungalows, the same square houses of stucco or tapestry brick. The shcps show the same standardized, nationally advertised wares; the newspapers of sections three thousand miles apart have the same "syndicated features"; the boy in Arkansas displays just such a flamboyant ready-made suit as is found on just such a boy in Delaware, both of them iterate the same slang phrases from the same sporting-pages, and if one of them is in college and the other is a barber, no one may surmise which is which.

STUDY QUESTIONS

Organization and Content

1. The heroine of Sinclair Lewis' famous novel of 1920, *Main Street,* lived in a small Midwestern town named Gopher Prairie. What then is meant by Gopher Prairies in sentence 1?
2. What propositions are being argued here?
3. Note the use of analysis in establishing the issues of the argument. List the issues.
4. Which issues are supported by concrete examples in paragraph 1?
5. What is the topic or dominant idea of paragraph 2?
6. How many different examples are used to support it?
7. What ironical or even paradoxical idea is expressed in sentence 4, paragraph 2?

Sentence Structure

1. Lewis uses several lists in this selection. Explain how the listed material is organized and made clear with semicolons and/or commas in sentence 2, paragraph 1, and sentences 3 and 5, paragraph 2.
2. What repeated words make parallel elements clear?
3. Why is the last element of sentence 2, paragraph 1, so much longer than the preceding elements?

Diction

1. Look up *sobriety, stucco, syndicated, flamboyant, iterate.*
2. What words in paragraph 1 have unfavorable connotations? If these words are omitted, is there any change in the effectiveness of the examples used?

Assignment

1. Imitate Lewis by writing on the same topic, but use up-to-date examples.
2. If you believe that there is now a greater variety in American towns or cities, write an argument giving abundant examples for proof.

3. Give examples to prove that prejudice is widespread in America; or give examples to prove that prejudice is lessening.
4. Similarly, using examples, write on decency or corruption in American life.

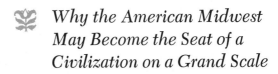

Why the American Midwest May Become the Seat of a Civilization on a Grand Scale

ALFRED NORTH WHITEHEAD AND LUCIEN PRICE

1   "In the Midwest, climate, soil, and food—those three preconditions to a flourishing civilization—are favourable. Man's earliest essays in recorded civilizations occur in hot climates where food is abundant and clothes and shelter next to needless. Rice, in large part, sustained the civilization of India; in Mesopotamia a civilized society arose on grain; in Egypt the food staple was mainly the date; in Central and South America among the Aztecs and Incas it was maize and the banana. But over-population, made possible by cheap food, cheapens labour and opens the way to political despotism; and although the wealth, and hence the leisure requisite for culture may result from cheap labour, the consequent loss of liberty stultifies the intellect. Thus it was that in Europe, a colder climate, where food, clothes, and shelter are harder to get, and where proliferation of the human species is not so exuberant but individuality is more pronounced, our northern civilization ventured into rational thought, thought less shackled by religious superstition, and finally produced that energetic and self-reliant creature, European man."

2   "Nearly every variety of European man is somewhere in our Midwest."

3   "It has a human soil further favourable to a new civilization: not only is it a self-selected stock; the country people and the people in small towns still hold a favourably large proportion as compared with the population of cities. Man's best thinking is done either by persons living in the country or in small communities, or else by those who, having had such environment in early life, enrich their

experience by life in cities; for what is wanted is contact with the elemental processes of nature during those years of youth when the mind is being formed."

4   "How often have I noticed that as between country boys or boys from small towns, and city boys or boys brought up in the suburbs," I said, "how much more self-reliant and resourceful the country-bred lads are. Suppose they lose their jobs: the city or suburban boy, who is usually from the white-collar class, is generally upset and feels rather helpless; your country boy will be cool as a cucumber. What of it? He has earned his living by working with his hands, and he could do it again if necessary."

5   "Urbanization," Whitehead continued, "is a weakness in much of our modern thinking, especially about social problems. Thought is taken primarily for the cities when perhaps it isn't the cities that so much matter. Smart plays are written for blasé audiences in a metropolis; eccentric poetry and clever novels are concocted about dwellers in crowded streets who, poor souls, are cut off through most of the year from contact with the soil, the woods, and the sea, and who perhaps never did a day's hard manual labor in their lives; and to whom the very changes of the weather are but feebly perceptible. They are deprived of that discipline which is imposed by daily contact with the leisurely growth of crops, by the anxiety that those crops should be so at the mercy of nature's caprice, and yet also the reassuring experience of nature's bounty in the long term."

STUDY QUESTIONS

Organization and Content

For many years Lucien Price recorded his conversations with Alfred North Whitehead, noted twentieth-century mathematician and philosopher. In this selection Whitehead spoke paragraphs 1, 3, and 5; and Price 2 and 4.

1. What advantage do hot climates have for the development of civilization? Cold climates like Europe's?
2. Is any reason given for believing that country people do better thinking than city people?
3. Why did Whitehead believe that "urbanization is a weakness . . ."?
4. Indicate what part of the argument is set forth in each paragraph.
5. Put the whole argument together in logical fashion.

Sentence Structure

1. Note that in sentences 1 and 2 the greatest emphasis is thrown on adjectives, the last words in the sentences. How is this emphasis achieved?

2. How is sentence 3 arranged so as to emphasize certain nouns?
3. What words receive chief emphasis in sentence 4?
4. Show how parallel grammatical elements function in sentence 5.
5. Rearrange sentence 5 with "European man" in other positions. What is the effect of shifting it from the final position?
6. How is contrast achieved in the sentence structure of sentence 3 of paragraph 5?
7. Explain the parallel elements of the last sentence.

Diction

1. Look up *staple* (noun), *stultifies, proliferation, elemental, urbanization, blasé, metropolis, eccentric, concocted, discipline, caprice.*
2. What is the common element in *proliferate, prolific,* and *proletariat?*
3. What other words are based on the root of *urbanization? Metropolis? Eccentric?*

Assignment

Perhaps you would like to argue on the other side from Whitehead—that city people have advantages over country people for the advance of civilization. Present evidence in two paragraphs.

You might argue in more detail that nature's influence is good for a person; or, on the other side, that nature has an unfavorable influence.

Perhaps you might show why you believe that some other region—the Pacific Coast, the South, or New England—is more likely to be the seat of a great civilization than the Midwest. Be sure to present your evidence in a logical and orderly manner.

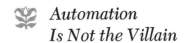 *Automation Is Not the Villain*

PETER F. DRUCKER

1 Everyone seems to know why the American worker has such fear of automation: it creates unemployment. A good many people— labor leaders, politicians, some businessmen—even know how great the damage is: 1.5 to 2 million jobs destroyed by automation each year. This is a widely quoted figure, and the late President Kennedy . . . gave it his blessing by saying "that approximately 1.8 mil-

lion persons holding jobs are replaced every year by machines."
(Neither he nor President Johnson ever repeated this figure,
however.)

2   The worker's fears are real. There are social changes under
way which deeply affect traditional American values regarding manual work and its contribution, and which tend to undermine the status
and self-respect of the manual worker. But in blaming "automation"
for them, the worker blames a phantom.

3   Of course, automation has caused job losses in a good many
plants and industries. But automation and other technological changes,
according to all the evidence, have had no unusual, let alone destructive, impact on the total number of jobs available, on workers'
wages or even on job security. The *real* villain is the tremendous
upgrading in the country's educational level—something the worker,
like most Americans, thoroughly approves of. As one of its totally
unexpected byproducts, the uneducated or less educated—a 10 to
20 per cent minority of our young people but still a large total number, especially of young Negroes—are losing ground in status and
opportunities.

4   That "automation" is just today's fashionable scapegoat—perhaps because it is a new and mysterious word—does not make any
less real the social and psychological changes the worker fears. Nor
does it make them less serious. They deserve to be understood; and
they need to be tackled.

5   There are dozens of definitions of "automation," no two alike
and most quite technical. The public, however, has come to call "automation" whatever, in President Kennedy's words, "replaces jobs by
machines" (and what used to be called "mechanization" in earlier
and less sophisticated days). Are people and their jobs actually being
replaced by the machine on a large scale?

6   If automation destroyed anything like 1.5 to 2 million jobs a
year, unemployment today, after a decade of automation, would rival
that of the Great Depression when one out of every three Americans
was out of work. Of our present civilian labor force in America of
74 millions, some 20 millions would be unemployed. Unemployment
of this magnitude has indeed been predicted by all the voices of
"automation job destruction" since 1949. Actually unemployment
stands at 3.5 million or some 5 per cent of the labor force; it has
been falling, slowly, rather than increasing, these last few years.

7   Almost every year since World War II we have added more
new jobs to the American economy than in the year before; the figure
has risen from 600,000 or so in the late forties to 1.5 million new
jobs a year in the last three years. Only during the near-recession

years 1957–60, at the end of the Eisenhower Administration, did we not add each year as many new jobs as we added people to the work force.

8   In the last four years, since the U.S. economy began to grow again, the blue-collar manufacturing jobs that automation supposedly devours have been growing particularly fast—by 1,600,000 altogether since 1961; that is, at twice the rate of the other job classes. There has been no drop in the past 10 or 15 years either in the proportion of the American labor force employed on the factory floor (a third of total employment in the country) or in the number of manhours per week needed to get the nation's work done. The average weekly take-home pay of the factory worker is at an all-time peak and likely to grow further in 1965 as a result of sharp pay raises in the new union contracts.

9   "Automation," everyone is being told, "destroys jobs for good and throws their holders on the scrap heap of industry." But there is almost no long-term chronic unemployment in this country. Fewer than half a million men and women have been out of work for more that six months. In the employment of husbands and fathers, the breadwinners of this country, we actually have been running at full employment all along.

10   Under "full employment," according to labor economists, 97 out of every 100 people in the work force have jobs—for in this extremely restless society of ours, where one man in seven changes his job every year (most of them voluntarily), there are always quite a few people between jobs. But all through the fifties up to the present, 97 out of every 100 adult married men in the labor force have always had jobs.

11   The hard core of our present unemployment is made up of teen-agers, especially teen-age Negroes. It is quite unlikely that automation has much to do with their plight. One million youngsters who are counted as "unemployed" either are full-time students who want—and often need—part-time jobs; or they are "dropouts," below the age at which our various state laws permit full-time factory work. These young people in the past would have held jobs as delivery boys in the grocery stores, as car washers in filling stations, as bus boys in summer resorts.

12   Why the jobs have apparently become scarce is hotly debated. The reason may be money; the unskilled teen-ager may have "priced himself out of the market." Residential segregation certainly plays a large part in the unemployment of the teen-age Negro boy; while he lives in the city slum, the job opportunities are out in the suburbs. That proportionately twice as many women work today as 30 or 40

years ago may have a bearing; messengers, receptionists, file clerks used to be largely adolescent boys a generation ago—they are mostly women now.

13   But that the jobs have been "automated away" is *clearly not* a major reason for teen-age unemployment. Otherwise, we could not explain why most of these teen-age unemployed find jobs when they become adults; that is, when they are available for full-time work. After 20, there is a dramatic drop in the joblessness rate, even among Negroes.

14   There is one clue as to where this amazing figure of "1.5 to 2 million jobs destroyed by automation every year" originally came from. That many jobs do indeed disappear from the American economy every year—"*from all causes.*" This seems like a lot. But while we have not truly reliable historical data, the most experienced and most respected labor economists in the country, the professionals in the United States Department of Labor, are convinced that we are today liquidating jobs at a *lower* rate than at most times in the past. Certainly, they would say, we are not liquidating jobs at a higher rate.

15   At the same time, we create each year new jobs—again "from all causes"—at the rate of 2.5 to 3.5 millions. This gives us the net annual growth in total jobs of 1 to 1.5 million a year that has already been mentioned. And Labor Department economists believe that we create new jobs at a somewhat higher rate than we did in past periods, even those of great business activity.

STUDY QUESTIONS

Organization and Content

1. Put the thought of paragraphs 1–5 into one sentence. What is the function of these paragraphs? Of paragraphs 6–10? What special phase of the matter is discussed in paragraphs 11–13? What conclusion is reached in paragraph 15?
2. According to Drucker, what is the real force in American society that causes the workers' fears? How does it affect manual workers? Where does he assert that automation is not creating national unemployment?
3. What concession does Drucker make in paragraph 3? Is it better to make concessions early or late in an argument?
4. After the concession what positive assertion does Drucker make concerning the nature of unemployment and its cause in the United States? What three things have been little affected by technological changes?

5. In paragraph 4 Drucker implies that he will try to deal in what way with his topic?
6. What is the purpose of the first two sentences of paragraph 5? The purpose of the third sentence?
7. For what purpose does Drucker use statistical evidence in paragraph 6? Why are paragraphs 6 and 8 particularly impressive in the argument?
8. What three points about unemployment does Drucker make in paragraph 9? How does he define "full employment"?
9. What three possible reasons are suggested for the increase in teen-age unemployment?
10. What surprising reversals of common opinion does Drucker's evidence support?

Sentence Structure

1. Drucker tends to vary sentence length. Analyze the sentences of paragraphs 2, 3, and 4, to see how long and how complicated his longer sentences are. Is there anything in their structure to cause reading difficulty?
2. Point out parallel clauses in sentence 2, paragraph 2; interrupters set off by commas in sentence 2, paragraph 3; the use of dashes in the next three sentences.
3. What is the antecedent of *it* in sentence 2, paragraph 4? How does Drucker throw emphasis on certain words in sentences 2 and 3, paragraph 4?
4. What is the purpose of the question at the end of paragraph 5?
5. Drucker begins several sentences with *but*. Why?
6. Sentences 2, 3, and 4, paragraph 12, have the same basic pattern. In each one, what does the part after the semicolon tell us? Why is it effective to use the same pattern in these three sentences?

Diction

1. Is your dictionary recent enough to contain a definition of *automation?* If so, how does the definition compare with Drucker's?
2. Look up *phantom, status, scapegoat, sophisticated, economy, chronic.*
3. Does Drucker use too many colloquialisms? Are there any places where his vocabulary seems too formal or too technical?

Assignment

Essentially, Drucker's argument is a rebuttal of the idea that automation has created national unemployment. Write a similar argument as a rebuttal of some belief uncritically held by many people. Some suggestions:

1. Human beings live happier lives than animals do.
2. Women are generally less capable than men.
3. Young people today are generally wicked and destructive.
4. Fraternity or sorority membership is a criterion of excellence.

🌻 *Acceptance of Law or Destruction of Mankind*

BERTRAND RUSSELL

1   Modern warfare, so far, has not been more destructive of life than the warfare of less scientific ages, for the increased deadliness of weapons has been offset by the improvement in medicine and hygiene. Until recent times, pestilence almost invariably proved far more fatal than enemy action. When Sennacherib besieged Jerusalem, 185,000 of his army died in one night, "and when they arose early in the morning, behold they were all dead corpses" (II Kings xix. 35). The plague in Athens did much to decide the Peloponnesian War. The many wars between Syracuse and Carthage were usually ended by pestilence. Barbarossa, after he had completely defeated the Lombard League, lost almost his whole army by disease, and had to fly secretly over the Alps. The mortality rate in such campaigns was far greater than in the two great wars of our own century. I do not say that future wars will have as low a casualty rate as the last two; that is a matter to which I will come shortly. I say only, what many people do not realize, that up to the present science has not made war more destructive.

2   There are, however, other respects in which the evils of war have much increased. France was at war, almost continuously, from 1792 to 1815, and in the end suffered complete defeat, but the population of France did not, after 1815, suffer anything comparable to what has been suffered throughout Central Europe since 1945. A modern nation at war is more organized, more disciplined, and more completely concentrated on the effort to secure victory, than was possible in pre-industrial times; the consequence is that defeat is more serious, more disorganizing, more demoralizing to the general population, than it was in the days of Napoleon.

3   But even in this respect it is not possible to make a general rule. Some wars in the past were quite as disorganizing and as destructive of the civilizations of devastated areas as was the Second World War. North Africa has never regained the level of prosperity that it enjoyed under the Romans. Persia never recovered from the Mongols nor Syria from the Turks. There have always been two kinds

of wars, those in which the vanquished incurred disaster, and those in which they only incurred discomfort. We seem, unfortunately, to be entering upon an era in which wars are of the former sort.

4   The atom bomb, and still more the hydrogen bomb, have caused new fears, involving new doubts as to the effects of science on human life. Some eminent authorities, including Einstein, have pointed out that there is a danger of the extinction of all life on this planet. I do not myself think that this will happen in the next war, but I think it may well happen in the next but one, if that is allowed to occur. If this expectation is correct, we have to choose, within the next fifty years or so, between two alternatives. Either we must allow the human race to exterminate itself, or we must forgo certain liberties which are very dear to us, more especially the liberty to kill foreigners whenever we feel so disposed. I think it probable that mankind will choose its own extermination as the preferable alternative. The choice will be made, of course, by persuading ourselves that it is not being made, since (so militarists on both sides will say) the victory of the right is certain without risk of universal disaster. We are perhaps living in the last age of man, and, if so, it is to science that he will owe his extinction.

5   If, however, the human race decides to let itself go on living, it will have to make very drastic changes in its way of thinking, feeling, and behaving. We must learn not to say: "Never! Better death than dishonor." We must learn to submit to law, even when imposed by aliens whom we hate and despise, and whom we believe to be blind to all considerations of righteousness. Consider some concrete examples. Jews and Arabs will have to agree to submit to arbitration; if the award goes against the Jews, the President of the United States will have to insure the victory of the party to which he is opposed, since, if he supports the international authority, he will lose the Jewish vote in New York State. On the other hand, if the award goes in favor of the Jews, the Mohammedan world will be indignant, and will be supported by all other malcontents. Or, to take another instance, Eire will demand the right to oppress the Protestants of Ulster, and on this issue the United States will support Eire while Britain will support Ulster. Could an international authority survive such a dissension? Again: India and Pakistan cannot agree about Kashmir, therefore one of them must support Russia and the other the United States. It will be obvious to anyone who is an interested party in one of these disputes that the issue is far more important than the continuance of life on our planet. The hope that the human race will allow itself to survive is therefore somewhat slender.

6   But if human life *is* to continue in spite of science, mankind

will have to learn a discipline of the passions which, in the past, has not been necessary. Men will have to submit to the law, even when they think the law unjust and iniquitous. Nations which are persuaded that they are only demanding the barest justice will have to acquiesce when this demand is denied them by the neutral authority. I do not say that this is easy; I do not prophesy that it will happen; I say only that if it does not happen the human race will perish, and will perish as a result of science.

STUDY QUESTIONS

Organization and Content

1. Point out the topic sentences of paragraphs 1–3.
2. With what kind of material does Russell support the ideas in the topic sentences?
3. What points in his argument has Russell tried to make in the first three paragraphs?
4. In paragraph 1 mention is made of conditions in the past, the present, and the future. What determined the order in which the author took up these conditions?
5. What new idea is brought out in paragraph 4?
6. Note that in paragraph 4 Russell presents his readers with a dilemma (either . . . or). Explain what logical force this presentation of alternatives is intended to have.
7. What is the relation of paragraph 5 to paragraph 4?
8. Why does Russell mention the Jews, Eire, and Pakistan?
9. Paragraph 5 ends rather pessimistically; to what extent is a contrasting optimism apparent in paragraph 6?
10. Complete the following statement: The proposition that Russell is arguing may be stated as follows: —————.
11. What issues does Russell deal with in his argument?

Sentence Structure

1. Russell uses few sentences in paragraph 1 in which clauses are connected with coordinating conjunctions. What purpose of this paragraph probably caused him to put sentences in the form that he used?
2. Paragraph 2 has three sentences. What considerations would determine the pattern and the length of each sentence?
3. Sentences 2 and 3 of paragraph 2 are long. Why are the sentences of paragraph 3 so much shorter?
4. Point out the ways in which transitional links are made between sentences in paragraph 4.
5. In paragraph 5 how does Russell introduce concrete examples?
6. In what different ways does he move from one concrete example to another?

7. How is a contrasting idea introduced at the beginning of paragraph 6?
8. Is sentence 2 of paragraph 6 arranged so as to provide enough emphasis?
9. The last sentence has three parts. Explain how the arrangement of words in the three parts makes this a very emphatic sentence.

Diction

1. Are there differences of meaning between: *medicine* and *hygiene; pestilence* and *plague; mortality* and *casualty; extermination* and *extinction; dispute* and *dissension; injustice* and *iniquity?*
2. Look up *vanquished, eminent, arbitration.*
3. Is it because the extermination of the human race seems so horrible that Russell adopts an ironic tone in the second half of his argument? Consider the irony in paragraph 4 from: ". . . we must forgo certain liberties which are very dear to us, more especially the liberty to kill foreigners whenever we feel so disposed." Explain the effect of the connotations of words here which produces a shock in the last part of the sentence.
4. Similarly, when Russell says, "The choice will be made, of course . . . ," what is the effect of the "of course"?
5. What is the effect in paragraph 5 of including in one sentence: *submit, imposed, aliens, hate, despise, blind?*
6. What is the great significance of *interested party* later in paragraph 5? How does the diction of the last two sentences of paragraph 5 produce an ironic effect?

Assignment

Write two or three paragraphs using Russell's technique of argument—an argument, that is, in terms of alternatives. Some possibilities:

1. Either we must pay college professors higher salaries, or college education will be greatly weakened.
2. Either we must admit to college all who wish to attend, or the public will remain dangerously ignorant.
3. Either we must drastically limit college admissions to the best students, or the quality of college training will be seriously diluted.
4. Either we must lessen the cost of political campaigns, or we shall be governed by rich men only.
5. Either the public must provide increased funds for medical research, or we must accept higher mortality rates for cancer and other diseases.
6. Either engineers and others with highly specialized training must have a broader education, or they will be unable to participate in our public life.
7. Either we must admit more foreign students to our colleges and send more of our native students abroad, or expect that effective international understanding will be dangerously delayed.
8. Either we must revise our police procedures, or expect further increases in crime.

Be sure to support the issues of your argument with good evidence.

Romance Is a Poor Basis for Marriage

Denis de Rougemont
(Montgomery Belgion, trans.)

1   The better to see our situation, let us look at America—that other Europe which has been released from both the routine practices and traditional restraints of the old. No other known civilization, in the 7000 years that one civilization has been succeeding another, has bestowed on the love known as *romance* anything like the same amount of daily publicity by means of the screen, the hoarding, the letter-press and advertisements in magazines, by means of songs and pictures, and of current morals and of whatever defies them. No other civilization has embarked with anything like the same ingenuous assurance upon the perilous enterprise of making marriage coincide with love thus understood, and of making the first depend upon the second.

2   During a telephone strike in 1947, the women operators in the county town of White Plains, near New York, received the following call: "My girl and I want to get married. We're trying to locate a justice of the peace. Is it an emergency?" The women telephone operators decided forthwith that it was. And the newspaper which reported the item headed it: "Love is Classified as an Emergency." This commonplace newspaper cutting provides an example of the perfectly natural beliefs of Americans, and that is how it is of interest. It shows that in America the terms "love" and "marriage" are practically equivalent; that when one "loves" one must get married instantly; and, further, that "love" should normally overcome all obstacles, as is shown every day in films, novels, and comic-strips. In reality, however, let romantic love overcome no matter how many obstacles, and it almost always fails at one. That is the obstacle constituted by time. Now, either marriage is an institution set up to be lasting—or it is meaningless. That is the first secret of the present breakdown, a breakdown of which the extent can be measured simply by reference to divorce statistics, where the United States heads the list of countries. To try to base marriage on a form of love which is unstable by definition is really to benefit the State of Nevada. To insist that

no matter what film, even one about the atomic bomb, shall contain a certain amount of the romantic drug—and romantic more than erotic—known as "love interest," is to give publicity to the germs that are making marriage ill, not to a cure.

3   Romance feeds on obstacles, short excitations, and partings; marriage, on the contrary, is made up of wont, daily propinquity, growing accustomed to one another. Romance calls for "the far-away love" of the troubadours; marriage, for love of "one's neighbour." Where, then, a couple have married in obedience to a romance, it is natural that the first time a conflict of temperament or of taste becomes manifest the parties should each ask themselves: "Why did I marry?" And it is no less natural that, obsessed by the universal propaganda in favour of romance, each should seize the first occasion to fall in love with somebody else. And thereupon it is perfectly logical to decide to divorce, so as to obtain from the new love, which demands a fresh marriage, a new promise of happiness—all three words, "marriage," "love," "happiness," being synonyms. Thus, remedying boredom with a passing fever, "he for the second time, she for the fourth," American men and women go in quest of "adjustment." They do not seek it, however, in the old situation, the one guaranteed—"for better, for worse"—by a vow. They seek it, on the contrary, in a fresh "experience" regarded as such, and affected from the start by the same potentialities of failure as those which preceded it. That is how divorce assumes in the United States a less "disastrous" character, and is even more "normal," than in Europe. There where a European regards the rupture of a marriage as producing social disorder and the loss of a capital of joint recollections and experiences, an American has rather the impression that "he is putting his life straight," and opening up for himself a fresh future. The economy of saving is once again opposed to that of squandering, as the concern to preserve the past is opposed to the concern to make a clean sweep in order to build something tidy, without compromise. But any man opposed to compromise is inconsistent in marrying. And he who would draw a draft on his future is very unwise to mention beforehand that he wishes to be allowed not to honour it; as did the young millionairess who told the newspaper men on the eve of her marriage: "It's marvellous to be getting married *for the first time!*" A year later, she got divorced.

4   Whereupon a number of people propose to forbid divorce, or at least to render it very difficult. But it is marriage which, in my opinion, has been made too easy, through the supposition that let there be "love" and marriage should follow, regardless of outmoded conventions of social and religious station, of upbringing and sub-

stance. It is certainly possible to imagine new conditions which candidates for marriage—that true "co-existence" which should be enduring, peaceable, and mutually educative—should fulfil. It is possible to exact tests or ordeals bearing on whatever gives any human union its best chances of lasting: aims in life, rhythms of life, comparative vocations, characters, and temperaments. If marriage—that is to say, lastingness—is what is wanted, it is natural to ensure its conditions. But such reforms would have little effect in a world which retained, if not true passion, at least the nostalgia of passion that has grown congenital in Western man.

5   When marriage was established on social conventions, and hence, from the individual standpoint, on chance, it had at least as much likelihood of success as marriage based on "love" alone. But the whole of Western evolution goes from tribal wisdom to individual risk; it is irreversible, and it must be approved to the extent it tends to make collective and native destiny depend on personal decision.

STUDY QUESTIONS

Organization and Content

1. Why does the author focus paragraph 1 on America?
2. Why does he tell the story of the telephone operators in paragraph 2? Which sentence brings out his purpose?
3. In the second half of paragraph 2, what objection to romance does the author raise?
4. In sentence 10 of paragraph 2, what effect in the argument does the *either-or* statement have? Is it acceptable to you?
5. Paragraph 3 points out contrasts. List them.
6. Paragraph 4 shows the author rather dubious about reforms. Why?
7. To what extent does the author make concessions in paragraph 5?
8. The author makes use of specific examples, of definitions, of reasoning from assumptions. Which of these means of argument is the most effective?
9. In what terms does the author define *romance* and *marriage?*
10. How are America and Europe represented? Does the effectiveness of the argument depend at all upon one's attitude toward America or Europe?
11. Set down De Rougemont's argument in the form of a syllogism, with major premise, minor premise, and conclusion.

Sentence Structure

1. Explain the reason for the structure of sentences 1 and 2 of paragraph 3.
2. Indicate by what means sentences 3–6 of paragraph 3 are linked.

3. What terms show that the author in sentences 3–6 is drawing conclusions from the ideas in sentences 1 and 2 of paragraph 3?
4. Why is the last sentence of paragraph 3 so short?
5. Are there too many "interrupters" in the sentences of paragraph 4?

Diction

1. Look up *romance, hoarding, ingenuous, erotic, wont, propinquity, troubadour, obsessed, economy, nostalgia, congenital.*
2. Why do so many words have quotation marks around them?
3. Which of De Rougemont's terms are metaphors?

Assignment

De Rougemont's argument may make you wish to reply to it by writing a defense of marriage based on romance. If you choose to do so, state clearly on what issues you base your counter argument.

Perhaps you prefer to imitate the work of De Rougemont in an argument that says *this* is better than (or preferable to) *that.* Some possibilities:

1. A campus with plenty of grass and trees and without automobiles is preferable to a campus with large areas given up to parking lots and many automobiles.
2. It is better to read much (100 books a year, for example) than to read little, as most Americans do.
3. It is better to play a musical instrument (or sing) than to attend concerts.
4. For nonscience students it would be better to read books about the history of science and the significance of science than to take a course in laboratory science.

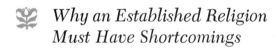 *Why an Established Religion Must Have Shortcomings*

SOAME JENYNS

An Established Religion must be liable to many imperfections from its own nature, and the nature of man; in its original constitution, it must lean to the errors and prejudices of the times; and, how much soever it is then approved, it cannot long preserve that approba-

From Soame Jenyns, *Works* (London, 1790).

tion, because, human science being continually fluctuating, mankind grow more or less knowing in every generation, and consequently must change their opinions on religious, as well as on all other subjects; so that however wisely any Established System may be formed at first, it must, from the natural increase of human knowledge, be found or thought to be erroneous in the course of a few years: and yet the change of national religions cannot keep pace with the alterations of national opinions, because such frequent reviews and reformations would totally unhinge men's principles, and subvert the foundations of all religion and morality whatever. It must likewise be corrupted by the very establishment which protects it, because by that it will be mixed with the worldly pursuits of its degenerate votaries; and it must be extremely dissimilar to its original purity, or it would be incapable of being established; for pure and genuine Christianity never was, nor ever can be the National Religion of any country upon earth. It is a gold too refined to be worked up with any human institution, without a large portion of alloy; for, no sooner is this small grain of mustard seed watered with the fertile showers of civil emoluments, than it grows up into a large and spreading tree, under the shelter of whose branches the birds of prey and plunder will not fail to make for themselves comfortable habitations, and thence deface its beauty and destroy its fruits.

STUDY QUESTIONS

Organization and Content

1. Be sure you know what is meant by an Established Religion.
2. State the proposition that Jenyns is arguing.
3. State the two issues on which he undertakes to convince us.
4. What is the function of the statement in sentence 1 immediately after the colon—"and yet the change . . ."?
5. How does sentence 2 support the argument? Does it have any connection with sentence 1?
6. In what way does sentence 3 have a bearing on the discussion?
7. Sentence 3 mentions gold, mustard seed, and a tree; of what use are they in the argument? Are they metaphors, analogies, illustrations, data, evidence, or historical examples?

Sentence Structure

1. Is any of the three sentences of the paragraph too long?
2. Though the sentences have several parts, by what means has the author tried to make them easy to understand?

3. What principle of structure do all three sentences follow?
4. This paragraph was written in the eighteenth century. Would a twentieth-century writer write the sentences in any different way?

Diction

1. Look up *approbation, science, fluctuating, erroneous, subvert, degenerate votaries, civil emoluments.*
2. From what language do these words come? Judging by his vocabulary and sentence structure, what would you suppose about the author's education?
3. Does the author use a learned or a popular vocabulary?
4. Which sentence contains the greatest number of concrete terms?
5. What are the connotations of "fertile showers," "prey and plunder," "deface . . . and destroy"?

Assignment

Write one or two paragraphs in which you convince a reader why, under given conditions, a certain thing was bound to happen. Some suggestions:

1. Why the number of people engaged in farming in the United States declined in the twentieth century
2. Why railroads in the United States are a declining industry
3. Why California has grown rapidly in population
4. Why many American college students are poorly prepared for college
5. Why American mass-produced articles have shortcomings
6. Why your church has shortcomings
7. Why your college has shortcomings
8. Why the people of a region (South, East, West) have developed certain recognizable qualities

Remember that you do not have to demonstrate that the thing has happened but to convince a reader why it had to happen.

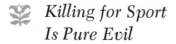 *Killing for Sport Is Pure Evil*

Joseph Wood Krutch

1   To me it is inconceivable how anyone should think an animal more interesting dead than alive. I can also easily prove to my own satisfaction that killing "for sport" is the perfect type of pure evil for which metaphysicians have sometimes sought.

From Joseph Wood Krutch, *The Great Chain of Life.* Reprinted by permission of the publisher, Houghton Mifflin Company.

2   Most wicked deeds are done because the doer proposes some good to himself. The liar lies to gain some end; the swindler and the thief want things which, if honestly got, might be good in themselves. Even the murderer may be removing an impediment to normal desires or gaining possession of something which his victim keeps from him. None of these usually does evil for evil's sake. They are selfish or unscrupulous, but their deeds are not gratuitously evil. The killer for sport has no such comprehensible motive. He prefers death to life, darkness to light. He gets nothing except the satisfaction of saying, "Something which wanted to live is dead. There is that much less vitality, consciousness, and, perhaps, joy in the universe. I am the Spirit that Denies." When a man wantonly destroys one of the works of man we call him Vandal. When he wantonly destroys one of the works of God we call him Sportsman.

3   The hunter-for-food may be as wicked and as misguided as vegetarians sometimes say; but he does not kill for the sake of killing. The rancher and the farmer who exterminate all living things not immediately profitable to them may sometimes be working against their own best interests; but whether they are or are not they hope to achieve some supposed good by their exterminations. If to do evil not in the hope of gain but for evil's sake involves the deepest guilt by which man can be stained, then killing for killing's sake is a terrifying phenomenon and as strong a proof as we could have of that "reality of evil" with which present-day theologians are again concerned.

STUDY QUESTIONS

Organization and Content

1. Be sure to state correctly the proposition that Krutch is arguing. Note that it is not: Sportsmen are bad men, or a law should be passed protecting animals from sportsmen; the proposition of his argument is more abstract.
2. If sentence 1 is Krutch's major premise, what are the minor premise and conclusion of the syllogism he is relying on for support of his argument? (Krutch says "an animal"; presumably a proper example would be a leopard, rhinoceros, blacksnake, or bluejay.)
3. Krutch groups liar, swindler, thief, and murderer together because they have something in common. What is it? According to sentence 5, paragraph 2, what quality is absent from all of their deeds?
4. Paragraph 2 is divided into two parts. What is the main idea of each part, and how are the two parts related?

5. In Krutch's argument what are life and death to be equated with? In the argument how are these equations related to sentence 1, paragraph 2?
6. What idea do sentences 11 and 12, paragraph 2, ironically illustrate? What contrast provides the basis for irony?
7. On what issues is the argument continued in paragraph 3? What is the significance of the final sentence?
8. To what extent is Krutch's argument based on evidence and to what extent on reasoning?

Sentence Structure

1. Why is the structure of sentence 2, paragraph 2, appropriate to the ideas expressed there? Why is the murderer named last and in a new sentence, and how does Krutch place emphasis on the murderer?
2. Sentences 6–8, paragraph 2, have the same basic structure. What is it, and why is it suitable? What transitional device links these three sentences?
3. Point out repetition and parallelism in sentences 11 and 12, paragraph 2. Why are these devices effective here?
4. How does Krutch gain strong contrast in sentences 1 and 2, paragraph 3?

Diction

1. Look up *metaphysicians, gratuitously, wantonly, Vandal, phenomenon, theologians.*
2. What do the words *gratuitously* and *wantonly* contribute to Krutch's argument?
3. Explain the allusion behind the meaning of *Vandal.*

Assignment

1. If you took the side of a "sportsman," could you suggest any "good" as he sees the matter, and formulate an argument opposing Krutch?
2. Perhaps you do not agree with Krutch's sentence 1. If so, justify your position.
3. Krutch condemns the sportsman for saying with satisfaction, "Something which wanted to live is dead." You might explore the questions: "Is every death an evil? What killings can be justified?" What proposition would you finally be willing to argue for?
4. Imitate Krutch by writing an argument on one of the following topics: Loss of freedom is the greatest evil; vivisection is an evil—or a good—in our society; a world that permits starvation is evil; a world that permits unlimited births is evil.

🌷 *The Size of the United States Senate and the Terms of the Senators*

JAMES MADISON

1   IV. The number of senators and the duration of their appointment come next to be considered. In order to form an accurate judgment on both these points it will be proper to inquire into the purposes which are to be answered by a senate; and in order to ascertain these it will be necessary to review the inconveniences which a republic must suffer from the want of such an institution.

2   *First.* It is a misfortune incident to republican government, though in a less degree than to other governments, that those who administer it may forget their obligations to their constituents and prove unfaithful to their important trust. In this point of view, a senate, as a second branch of the legislative assembly, distinct from, and dividing the power with, a first, must be in all cases a salutary check on the government. It doubles the security to the people by requiring the concurrence of two distinct bodies in schemes of usurpation or perfidy, where the ambition or corruption of one would otherwise be sufficient. This is a precaution founded on such clear principles, and now so well understood in the United States, that it would be more than superfluous to enlarge on it. I will barely remark that, as the improbability of sinister combinations will be in proportion to the dissimilarity in the genius of the two bodies, it must be politic to distinguish them from each other by every circumstance which will consist with a due harmony in all proper measures and with the genuine principles of republican government.

3   *Secondly.* The necessity of a senate is not less indicated by the propensity of all single and numerous assemblies to yield to the impulse of sudden and violent passions and to be seduced by factious leaders into intemperate and pernicious resolutions. Examples on this subject might be cited without number, and from proceedings within the United States as well as from the history of other nations. But a position that will not be contradicted need not be proved. All that need be remarked is that a body which is to correct this infirmity ought itself to be free from it, and consequently ought to

From Alexander Hamilton, James Madison, and John Jay, *The Federalist* (1788).

be less numerous. It ought, moreover, to possess great firmness, and consequently ought to hold its authority by a tenure of considerable duration.

4   *Thirdly.* Another defect to be supplied by a senate lies in a want of due acquaintance with the objects and principles of legislation. It is not possible that an assembly of men called for the most part from pursuits of a private nature, continued in appointment for a short time and led by no permanent motive to devote the intervals of public occupation to a study of the laws, the affairs, and the comprehensive interests of their country, should, if left wholly to themselves, escape a variety of important errors in the exercise of their legislative trust. It may be affirmed, on the best grounds, that no small share of the present embarrassments of America is to be charged on the blunders of our governments, and that these have proceeded from the heads rather than the hearts of most of the authors of them. What indeed are all the repealing, explaining, and amending laws, which fill and disgrace our voluminous codes, but so many monuments of deficient wisdom, so many impeachments exhibited by each succeeding against each preceding session, so many admonitions to the people of the value of those aids which may be expected from a well-constituted senate?

5   A good government implies two things: first, fidelity to the object of government, which is the happiness of the people; secondly, a knowledge of the means by which that object can be best attained. Some governments are deficient in both these qualities, most governments are deficient in the first. I scruple not to assert that in American governments too little attention has been paid to the last. The federal Constitution avoids this error; and what merits particular notice, it provides for the last in a mode which increases the security for the first.

6   *Fourthly.* The mutability in the public councils arising from a rapid succession of new members, however qualified they may be, points out, in the strongest manner, the necessity of some stable institution in the government. Every new election in the States is found to change one half of the representatives. From this change of men must proceed a change of opinions; and from a change of opinions, a change of measures. But a continual change even of good measures is inconsistent with every rule of prudence and every prospect of success. The remark is verified in private life and becomes more just, as well as more important, in national transactions. . . .

7   A *fifth* desideratum illustrating the utility of a senate is the want of a due sense of national character. Without a select and stable member of the government, the esteem of foreign powers will

not only be forfeited by an unenlightened and variable policy, proceeding from the causes already mentioned, but the national councils will not possess that sensibility to the opinion of the world which is perhaps not less necessary in order to merit than it is to obtain its respect and confidence.

8　　An attention to the judgment of other nations is important to every government for two reasons: the one is that, independently of the merits of any particular plan or measure, it is desirable, on various accounts, that it should appear to other nations as the offspring of a wise and honorable policy; the second is that in doubtful cases, particularly where the national councils may be warped by some strong passion or momentary interest, the presumed or known opinion of the impartial world may be the best guide that can be followed. What has not America lost by her want of character with foreign nations, and how many errors and follies would she not have avoided if the justice and propriety of her measures had, in every instance, been previously tried by the light in which they would probably appear to the unbiased part of mankind?

9　　Yet, however requisite a sense of national character may be, it is evident that it can never be sufficiently possessed by a numerous and changeable body. It can only be found in a number so small that a sensible degree of the praise and blame of public measures may be the portion of each individual, or in an assembly so durably invested with public trust that the pride and consequence of its members may be sensibly incorporated with the reputation and prosperity of the community. The half-yearly representatives of Rhode Island would probably have been little affected in their deliberations on the iniquitous measures of that State by arguments drawn from the light in which such measures would be viewed by foreign nations or even by the sister States, whilst it can scarcely be doubted that if the concurrence of a select and stable body had been necessary, a regard to national character alone would have prevented the calamities under which that misguided people is now laboring.

STUDY QUESTIONS

Organization and Content

1. This selection by James Madison is taken from *The Federalist*, the famous series of papers arguing for the adoption of the proposed American Constitution. In addition to the topics of discussion, what other thing is announced in paragraph 1?

2. In effect, Madison says that in order to understand A we must consider B; and in order to understand B we must consider C. What ideas do the letters represent in paragraph 1?
3. Explain what issue is discussed in each of the five parts into which Madison divides his argument.
4. In his second section Madison says that many examples might be cited from history of certain evils in legislatures. What proposal about the Senate has a bearing on these evils?
5. What makes Madison think that the Senate would pass wise laws? Is he assuming that it would pass wiser laws than the House of Representatives?
6. What bearing does the six-year term of Senators have on the issue raised in section 4?
7. Does Madison assert in section 5 that the make-up of the Senate will have an influence on foreign nations or that foreign nations will have an influence on the Senate?
8. Does the material of section 5 support the issue of the size of the Senate or of the term of Senators?
9. Complete the following statement: According to Madison, without a Senate a republic will be likely to suffer from —————.

Sentence Structure

1. Is the sentence structure of the selection chiefly of a formal kind or of an informal kind?
2. Are the sentences mostly long or short? Simple or complex?
3. Analyze the structure of sentences 1 and 2 of paragraph 2.
4. The structure pattern causes' what words to be emphasized in both sentences?
5. In paragraph 4 sentences 2 and 3 begin with an impersonal construction. What kind of effect does this type of beginning have on the latter part of the sentence?
6. Both paragraph 4 and paragraph 8 end with questions. What effect in the argument do these questions have?
7. What word does Madison repeat in paragraph 5 in order to hold the sentences of the paragraph together?
8. Point out examples of balance in the sentences of paragraph 5.
9. Show how the sentence structure is adapted to the course of logical thought in paragraph 6.

Diction

1. Look up *salutary, usurpation, perfidy, sinister, politic, propensity, seduced, factious, pernicious, infirmity, tenure, voluminous, impeachments, admonitions, fidelity, scruple, mutability, desideratum, sensible, durably, invested, iniquitous.*
2. Learn the meaning of the root in each of the following: *perfidy, sinister, seduced, tenure, admonitions, fidelity, mutability, sensible, durably, invested.*
3. From what language do the above words come that have three syllables or more?

4. What effect does the use of these longer words have on the style of the selection?
5. What terms would you use to describe Madison's *style?*
6. Do you think that his style was influenced most by his education, his being a lawyer, the age in which he lived (he was born in 1751), or the subject about which he was arguing?

Assignment

Following Madison's pattern of argument, write an argument to convince a reader:

1. That everyone who studies foreign languages, science, mathematics, or English ought to pursue the study for _____ years (a considerable time), for if he does not, then undesirable results will follow
2. That the United States should adopt a system like that of Canada and England according to which the term of the Chief Executive (Prime Minister) may end at any time that his party loses a vote on an important issue
3. That the President of the United States should have a longer term of office
4. That students in publicly supported colleges should have all expenses paid by the government provided that they make high scores on entrance examinations and maintain high grades in college
5. That every citizen of the United States, before being eligible to vote in any given election, should be required to demonstrate familiarity with the issues and with the careers of the candidates

 Cities Need Old Buildings

JANE JACOBS

1   Cities need old buildings so badly it is probably impossible for vigorous streets and districts to grow without them. By old buildings I mean not museum-piece old buildings, not old buildings in an excellent and expensive state of rehabilitation—although these

From *The Death and Life of Great American Cities,* by Jane Jacobs. © Copyright 1961 by Jane Jacobs. Reprinted by permission of Random House, Inc.

make fine ingredients—but also a good lot of plain, ordinary, low-value old buildings, including some rundown old buildings.

2   If a city area has only new buildings, the enterprises that can exist there are automatically limited to those that can support the high costs of new construction. These high costs of occupying new buildings may be levied in the form of rent, or they may be levied in the form of an owner's interest and amortization payments on the capital costs of the construction. However the costs are paid off, they have to be paid off. And for this reason, enterprises that support the cost of new construction must be capable of paying a relatively high overhead—high in comparison to that necessarily required by old buildings. To support such high overheads, the enterprises must be either (*a*) high profit or (*b*) well subsidized.

3   If you look about, you will see that only operations that are well established, high-turnover, standardized or heavily subsidized can afford, commonly, to carry the costs of new construction. Chain stores, chain restaurants and banks go into new construction. But neighborhood bars, foreign restaurants and pawn shops go into older buildings. Supermarkets and shoe stores often go into new buildings; good bookstores and antique dealers seldom do. Well-subsidized opera and art museums often go into new buildings. But the unformalized feeders of the arts—studios, galleries, stores for musical instruments and art supplies, backrooms where the low earning power of a seat and a table can absorb uneconomic discussions—these go into old buildings. Perhaps more significant, hundreds of ordinary enterprises, necessary to the safety and public life of streets and neighborhoods, and appreciated for their convenience and personal quality, can make out successfully in old buildings, but are inexorably slain by the high overhead of new construction.

4   As for really new ideas of any kind—no matter how ultimately profitable or otherwise successful some of them might prove to be—there is no leeway for such chancy trial, error and experimentation in the high-overhead economy of new construction. Old ideas can sometimes use new buildings. New ideas must use old buildings.

5   Even the enterprises that can support new construction in cities need old construction in their immediate vicinity. Otherwise they are part of a total attraction and total environment that is economically too limited—and therefore functionally too limited to be lively, interesting and convenient. Flourishing diversity anywhere in a city means the mingling of high-yield, middling-yield, low-yield and no-yield enterprises.

STUDY QUESTIONS

Organization and Content

1. Regarding buildings in cities, what assumptions do many people make that may cause the author's first statement to be surprising and challenging?
2. Why does the author include sentence 2, paragraph 1?
3. In effect, the author says in sentence 1, paragraph 2: "Let us assume that a city area contains only new buildings." What conclusion follows from this assumption?
4. Indicate the steps in the reasoning from sentence 1 to sentence 5, paragraph 2.
5. Where does the author give examples of well-subsidized operations that can support costs of new construction? What kinds of operations are mentioned in sentences 2 and 4, paragraph 3?
6. What contrasts are brought out in sentences 3, 4, and 6, paragraph 3?
7. What function does paragraph 3 perform in the argument?
8. What assumptions and what reasoning lie behind the final statement of paragraph 4: "New ideas must use old buildings"?
9. How do the concepts of "total attraction" and "flourishing diversity" influence the argument in paragraph 5?
10. What is the main issue on which the success of this argument depends?

Sentence Structure

1. Most of the sentences in paragraphs 1 and 2 begin with introductory dependent elements. Which of them are used mainly for transition and which mainly because of the reasoning?
2. Why are there more sentences in paragraph 3 that begin with the subject?
3. Show how parallel construction, especially with groups of two or three examples, is used in paragraph 3.
4. Would it be better to use commas (less separation) or parentheses (greater separation) than the dashes to set off the interrupter in sentence 1, paragraph 4?
5. How is emphatic contrast achieved in sentences 2 and 3, paragraph 4?

Diction

1. Look up *museum-piece, amortization, inexorably.*
2. Is the author's vocabulary extremely formal, informal, or technical?

Assignment

Write an argument on one of the following topics: A person's wardrobe always needs some old clothes; a scientific curriculum needs courses in history of science; it is best to have friends with a diversity of age, interests, and occupation; it is best to have a balance of utility and beauty in a house.

Argue for certain means of achieving diversity in: a flower garden; a personal collection of books; amusements; a recreational reading room in a library; house furnishings; diet.

❧ *Presidential Power Has Not Become Dangerously Personalized*

JAMES MACGREGOR BURNS

1   I do contend that as a result of the development of the presidential office, and as a result of tendencies to be explored in later chapters, the Presidency has developed settled processes of decision making that embody and reflect the kinds of interactions among the President and central decision makers that I have described. There is, in short, some pattern, some continuity, some predictability, some structure in the executive impulse in the modern Presidency. This conclusion runs counter to two important views, one intellectual, one popular.

2   The first view, held most notably by historians, is that the Presidency is too nearly a unique institution, its incumbents too varied and impenetrable as persons, the stream of forces impinging on it too tumultuous, mixed, and unpredictable, the whole political, social and ideological context too inchoate and changeable, to permit significant generalizations about presidential decision making. Presidential personality alone—the tremendous contrasts between a Hoover and a Roosevelt and a Truman and an Eisenhower and a Kennedy and a Johnson—would thwart any effort at systematic theory. All of us—including historians—actually do generalize about Presidents. Indeed, the theory of strong Presidents is a vitally important generalization in itself, as we have noted. But effective theory seeking to penetrate much below the level of such simplicities or pieties is hopeless, it is said.

From James MacGregor Burns, *Presidential Government: The Crucible of Leadership.* Reprinted by permission of the publisher, Houghton Mifflin Company.

3   This view stems of course from a certain view of history; it stems also—as it applies to the Presidency—from the era of Hamiltonian Presidents who have exercised great powers but in an unstable executive, political, and ideological environment. Presidents have been dependent on a small circle of advisers subject to sudden shifts in membership and attitude. It is only natural that a historian studying the Roosevelt administration should come away from it with a sinking sensation (or perhaps with a feeling of relief) that Roosevelt and his decision-making methods were so harum-scarum as to be ultimately inscrutable. He could react in the same way to seemingly more fixed relations between a President and one adviser. Wilson's relation with Colonel House was so intimate (they even used a private code in telephoning), so mutually dependent, and so informal and unofficial as to seem indestructible. That relationship had much of the quality of a man's relation to his mistress; its very lack of formality was both a strength and a weakness. Certainly it would be hard to generalize about such a relation—except to note that in the end it collapsed, as did that between Roosevelt and Corcoran, and that between Eisenhower and Adams.

4   But it is precisely here that the office—and the capacity to generalize about it—has changed. The modern President is less dependent on single outside advisers or on haphazard staff arrangements. The collective decision-making processes that have been built up in the Presidency are so strong in their own right, so durable, so rooted now in governmental and administrative practice, that the Presidency itself has come to be more bureaucratized (in the sense of routine, specialization, interdependence). Clearly there will be occasional Presidents who will suppress or distort the usual pattern of presidential decision making. But the continuing tendencies will be strong, and generalizations all the more permissible.

5   This view, however, runs counter to a second, more popular conception of the Presidency. This is the notion of "the lonely President"—the man who, though surrounded by many other men, is ultimately alone with his thoughts and his decisions. Immersed in his problems and the squabbles of his advisers, ultimately he rises, steps out of the Oval Office through one of the French doors, and paces up and down in the Rose Garden as he—very much alone—comes to the Final Decision.

6   This is a good scene for novels about the Presidency but a long way from reality. The President is never alone. He would not be President if he did not incorporate within himself the hopes, attitudes, policy preferences, interests, and goals of scores of central decision makers and of a host of interested politicians and voters outside. To be sure, there are some decisions that call for personal

intervention from him, that may arouse greater conflicts within himself, that threaten to strain the bonds between him and men he may esteem and need. But in such situations he will be leaning all the more heavily on other advisers or interests or publics—or on future historians. Loneliness as such is impossible in such a situation of interdependence—the concept is analytically meaningless.

7   It is also a misleading concept. For the more we are led to think in terms of the "lonely President," the more we bolster the fears of those alarmed about "one-man" presidential power, just as we bolster the case of the historians who conclude that the Presidency is impenetrable. If the great decisions—including the decisions about life and death—in the end are made by lonely Presidents wrestling with their consciences in the dark, then indeed we could share, for example, Professor Hyneman's fears about a "single individual with dominant political authority." No democrat would want his future, and his country's, settled by some unpredictable decision maker responding to inscrutable forces in some normless void. No democrat could tolerate a political institution so divorced from the expression of popular attitudes and choices, from constitutional machinery and safeguards, and above all from the advice and consent of the men immediately around him.

8   Thus I conclude that more centralized control has not meant more "one-man" control of the executive branch. The real danger, it seems to me, is just the reverse—whether we have created such an institutionalized Presidency that the President will be smothered by the machinery, whether he will lose the vitality, independence and inventiveness necessary for creative leadership. The question is whether the executive impulse, in helping to produce the modern Presidency, has begun to sacrifice the qualities that Hamilton wanted in the executive. We can dismiss the concept of the lonely President as a myth. But there is another, equally popular concept of the Presidency—"the President is many men." This notion is true—and embraces the real problem.

STUDY QUESTIONS

Organization and Content

1. What decision regarding presidential power has Burns reached? His decision, he says, needs defense against two opposing views. What are they?
2. Why does he call one of these views intellectual and the other popular? Where is the "intellectual" view first announced? What examples repre-

sent this view? In which sentences of paragraph 2 are the author's own views stated?

3. What idea do the references to Presidents Roosevelt, Wilson, and Eisenhower illustrate in paragraph 3? In sentence 7, paragraph 3, does Burns make so great a concession that it seriously weakens his argument? What is the significance of the second half of this sentence?

4. What evidence does Burns produce in paragraph 4? In which sentence does he make a concession, and how does he minimize the importance of the concession?

5. What is the difference between the "intellectual" view of the Presidency and the "popular" view?

6. On what two issues does Burns argue against the "popular" view? What three concessions does he make in paragraph 6? How does he then turn these concessions to his advantage in the argument?

7. Explain the reference to "future historians" in sentence 5, paragraph 6.

8. Why does Burns think the "popular" view is misleading? Why would no believer in democracy wish to adopt this view? If the Presidency were the kind of institution described in sentence 5, paragraph 7, what kind of political leader would the President properly be called?

9. On the basis of his evidence, what has Burns concluded? What is the purpose of most of paragraph 8? To what problem does it look ahead?

Sentence Structure

1. Some of Burns's sentences use repetition and parallel structures. Indicate them in sentence 2, paragraph 1; sentence 1, paragraph 2; sentence 5, paragraph 3; sentence 3, paragraph 4; sentence 4, paragraph 6.

2. What is the purpose of the dashes in sentences 2 and 3, paragraph 2; sentence 1, paragraph 3; sentence 3, paragraph 5; sentences 5 and 6, paragraph 6; sentence 3, paragraph 7?

3. What is the effect of the shortest sentences of paragraphs 6 and 7?

4. Why repeat "No democrat" in sentence 5, paragraph 7?

Diction

1. Look up *unique, incumbents, impenetrable, impinging, context, inchoate, pieties, ideological, inscrutable, host, democrat.*

2. Why use capitals on "Final Decision" in paragraph 5?

3. What are the connotations of *unpredictable, inscrutable,* and *void* in sentence 4, paragraph 7? What influence do these connotations have on the argument?

4. Has Burns made greater use of concrete terms or abstract terms? Why?

Assignment

State the proposition and the issues for an argument on one of the following topics and then write the argument in imitation of Burns's. Your argument may support the proposition, or it may serve as a rebuttal.

1. The principle of freedom of speech has become dangerously weakened in the United States.

2. The United States military establishment has acquired a dangerous amount of power in the American government.
3. State governments have become too unresponsive to citizens' needs.
4. Business corporations have become dangerously large and powerful in the modern world.
5. Young people have been allowed to have a dangerous amount of power and influence in the modern world.

 The Value of Liberty

JOHN STUART MILL

1   He who lets the world, or his own portion of it, choose his plan of life for him, has no need of any other faculty than the ape-like one of imitation. He who chooses his plan for himself, employs all his faculties. He must use observation to see, reasoning and judgment to foresee, activity to gather materials for decision, discrimination to decide, and when he has decided, firmness and self-control to hold to his deliberate decision. And these qualities he requires and exercises exactly in proportion as the part of his conduct which he determines according to his own judgment and feelings is a large one. It is possible that he might be guided in some good path, and kept out of harm's way, without any of these things. But what will be his comparative worth as a human being? It is really of importance, not only what men do, but also what manner of men they are that do it. Among the works of man, which human life is rightly employed in perfecting and beautifying, the first in importance surely is man himself. Supposing it were possible to get houses built, corn grown, battles fought, causes tried, and even churches erected and prayers said, by machinery—by automatons in human form—it would be a considerable loss to exchange for these automatons even the men and women who at present inhabit the more civilised parts of the world, and who assuredly are but starved specimens of what nature can and will produce. Human nature is not a machine to be built after a model, and set to do exactly the work prescribed for it, but a tree, which requires to grow and develop itself on all sides, according to the tendency of the inward forces which make it a living thing.

From John Stuart Mill, *On Liberty* (1859).

2   It is not by wearing down into uniformity all that is individual in themselves, but by cultivating it, and calling it forth, within the limits imposed by the rights and interests of others, that human beings become a noble and beautiful object of contemplation; and as the works partake the character of those who do them, by the same process human life also becomes rich, diversified, and animating, furnishing more abundant aliment to high thoughts and elevating feelings, and strengthening the tie which binds every individual to the race, by making the race infinitely better worth belonging to. In proportion to the development of his individuality, each person becomes more valuable to himself, and is therefore capable of being more valuable to others. There is a greater fulness of life about his own existence, and when there is more life in the units there is more in the mass which is composed of them. As much compression as is necessary to prevent the stronger specimens of human nature from encroaching on the rights of others cannot be dispensed with; but for this there is ample compensation even in the point of view of human development. The means of development which the individual loses by being prevented from gratifying his inclinations to the injury of others, are chiefly obtained at the expense of the development of other people. And even to himself there is a full equivalent in the better development of the social part of his nature, rendered possible by the restraint put upon the selfish part. To be held to rigid rules of justice for the sake of others, develops the feelings and capacities which have the good of others for their object. But to be restrained in things not affecting their good, by their mere displeasure, develops nothing valuable, except such force of character as may unfold itself in resisting the restraint. If acquiesced in, it dulls and blunts the whole nature. To give any fair play to the nature of each, it is essential that different persons should be allowed to lead different lives. In proportion as this latitude has been exercised in any age, has that age been noteworthy to posterity. Even despotism does not produce its worst effects, so long as individuality exists under it; and whatever crushes individuality is despotism, by whatever name it may be called, and whether it professes to be enforcing the will of God or the injunctions of men.

3   Having said that the individuality is the same thing with development, and that it is only the cultivation of individuality which produces, or can produce, well-developed human beings, I might here close the argument: for what more or better can be said of any condition of human affairs than that it brings human beings themselves nearer to the best thing they can be? Or what worse can be said of any obstruction to good than that it prevents this? Doubtless, how-

ever, these considerations will not suffice to convince those who most
need convincing; and it is necessary further to show, that these developed human beings are of some use to the undeveloped—to point
out to those who do not desire liberty, and would not avail themselves
of it, that they may be in some intelligible manner rewarded for
allowing other people to make use of it without hindrance.

4   In the first place, then, I would suggest that they might possibly learn something from them. It will not be denied by anybody,
that originality is a valuable element in human affairs. There is always
need of persons not only to discover new truths, and point out when
what were once truths are true no longer, but also to commence
new practices, and set the example of more enlightened conduct,
and better taste and sense in human life. This cannot well be gainsaid
by anybody who does not believe that the world has already attained
perfection in all its ways and practices. It is true that this benefit
is not capable of being rendered by everybody alike: there are but
few persons, in comparison with the whole of mankind, whose experiments, if adopted by others, would be likely to be any improvement
on established practice. But these few are the salt of the earth; without
them, human life would become a stagnant pool. Not only is it they
who introduce good things which did not before exist; it is they
who keep the life in those which already exist. If there were nothing
new to be done, would human intellect cease to be necessary? Would
it be a reason why those who do the old things should forget why
they are done, and do them like cattle, not like human beings? There
is only too great a tendency in the best beliefs and practices to degenerate into the mechanical; and unless there were a succession of persons whose ever-recurring originality prevents the grounds of those
beliefs and practices from becoming merely traditional, such dead
matter would not resist the smallest shock from anything really alive,
and there would be no reason why civilisation should not die out,
as in the Byzantine Empire. Persons of genius, it is true, are, and
are always likely to be, a small minority; but in order to have them,
it is necessary to preserve the soil in which they grow. Genius can
only breathe freely in an *atmosphere* of freedom. Persons of genius
are, *ex vi termini*, more individual than any other people—less capable, consequently, of fitting themselves, without hurtful compression,
into any of the small number of moulds which society provides in
order to save its members the trouble of forming their own character.
If from timidity they consent to be forced into one of these moulds,
and to let all that part of themselves which cannot expand under
the pressure remain unexpanded, society will be little the better for
their genius. If they are of a strong character, and break their fetters,

they become a mark for the society which has not succeeded in reducing them to commonplace, to point out with solemn warning as "wild," "erratic," and the like; much as if one should complain of the Niagara River for not flowing smoothly between its banks like a Dutch canal.

5   I insist thus emphatically on the importance of genius, and the necessity of allowing it to unfold itself freely both in thought and in practice, being well aware that no one will deny the position in theory, but knowing also that almost every one, in reality, is totally indifferent to it. People think genius a fine thing if it enables a man to write an exciting poem, or paint a picture. But in its true sense, that of originality in thought and action, though no one says that it is not a thing to be admired, nearly all, at heart, think that they can do very well without it. Unhappily this is too natural to be wondered at. Originality is the one thing which unoriginal minds cannot feel the use of. They cannot see what it is to do for them: how should they? If they could see what it would do for them, it would not be originality. The first service which originality has to render them, is that of opening their eyes: which being once fully done, they would have a chance of being themselves original. Meanwhile, recollecting that nothing was ever yet done which some one was not the first to do, and that all good things which exist are the fruits of originality, let them be modest enough to believe that there is something still left for it to accomplish, and assure themselves that they are more in need of originality, the less they are conscious of the want.

STUDY QUESTIONS

Organization and Content

1. In what sentences of paragraph 1 is the topic expressed?
2. What is the significance of the question in the middle of paragraph 1?
3. In the latter part of paragraph 1 Mill makes reference to machinery and a tree. How do these references help his argument?
4. Does paragraph 2 have a topic sentence?
5. What are the key words of paragraph 2?
6. In sentence 4 of paragraph 2 Mill seems to agree to some restrictions upon liberty. How can he justify such restrictions?
7. In his opinion what restrictions cannot be permitted?
8. What is the purpose of paragraph 3?
9. What issue is Mill trying to prove in paragraph 4?
10. According to Mill in paragraph 4, the loss of liberty would produce what bad effects?

11. In sentence 6 of paragraph 4 Mill uses metaphors of salt and of a pool. Explain them.
12. How does the point of paragraph 5 differ from that of paragraph 4?
13. Complete this statement: According to Mill everybody should grant freedom to other people because —————.

Sentence Structure

1. How is sentence 2 of paragraph 1 arranged so as to emphasize a contrast with sentence 1?
2. In sentence 3 a number of qualities and activities are listed. What grammatical relationship governs the list, and what determines the order of the list?
3. Sentence 9 is an interesting one. The infinitive *to get* has six objects (why is it effective to list so many separate things?), and the introductory dependent clause ends with the phrase *by machinery;* then, after the appositive set off by dashes comes the main clause. In the main clause what terms contrast with *machinery?* Why is it effective to end the dependent clause with *machinery?* Why is it skillful for Mill to place the phrase *for these automatons* directly after *to exchange?* Why does Mill wish to end his sentence with the two *who*-clauses modifying *men* and *women?* What important contrast is brought out by these parallel *who*-clauses? How many words does sentence 9 contain? Mill's arrangement of these words is a brilliant example of sentence management.
4. Show how sentence 10 uses the principle of contrast; of emphasis.
5. Explain the problems involved in the management of sentence 1 of paragraph 2.
6. Show how the two interrogative sentences of paragraph 3 involve parallelism and contrast.
7. What is the significance of these two questions in relation to Mill's assumptions in his argument?
8. Explain the effectiveness of the several infinitives in sentence 3 of paragraph 4.
9. Many of Mill's sentences are quite long. What is the effect of the several shorter sentences in paragraph 5?

Diction

1. Look up *discrimination, animating, aliment, encroaching, acquiesce, latitude, despotism, professes, injunction, obstruction, gainsaid.*
2. To what extent do the following terms of Mill's arouse feelings in the reader—and what feelings: *ape-like, salt of the earth, stagnant pool, like cattle, dead matter, Niagara River, Dutch canal?*
3. How does Mill's discussion gain from the connotations of such terms as *machine, automaton, tree, living thing?*
4. Note some of Mill's metaphors, such as *cultivating, dulls and blunts* (paragraph 2), *preserve the soil, moulds, fetters* (paragraph 4), and try replacing them with nonmetaphorical terms. What is the effect? Gain? Loss?
5. *Ex vi termini* means "by force of the term."

6. Compare Mill's style with that of Madison. Which is the more formal, the more lively, the more serious, the more dignified, the more emotional, the more intellectual, the more realistic, the more concrete, the more complex, the more demanding?

Assignment

Just as some people do not really wish to give to others the liberty that will allow them to develop in their individual ways, so some people criticize and grumble about certain institutions and concepts. Write an argument similar to Mill's to defend one of these institutions or concepts against those who "think that they can do very well without it." One might write on the value of:

1. Tradition
2. Higher education
3. The family
4. Religion

5. The sovereignty of the federal government
6. A system of taxation for society
7. Beauty

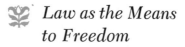 *Law as the Means to Freedom*

A. DELAFIELD SMITH

1   We need to see what the true meaning and function of law is, not in terms of authority, which is so commonly mistaken for law, but in terms of the rule of law in the ideal sense as a guide and challenge to the human will.

2   The best example of how law, in the ideal sense, works, how it evokes the sense of freedom and stimulates the individual is the survey of a game. Have you ever asked yourself why the participation in a game is so excellent a medium for self-expression and character development? This question is often superficially answered in terms of the rein given to the competitive instincts of the individual and his "zest" for conquest. But have you ever considered that here, in a game, and perhaps here alone, we human beings really do act almost completely under the aegis of law? That, rather than competition, is the real source of the game's restorative value for the human

From *The Right to Life* by A. Delafield Smith (Chapel Hill, N.C.: The University of North Carolina Press, 1955).

spirit. Analyze the process step by step and you must be convinced that this is the truth.

3   Your first step upon entering a game is the assumption of a distinct personality. You become clothed in a personality defined by the rules of the game. You assume a legal or game personality. You may describe yourself as a first baseman, as a right guard, or as a dealer. But however you describe yourself you will see that what you have described is a legal status—one of the focal points in a legal pattern with rights and obligations suitable to the position. These rights and duties are defined by the rules under whose empery you have thus put both yourself and all others with whom you have dealings. Your status, your rights, your obligations, all are secure, for the rules of the game are almost sure to be followed. The game indeed is defined by its rules. These are purely abstract. They are wholly free of will and dictation. They are pure rules of action composed usually in some physical setting which they serve to interpret and fashion till it becomes an arena of human action, just as, for example, the rules of the highway, in relation to the highway pattern itself, provide individuals with an arena on which they can operate successfully. Now the rules of the game have many functions. They, in fact, define the very goals that the players seek. One wins only in the context of the rules of the game. They determine inexorably the consequences of the player's action, every play that he makes. He acts solely in relation to the rules. Their empery is accepted like a fact or a circumstance. Finally, they challenge and stimulate him for he uses the rules to win. The game is otherwise unmanaged. An umpire or a referee is but an interpreter of the rules. He *can* be wrong. Such is the conception. This, then, may furnish an introduction to the real function of law in society.

4   Law gave birth to the concept of freedom. True it is that you can have no security in a situation in which every person and everything around you acts capriciously, unpredictably, or, in other words, lawlessly; but the point I wish to make is that while you would have no security in such an environment, it is more significant that you would have no freedom in such an environment. The reason you could not be free in such a situation is that you could not get anywhere you wanted to go or successfully do anything you wanted to do. You could make no plan in the expectation of carrying it out. You cannot possibly carry out any aim or goal of your own unless you have some basis for calculating what results may follow from any given act or activity of your own. Unless you can determine in advance what are the prospects and limitations of a given course of behavior, you cannot act intelligently. Whatever intelligence you

may have will do you no good. You cannot adjust your own step to anyone else's step nor can you relate your conduct to any series of events or occurrences outside yourself except to the extent that they follow a pattern that you can learn about in advance of your action.

5   The only way to promote freedom is to devise a set of rules and thus construct a pattern which the various members of that society can follow. Each can then determine his own acts in the light of his knowledge of the rules. On this basis each can predict his field of action in advance and what results are likely to ensue from his acts; and so he gains freedom to plan and to carry out his plans. The more you attempt to administer society, however, the less free it becomes. There is opportunity for freedom of choice only in acting subject to the rules, and then only if the rules are freed of any element of will or dictation. If these rules are just rules that tell you what method or act will yield what results, like the rules of a game, you can then freely determine your own play. You can use the rules to win the game. The more abstract and objective the rule, the freer is the individual in the choice of his alternatives. The rules must be so written as to cover every possible eventuality of choice and action.

STUDY QUESTIONS

Organization and Content

1. The assignment which Smith gave himself may look quite difficult: to convince people, most of whom have probably thought of law in terms of restriction, that law is the means to freedom; many people would think this a paradoxical idea. Smith approaches this challenging assignment by means of an analogy. In which sentence does he announce that he is going to make use of the analogy?
2. Paragraph 1 has what function?
3. In order to "clear the ground," what false idea does the author try to eliminate in paragraph 2?
4. What is he ready to do in paragraph 3?
5. Paragraph 3 has more than 20 sentences. To what are they devoted?
6. Which sentence is the topic sentence of paragraph 3? Why does the author mention the "rules of the highway"?
7. Explain the analogy used by Smith. Does his analogy hold? Are there important likenesses between the analogy and the situation he is discussing? Are there any significant differences?
8. How important is this analogy to his argument?
9. What idea essential to the argument is brought out in paragraph 4?
10. Does paragraph 4 have any connection with the analogy?

11. Is the first sentence of paragraph 5 a conclusion drawn from the preceding discussion, or is it simply an assertion of the proposition that the author is trying to prove?
12. On what evidence is he justified in saying, "The more abstract and objective the rule, the freer is the individual in the choice of his alternatives"?
13. He also says in paragraph 5, "The more you attempt to administer society, . . . the less free it becomes." Is this idea brought out in, or covered by, the analogy?
14. Contrast Smith's argument with Madison's in regard to methods used.

Sentence Structure

1. Many of the sentences of this selection are addressed to "you." Why? What is the effect of thus addressing the reader? Is there any advantage for the author in doing so?
2. Indicate how repetition of certain terms supplies transition in paragraphs 3 and 4.
3. Compare Smith's sentence style with that of John Stuart Mill. Which is the more formal, the more lively, the more dignified, the more concrete, the more emotional, the more complex, the more demanding?

Diction

1. Look up *aegis, assumption, empery, abstract, arena, context, inexorably, administer, objective, eventuality.*
2. Both Smith and James Madison were trained as lawyers. Compare their arguments to answer the question: To what extent has their legal training influenced their choice of diction?

Assignment

Write an argument in which you, like Smith, use an analogy. Some suggestions are:

1. Education should be carefully controlled; teachers should know exactly what operation to perform day by day (for educating a person is like turning out a product in a factory).
2. Education is best when students have much freedom (for education is like the growth of a tree; all the tree needs is a chance at things that are good for it, without unnecessary obstacles).
3. Students should have (or not have) freedom in choosing courses (for a college is like a great city with a wealth of things and experiences at the disposal of the inhabitants).
4. Students should have freedom in choosing courses (for studying some subject that one dislikes is like climbing a mountain).
5. It is good (or not good) to make oneself into a sophisticated person (for doing so is like baking and decorating a cake, or trimming a Christmas tree).
6. We should encourage more discipline in every phase of our society (for in Japanese flower-arranging, effects of grace and simplicity are obtained by disciplined training; or, as Alexander Pope wrote:

> True ease in writing comes from art, not chance,
> As those move easiest who have learned to dance).

7. No politician can be a completely good man; a politician should be prepared to have to make compromises and even to do some things that he knows are not good, in order to be able to accomplish the good things that he regards as most important (for a basketball player though committing many fouls may make enough goals to insure that his team will win).

Religion Is Important for Man's Survival Now

LEWIS MUMFORD

1   Not the least important force we must mobilize, in the interests of survival, is an ancient one: that of religion. Both Benjamin Kidd a generation ago, and Henri Bergson in our own time, interpreted religion as a self-preservative effort, on the part of life, to guard man against the discouraging effects of his own achievements in knowledge. There is a profound truth in these interpretations. Though most of the classic religions have dwelled on the familiar facts of man's limitations and frustrations, centered in the ultimate mystery of death, they have all guarded life itself, as zealously as the vestals guarded fire. Hinduism, Confucianism, Buddhism, Judaism, Christianity, even Mohammedanism, have sought to curb man's impulses to destruction and disintegration: each of them interdicts random killing, each of them encourages procreation, each of them has sought to foster love.

2   In this moment of common peril, we should do well to overlook the hypocrisies and failures of the orthodox: their very superstitions have nevertheless kept the ignorant, the willful, and the destructive under some limited sense of order and some minimum system of control. If the symbols of religion do not always stand up under rational examination, if their myths are more mysterious than the mysteries they would explain, that is not necessarily a proof of their inability to penetrate and control the irrational elements in man. Re-

ligion's function, in fact, is to redress man's pride in his intellect, to reduce his conceit and his complacence, so that he will be better fortified to face the ordeal of reality. Mankind is a-float on a frail life-raft. Religion understands the monsters of the deep and the storms that come up in the night.

3   Religion reminds man of his creatureliness and his creativeness, his impotence and his power, his cosmic littleness and his cosmic preciousness—for the tiny spark of consciousness man carries in his soul may be, up to now, the final event toward which the so-called physical universe has moved. Religion's cosmic time sense, achieved long before astronomy sustained the intuition with exact calculations, is a brake against the possibility that man might sacrifice his own long future to some temporary gratification or some temporary triumph. Here is a latent power for man's self-preservation: on the whole, theologians have made a more prompt response to the atomic bomb than any other group except the atomic physicists themselves, though they have still to show the capacity for unified effort that will make a wider renewal possible.

4   Morality is Sancho Panza to religion's Don Quixote; for morality develops out of the customs of the tribe and those customs, too, are usually life-preservative ones, though they may clash with those of other tribes. Modern man, proud of his fearless investigation of every part of the universe, conscious of his increasing powers to control his circumstances, has shown something less than forbearance to those primitive cultures whose daily acts are limited by taboos. But in throwing off the irrational object of most taboos, modern man has also forfeited the very habit of inhibition that the taboo imposed. He has thus forgotten one of the most essential secrets of man's advance: the practice of restraint. Whereas the older midbrain is the seat of man's instinctual energies and his explosive emotions, the newer forebrain, which takes care of his higher behavior, is also the seat of his inhibitions. Without the development of these inhibitions man's untempered curiosity might, long before this, have proved suicidal.

5   In little matters, modern man acknowledges taboos: he does not spit in a subway car, blow his nose in public without using a handkerchief, or enter a house with a quarantine notice posted on its door. But in general, his plan of life has resulted, not in exchanging taboos for rational restraints, but in exchanging taboos for equally irrational habits of relaxation. For the last two hundred years a long succession of thinkers, from Diderot and Rousseau onward, have urged man to throw off his ancient taboos: to act on his impulses, yield to his desires, abandon measure in his gratification. If man

were wholly rational and wholly good, these counsels would perhaps
have been profitable: but Dostoyevsky, who understood the demonic
in man, pointed out long ago the dangers of this moral nihilism;
and in our day those dangers have assumed cosmic dimensions.

6   Morality, in the elementary form of accepted inhibitions, is the
first step toward the conscious control of the powers man now commands: without this lowest form of morality, engrained in habit, no
higher form can be practiced. What Irving Babbitt called the inner
check—the vital restraint—is essential to our survival. Promptly we
must reverse Blake's dictum—we must bless braces and damn relaxes.

7   This moral tightening of the bit comes very hard to modern
man; for it is no exaggeration to say that he has attempted in the
past generation to live by the pleasure principle: he has tried to
establish a regime of limitless gratifications without accepting depriva-
tions or penalties. The very quantification of life through machine
production has lifted many natural limits that once prevailed. So
self-indulgent have we become that even a temporary shortage of
cigarettes in America evoked a response far more irrational in character than any religious taboo on smoking would be: in the midst of
a biting blizzard, crowds waited in line for a whole hour in order
to purchase their quota of cigarettes. The indecent haste with which
the American Government threw off the rationing of foods after the
Japanese surrender, at a time when the rest of the war-battered world
was close to starvation, is an indication of a popular unwillingness
to exercise self-control: an unwillingness most prevalent in the very
circles that exercise most political influence.

8   Morally, such people are as unfit for the control of atomic power
as a chronic alcoholic would be for the inheritance of a vast stock
of whiskey. Those who have lost respect for taboos of any kind are
most in need of their self-preservative principle.

9   Now, experience demands that we should recognize the place
of negative stimuli in human development. Pains, abstentions, renun-
ciations, inhibitions, are perhaps as essential for human development
as more positive nurture. During the war, fighting men learned this
lesson; it gave them power to confront danger and surmount it; and
where civilians were placed under the same stresses, as in cities that
endured aerial bombardment, they learned the same hard lesson. The
imaginative widening of this experience among people who are still
unchastened is an essential measure. To recover the very habit of
restraint, to subject every act to measure, to place limits even on
goods that may be offered in limitless quantities—this is the communal response we must make to the challenge of both physical and
moral disintegration. The very processes of democracy, which it is

so essential to extend to world organization, demand a high degree of conscious moderation. That is possibly why the most restrained of peoples, the English, are also the best exemplars of democratic processes. Every civilian must master, as the price of society's survival, the lesson that military organization teaches the soldier: group survival requires the acceptance of sacrifice.

STUDY QUESTIONS

Organization and Content

1. What constructive aspect of religion is emphasized in paragraph 1?
2. Does paragraph 2 indicate that Mumford approves of religious superstitions?
3. According to paragraphs 1 and 2, what is the relation between religion and intellect and knowledge?
4. Sentence 1 of paragraph 3 stresses certain contrasts. What do these contrasts and "religion's cosmic time sense" have to do with man's survival?
5. Interpret the metaphor involving the idealistic knight Don Quixote and his fat, earthy squire Sancho Panza. According to paragraph 4, how has science tended to weaken morality?
6. Are the acknowledged "taboos" mentioned in paragraph 5 really rational restraints? If they are, does this fact affect Mumford's argument in any way?
7. Why does Mumford believe that the counsels of such men as Diderot, Rousseau, and William Blake have not been profitable?
8. Does Mumford exaggerate when he asserts that the dangers of moral nihilism have now assumed *cosmic* dimensions?
9. Paragraph 6 emphasizes the "lowest form of morality"; of what value is it in the argument?
10. What difficulties are represented by machine production and the pleasure principle?
11. Why is paragraph 8 so short? What issue in the argument does this paragraph deal with?
12. In paragraph 9 in what way are "people who are still unchastened" to be paralleled with fighting men and civilians?
13. What do the English people exemplify in this paragraph?
14. State Mumford's argument so as to bring out the logical connections among the points.
15. List the issues of his argument.

Sentence Structure

1. In every paragraph except paragraph 8 there is at least one sentence with a colon; paragraph 7 has three such sentences. For what purpose are the colons used?

2. Does this regular use of the colon constitute a mannerism of style in Mumford's work?
3. In terms of structure what does sentence 5 of paragraph 1 have in common with sentence 1 of paragraph 2?
4. Does Mumford repeat ideas (using parallel grammatical elements) more than is necessary? (Consider sentences 2 and 3 of paragraph 2, sentence 1 of paragraph 3, sentences 2 and 5 of paragraph 9.)
5. To what extent does Mumford interrupt his sentences to place parenthetical material in the middle—as in sentence 2 of paragraph 1, sentence 2 of paragraph 3, sentence 2 of paragraph 4?
6. Which sentences in paragraphs 1, 2, and 4 are shortest? What is the effect of these short sentences?
7. Classify the sentences of each paragraph according to whether they begin with subjects or with dependent material. Are there too many sentences of either kind in any paragraph?
8. Does Mumford write with sufficient variety of sentence structure, or not?

Diction

1. Look up *mobilize, vestals, interdict, hypocrisy, irrational, impotence, cosmic, intuition, latent, theologians, morality, inhibition, measure, nihilism, quantification, unchastened.*
2. From what languages do these words come?
3. Do some research on the men to whom Mumford alludes.
4. Note the connotations of certain terms: "frail life-raft," "monsters of the deep," in paragraph 2, "tightening of the bit" in paragraph 7. What do these metaphors accomplish in the argument?
5. Is Mumford's vocabulary prevailingly abstract or concrete?
6. How are *creatureliness* and *creativeness* related in their origin? How do they contrast in their meanings?

Assignment

You may wish to take issue with Mumford; there are various questions which might be raised and which might be developed into counterarguments—for example:

1. Is it not true that human beings are wicked and that every man has his price? Therefore, such efforts as Mumford advises are doomed to failure.
2. Considering the worldliness of modern religion—how women dress up for church and how much emphasis is put on recreation in church activities—is it true that religion has retained its alleged powers for good?
3. Considering the great emphasis on money raising in churches, is it not true that modern religion has become too commercialized to be an effective curb upon man's desires and powers?
4. Would it be honest to favor religion only for a special benefit it may provide, meanwhile overlooking "the hypocrisies and failures of the orthodox"?
5. Mumford mentions several different religions in paragraph 1. If you

have special knowledge of some of these, you might argue that one of them has a greater power than the others for Mumford's purposes.
6. If you are less willing than Mumford to ignore the rational inadequacy of religious symbols, you might argue that the study of the classics and of philosophy has equal value with religion for developing moderation and control of instinctual impulses.

Report of the Commission on the Humanities

BARNABY C. KEENEY AND OTHERS

STATEMENT AND RECOMMENDATION

"The Commission on the Humanities recommends the establishment by the President and the Congress of the United States of a National Humanities Foundation. . . ."

I.

1 The humanities are the study of that which is most human. Throughout man's conscious past they have played an essential role in forming, preserving, and transforming the social, moral, and aesthetic values of every man in every age. One cannot speak of history or culture apart from the humanities. They not only record our lives; our lives are the very substance they are made of. Their subject is every man. We propose, therefore, a program for all our people, a program to meet a need no less serious than that for national defense. We speak, in truth, for what is being defended—our beliefs, our ideals, our highest achievements.

2 The humanities may be regarded as a body of knowledge and insight, as modes of expression, as a program for education, as an underlying attitude toward life. The body of knowledge is usually taken to include the study of history, literature, the arts, religion, and philosophy. The fine and the performing arts are modes of expressing thoughts and feelings visually, verbally, and aurally. The

From Barnaby C. Keeney and Others, *Report of the Commission on the Humanities.* Reprinted with permission of the sponsors, the American Council of Learned Societies, the Council of Graduate Schools in the United States, and the United Chapters of Phi Beta Kappa.

method of education is one based on the liberal tradition we inherit from classical antiquity. The attitude toward life centers on concern for the human individual: for his emotional development, for his moral, religious, and aesthetic ideas, and for his goals—including in particular his growth as a rational being and a responsible member of his community.

3   This Commission conceives of the humanities, not merely as academic disciplines confined to schools and colleges, but as functioning components of society which affect the lives and well-being of all the population. It regards the arts, both visual and performing, as part of the humanities and indeed essential to their existence. The arts differ in important ways from the conventional academic disciplines, but the Commission is confident that in any practical matter affecting the two these differences will readily be recognized and appropriate means devised for supporting each. The Commission further considers that science, as a technique and expression of intellect, is in fact closely affiliated with the humanities. Whatever scientists may learn concerning the physical world is or should be of profound interest to the humanist, just as the findings of behavioral scientists—whether they issue in social theories and inspire social action or merely make humans understandable—fall within the humanist's purview. The natural sciences, the social sciences, and the humanities are of their nature allies.

4   The Commission warmly supports the statement relating science to other intellectual activity in the report of the President's Advisory Committee of November 15, 1960 (page 3):

> . . . While this report centers on the needs of science, we repudiate emphatically any notion that science research and scientific education are the only kinds of learning that matter to America. The responsibility of this Committee is limited to scientific matters, but obviously a high civilization must not limit its efforts to science alone. Even in the interests of science itself it is essential to give full value and support to the other great branches of man's artistic, literary, and scholarly activity. The advancement of science must not be accomplished by the impoverishment of anything else, and the life of the mind in our society has needs which are not limited by the particular concerns which belong to this Committee and this report.

5   Science is far more than a tool for adding to our security and comfort. It embraces in its broadest sense all efforts to achieve valid and coherent views of reality; as such, it extends the boundaries of experience and adds new dimensions to human character. If the interdependence of science and the humanities were more generally under-

stood, men would be more likely to become masters of their technology and not its unthinking servants.

6   Even the most gifted individual, whether poet or physicist, will not realize his full potential or make his fullest contribution to his times unless his imagination has been kindled by the aspirations and accomplishments of those who have gone before him. Humanist scholars have therefore a special responsibility in that the past is their natural domain. They have the privilege and obligation of interpreting the past to each new generation of men who "necessarily must live in one small corner for one little stretch of time." They preserve and judge the fruits of humanity's previous attempts to depict, to rationalize, and to transcend the world it inhabits. The arts and letters, and the study of them, are therefore where we look most directly for enrichment of the individual's experience and his capacity for responding to it. Through the humanities we may seek intellectual humility, sensitivity to beauty, and emotional discipline. By them we may come to know the excitement of ideas, the power of imagination, and the unsuspected energies of the creative spirit.

7   Over the centuries the humanities have sustained mankind at the deepest level of being. They prospered in Greece and Rome, in the Middle Ages, in the Renaissance, and in the Enlightenment. Architecture, sculpture, poetry, and music flourished, and with the growth of colleges and universities the liberal arts took shape as a body of cumulative knowledge and wisdom. In the formative years of our own country it was a group of statesmen steeped in the humanities who fused their own experience with that of the past to create the enduring Constitution of the Republic.

8   During our early history we were largely occupied in mastering the physical environment. No sooner was this mastery within sight than advancing technology opened up a new range of possibilities, putting a new claim on energies which might otherwise have gone into humane and artistic endeavors. The result has often been that our social, moral, and aesthetic development lagged behind our material advance. Yet we have every reason to be proud of our artists and scholars, and new techniques have frequently served to make their work more widely available; but this is not enough. Now more than ever, with the rapid growth of knowledge and its transformation of society's material base, the humanities must command men of talent, intellect, and spirit.

9   The state of the humanities today creates a crisis for national leadership. While it offers cultural opportunities of the greatest value to the United States and to mankind, it holds at the same time a danger that wavering purpose and lack of well-conceived effort may

leave us second-best in a world correspondingly impoverished by our incomplete success. The challenge is no less critical and direct than the one we have already met with our strong advocacy of healthy and generously supported science. It must be met in turn with equal vision and resolve.

II. America's Need
of the Humanities

10   Many of the problems which confront the people of the United States necessarily involve the humanities. They are of nationwide scope and interest. Each is of concern to every citizen, and the way in which each is solved will be of consequence to him. Among them are the following:

11   1. All men require that a vision be held before them, an ideal toward which they may strive. Americans need such a vision today as never before in their history. It is both the dignity and the duty of humanists to offer their fellow-countrymen whatever understanding can be attained by fallible humanity of such enduring values as justice, freedom, virtue, beauty, and truth. Only thus do we join ourselves to the heritage of our nation and our human kind.

12   2. Democracy demands wisdom of the average man. Without the exercise of wisdom free institutions and personal liberty are inevitably imperilled. To know the best that has been thought and said in former times can make us wiser than we otherwise might be, and in this respect the humanities are not merely our, but the world's best hope.

13   3. The United States is not a nation of materialists, but many men believe it to be. They find it hard to fathom the motives of a country which will spend billions on its outward defense and at the same time do little to maintain the creative and imaginative abilities of its own people. The arts have an unparalleled capability for crossing the national barriers imposed by language and contrasting customs. The recently increased American encouragement of the performing arts is to be welcomed, and will be welcomed everywhere as a sign that Americans accept their cultural responsibilities, especially if it serves to prompt a corresponding increase in support for the visual and the liberal arts. It is by way of the humanities that we best come to understand cultures other than our own, and they best to understand ours.

14   4. World leadership of the kind which has come upon the United States cannot rest solely upon superior force, vast wealth, or preponderant technology. Only the elevation of its goals and the

excellence of its conduct entitle one nation to ask others to follow its lead. These are things of the spirit. If we appear to discourage creativity, to demean the fanciful and the beautiful, to have no concern for man's ultimate destiny—if, in short, we ignore the humanities —then both our goals and our efforts to attain them will be measured with suspicion.

15   5. A novel and serious challenge to Americans is posed by the remarkable increase in their leisure time. The forty-hour week and the likelihood of a shorter one, the greater life-expectancy and the earlier ages of retirement, have combined to make the blessing of leisure a source of personal and community concern. "What shall I do with my spare time" all-too-quickly becomes the question "Who am I? What shall I make of my life?" When men and women find nothing within themselves but emptiness they turn to trivial and narcotic amusements, and the society of which they are a part becomes socially delinquent and potentially unstable. The humanities are the immemorial answer to man's questioning and to his need for self-expression; they are uniquely equipped to fill the "abyss of leisure."

III. Problems
of Academic Humanists

16   The American practitioners of the humanities—the professionals, so to speak—are now prevented in certain specific ways from realizing their full capacities and from attracting enough first-rate individuals into their ranks.

17   There is genuine doubt today whether the universities and colleges can insure that the purposes for which they were established and sometimes endowed will be fulfilled. The laudable practice of the federal government of making large sums of money available for scientific research has brought great benefits, but it has also brought about an imbalance within academic institutions by the very fact of abundance in one field of study and dearth in another. Much of the federal money for science requires a proportionate commitment of general university funds to sustain the higher level of activity in the scientific departments. Students, moreover, are no different from other people in that they can quickly observe where money is being made available and draw the logical conclusion as to which activities their society considers important. The nation's need for balanced education demands that this imbalance be remedied.

18   In public and private schools important steps have been taken to improve teaching methods in the sciences, in mathematics, and in languages. Similar steps have not been taken in the humane studies,

so that a student may often enter a college or university without adequate training in the humanities or, for that matter, a rudimentary acquaintance with them. Sound education requires that the schools open equally inviting doors into all fields of instruction, so that students may discover where their undeveloped talents lie. Today, moreover, young humanists need to be scientifically literate just as young scientists need to be aware of the world outside their specialty. Only a fully educated people will be capable of sound judgment in government, in business, or in their daily lives.

IV. The Humanities and the National Interest

19   These are our arguments for greater support and stronger development of the humanities. Societies traditionally support those things which their people regard as useful, and governments support those things which are thought to be in the national interest. The question arises: Is it then in the interest of the United States and of its federal government to give greater support to the humanities?

20   During our national life the activities of society as a whole and of government in particular have been greatly extended. Health was once considered a private problem; it is now a national one. The newer forms of transportation are heavily subsidized and, to some extent, controlled by the federal government. In World War II the federal government undertook an active role in technology and since then, as we have seen, it has greatly extended its activities in the fields of science. Education was once entirely the concern of private foundations or local government, but it has long since ceased to be so.

21   Traditionally our government has entered areas where there were overt difficulties or where an opportunity had opened for exceptional achievement. The humanities fit both categories, for the potential achievements are enormous while the troubles stemming from inadequate support are comparably great. The problems are of nationwide scope and interest. Upon the humanities depend the national ethic and morality, the national aesthetic and beauty or the lack of it, the national use of our environment and our material accomplishments—each of these areas directly affects each of us as individuals. On our knowledge of men, their past and their present, depends our ability to make judgments—not least those involving our control of nature, of ourselves, and of our destiny. Is it not in the national interest that these judgments be strong and good?

22   The stakes are so high and the issues of such magnitude that

the humanities must have substantial help both from the federal government and from other sources. It is for these reasons that the Commission recommends the establishment of a National Humanities Foundation to parallel the National Science Foundation, which is so successfully carrying out the public responsibilities entrusted to it.

STUDY QUESTIONS

Organization and Content

1. Section I of this argument has no title. Suggest a suitable title for it.
2. Where does definition play a part in Section I?
3. Note how paragraph 1 is balanced: sentences 1 and 2 balanced by 6 and 7, with sentences 3, 4, and 5 in the center. By what steps does the reader pass successively from sentence to sentence?
4. Sentence 1, paragraph 2, cites four ways of regarding the humanities. How are the four ways developed in the rest of the paragraph?
5. What is the relation of the humanities to the fine arts and the sciences?
6. What attitude does the Commission take toward science? In what ways is science important, and what limitations does it have?
7. What sort of enrichment do we get from the past?
8. How is paragraph 7 organized? How does it lead into paragraph 8?
9. How do paragraphs 8 and 9 attempt to justify support for the humanities?
10. Just what is the crisis mentioned in paragraph 9?
11. What is the function of paragraph 10?
12. What things are enumerated in paragraphs 11–15?
13. How do the first and last sentences of each paragraph in paragraphs 11–15 function?
14. What sort of "vision" is meant in paragraph 11?
15. In what way does Section III attempt to justify support for the humanities?
16. How does the discussion in Section III relate the situation of the humanities to recent assistance given to science and other studies?
17. Paragraph 19 states: "These are our arguments. . . ." Taking these arguments, or issues, to be those presented in paragraphs 6–9 and 11–18, which of them have the greatest importance?
18. Paragraph 19 is a transitional paragraph that looks back and then ahead. What is the function of sentence 3?
19. What specific question are paragraphs 19–21 intended to answer? In other words, if a member of Congress said, "I agree with paragraphs 1–18, but _____" what possible objection of his are paragraphs 20–21 trying to remove?
20. What analogies are used in paragraph 20?
21. How do sentences 4 and 5 support sentence 3, paragraph 21?

22. What examples can you suggest to illustrate *ethic, aesthetic,* and *use of environment* in paragraph 21?
23. What gives particular importance to paragraph 21? Why does it close with a question? What is the answer to the question?
24. What is the function of paragraph 22?
25. State the propositions of this argument and the issues on which the argument is centered.

Sentence Structure

1. Indicate how the groups of three items are handled in sentences 2 and 7, paragraph 1; sentences 6 and 7, paragraph 6.
2. On what principles of balance and emphasis is sentence 4, paragraph 1, constructed?
3. In what way is the last main element of sentences 6 and 7 related to the other parts of these sentences?
4. How is parallel structure employed in sentences 1, 2, and 5, paragraph 2? (Note especially the complicated pattern of sentence 5.)
5. Sentence 5, paragraph 3, has an approximate balance; show how it is organized.
6. Note the position, and explain the function, of *therefore* in sentences 2 and 5, paragraph 6.
7. Explain the varying lengths and rhythms of the four sentences of paragraph 14, and show their effect.
8. Explain the balance of parts in sentence 2, paragraph 19.
9. Explain the varied sentence constructions in which the four examples of paragraph 20 are presented.
10. Indicate the inverted sentence order and the role of parallel structure in the eloquent sentences 4 and 5, paragraph 21.

Diction

1. Look up the following words (numerals represent paragraphs): *disciplines, components, behavioral scientists, purview* (3); *repudiate* (4); *technology* (5); *potential* (noun), *transcend* (6); *humane* (8); *materialists, fathom* (13); *demean* (14); *narcotic* (adjective) (15); *ethic* (21).
2. Is the vocabulary of this report more abstract or less abstract than Mumford's?

Assignment

1. Develop an argument to prove that the "aspirations and accomplishments" of our forerunners can take us out of the "one small corner" in which we briefly live.
2. Develop an argument that music, art, and poetry can provide an "emotional discipline" for us.
3. Support the statement in paragraph 8 "that our social, moral, and aesthetic development lagged behind our material advance" with an argument contrasting material abundance, roads, machines, laboratories, and factories with the appearance of towns and cities and the chief activities of their citizens.

4. Argue in favor of the idea that Americans need "a vision today as never before in their history."
5. Argue that in a democracy the average man needs wisdom more than he does in countries with other forms of government.
6. Develop an argument in support of the idea that the United States "is not a nation of materialists."
7. Argue that the increase in leisure time is a serious problem.
8. Fill in with details an argument that the humanities are best equipped to fill leisure time.
9. Argue that knowledge of men's lives, past and present, increases our ability to make judgments.

*Index
of
Authors*

Index of Authors